MORAVIAN DAILY TEXTS

Bible Texts with Hymn Verses and Prayers for Every Day in the Year

2020

Two Hundred Ninetieth Year

The Moravian Church in America
1021 Center St., Bethlehem, PA 18018
459 S. Church St., Winston-Salem, NC 27101
www.moravian.org

Moravian Daily Texts 2020

Verse translation by Erdmute Frank. Compilation and copy editing by Susan Kiefner, with assistance from Mike Riess, Jill Bruckart and Anna French.

Cover photo by Mike Riess, IBOC.

Book design: Sandy Fay, Laughing Horse Graphics, Inc., Doylestown, Pa.

Printed by McNaughton & Gunn, Inc., Saline, Mich.

Printed in the United States of America

ISBN: 978-1-933571-86-7 paperback edition

NEW EVERY MORNING

"The steadfast love of the Lord never ceases, his mercies never come to an end; they are new every morning."
Lamentations 3:22,23

The first printed edition of the *Daily Texts* (Losungen) was published in Herrnhut, Saxony, in 1731. The title page of that edition quoted the passage from Lamentations and promised a daily message from God that would be new every morning. It was an outgrowth of a spiritual renewal of the Moravian Church (Unitas Fratrum) that dated from August 13, 1727.

In 1722 refugees from Bohemia and Moravia began arriving at the estate of Count Nicholas Ludwig von Zinzendorf (1700-1760), where he gave them a welcome and land on which to establish the settlement of Herrnhut ("Watch of the Lord").

Each day the settlers came together for morning and evening devotions, consciously placing their lives in the context of God's Word. On May 3, 1728, during the evening service, Count Zinzendorf gave the congregation a "watchword" for the next day. It was to be a "Losung" (watchword) to accompany them through the whole day.

Thereafter one or more persons of the congregation went daily to each of the 32 houses in Herrnhut to bring them the watchword for the day, and engage the families in pastoral conversations about the text.

From this oral tradition, the *Daily Texts* soon became fixed in printed form. Zinzendorf compiled 365 watchwords for the year and the first edition of the Losungen was published for 1731.

Even in the first editions there appeared the characteristic coupling of a Bible verse and hymn stanza. Zinzendorf called the hymns "collects" and considered them to be the answer of the congregation to the Word of God. The *Daily Texts* would be a great deal poorer without the mixture of God's Word and our human response.

The watchword soon became accompanied by a "doctrinal" text. The idea of an additional text grew out of a number of collections of texts from the Bible that were put together by Zinzendorf. Such additional lists (some of them for children) were used for special study within the groups in the community, and they came to be referred to as doctrinal texts.

For the *Daily Texts,* as for the whole Moravian Church, Count Zinzendorf's death (May 9, 1760), was a turning point.

His co-workers sensed the uniqueness of Zinzendorf's watchwords, textbooks, and lessons and had them published at Barby-on-the-Elbe in a four-volume collection 1762.

From then on the watchwords and doctrinal texts are distinguished by the way they are selected each year. The watchwords are chosen from various verse collections and, since 1788, they have been drawn by lot from a collection of around 2,000 suitable Old Testament texts. The doctrinal texts are not chosen by lot but are selected. The difference between the watchwords and doctrinal texts was explained in 1801 as follows: "The watchword is either a promise, an encouragement, an admonition or word of comfort; the doctrinal text contains a point of revealed doctrine."

By 1812 it was established that all watchwords would be drawn by lot from a selection of Old Testament texts, and the doctrinal texts would be selected from the New Testament. No doctrinal text is used more than once in a given year. By the end of the nineteenth century, the custom was established to relate the two texts in theme or thought.

Into all the world

Another characteristic of the *Daily Texts* that was already apparent in the early years of its publication was its worldwide distribution. Missionaries who went as "messengers" from Herrnhut after 1732 had a *Daily Texts (Losungen)* in their luggage. They felt united with their home congregation through the daily contemplation of the same Scripture passages.

The *Daily Texts* of 1739 lists a multitude of places around the globe where messengers were witnessing for the Savior. The introduction read:

> "The Good Word of the Lord, 1739, From all the Prophets for His congregations, and servants at Herrnhut, Herrnhaag, Herrendijk [Holland], Pilgerruh [Denmark], Ebersdof, Jena, Amsterdam, Rotterdam, London, Oxford, Berlin, Greenland, St. Croix, St. John and St. Thomas [Virgin Islands], Berbice [Guyana], Palestine, Surinam, Savannah in Georgia, among the Moors in Carolina, with the wild Indians in Irene

[an island in the Savannah River in Georgia], in Pennsylvania, among the Hottentots [South Africa], in Guinea, in Latvia, Estonia and Lithuania, Russia, on the White Sea, in Lappland, Norway, in Switzerland, [Isle of] Man, Hittland [Scotland], in prison, on pilgrimage, to Ceylon, Ethiopia, Persia, on visitation to the missionaries among the heathen, and elsewhere on land and sea."

This distribution of the Moravians into every continent in the known world seems all the more amazing when you consider that the settlement at Herrnhut was only 17 years old, and the first missionaries had gone out only seven years earlier in 1732.

Present membership of the worldwide Moravian Church is more than 1 million in 21 provinces. The *Daily Texts* has a press run of more than 1 million copies in the German language alone. This far surpasses the 25,000 members of the Moravian Church in all of Europe. Other language editions bring the total circulation of this small devotional book to over 1.5 million copies. The *Daily Texts* is now published in more than 50 languages and dialects.

The physical form of the *Daily Texts* varies considerably from country to country. Some, like this North American edition, have a separate page for the verses, hymns, and prayers of each day. Others have several days' texts printed on one page, which makes a thin, pocket-size volume. Some are beautiful examples of the printing and bookbinding arts. Others are simply photocopied and stapled together.

These external nonessentials pale beside the fact that this little book is probably the most widely read devotional guide in the world, next to the Bible. It forms an invisible bond between Christians on all continents, transcending barriers of confession, race, language, and politics. In its quiet way it performs a truly ecumenical service for the whole of Christendom.

North American editions

The printing of the *Daily Texts* in North America dates back at least to 1767, when the Losungen was printed "at Bethlehem on the Forks of the Delaware by Johan Brandmuller." The printer's imprint bears the date of 1767 as well and may have been an extra printing for the German version done at Barby-on-the-Elbe in Germany, where most of the printing was done for the Moravian Church those days.

During the crucial days of the Revolution, the German-language edition was printed in Philadelphia by Heinrich Miller, who had worked for Benjamin Franklin when he first came to America. The daily text for July 4, 1776, was from Isaiah 55:5 —"Behold, you shall call nations that you know not, and nations that knew you not shall run to you" (RSV).

English versions were printed in London as early as 1746, and the title page bears the imprint of "James Hutton near the Golden Lion in Fetter Lane." Hutton was the well-known London printer associated with the Moravian Church who was a friend of John and Charles Wesley in the formative years of their ministry.

The 1850s were crucial years for the Moravian Church in America as the congregations established in the United States broke away from direct control from the Moravian headquarters in Europe. Both German and English editions of the *Daily Texts* were regularly printed in Philadelphia or Bethlehem, Pennsylvania, and in a few years the custom was established to include the statistics of the provinces and districts of the Moravian Church in America.

The biblical texts for each day are chosen in Herrnhut, Germany, and then sent around the world to those who prepare the different language editions. Since 1959 the edition published in the United States has included a prayer for each day. For this North American edition, the hymns are chosen or written, and the prayers are written by Moravian clergy and laypersons from the United States and Canada. Each month is prepared by a different individual or couple, of a variety of ages, so that the prayers reflect the great diversity of devotion in the Moravian Church. We are grateful for the work and inspired words these writers offer and their contributions strengthen each year's edition of the *Moravian Daily Texts*.

DAILY TOPICS FOR PRAYER

On August 27, 1727, certain members of the Moravian Church in Herrnhut, Saxony, formed a remarkable prayer union known as the "Hourly Intercession." This provided that, for every hour of the day and night, one of the volunteer intercessors would, for one hour in private, bear on his or her heart and mind the interests and hopes of the Kingdom of God in the world. This wonderful intercession continued for over 100 years.

On August 27, 1872, a Moravian Prayer union was formed in England as a form of resuscitation of the Hourly Intercession, and today its members are found in all areas of the Moravian world. You are invited to join in this prayer covenant. The following prayer suggestions may be helpful:

Sunday: The Church At Worship. For her purity and peace, unity and power. For the congregation to which we belong or with which we worship. For the ministry of the word of God. For the winning of people into fellowship with Christ. For all church schools, youth ministries, and other church groups at work.

Monday: The Church At Work. For the church in its mission next door and in other lands. For new congregations and specialized ministries. For the workers and leaders in these endeavors. For the worker volunteers to carry out the mission of the church.

Tuesday: Home and School. For households. For the Christian education of the young, and that our children may be led to give themselves to Christ. For all schools and teachers. For young people enrolled in colleges and universities. For the training of ministers in theological seminaries.

Wednesday: For Those In Need. For all in special need, whether as aged, sick, poor, or homeless. For those in prison. For all victims of famine, oppression, aggression, and war.

Thursday: Our Nation and Our World. For those who govern and for those who are governed. For the guidance of God to all who are in authority. For unity of nations and all agencies for peace. For the whole human family and equal rights for all. For the guidance and blessing of God as humanity enters the future.

Friday: Our Own Church Fellowship. For the purity, zeal, and practice of the church as a witnessing fellowship of the love of God. That the church may be a light to the world wherever its congregations are found, and that it may be active in redeeming mission in these communities.

Saturday: The Witness of Christians. That all who confess the name of Christ may grow in the grace and knowledge of Jesus Christ as Lord and Savior.

"O thou King of kings and Lord of lords, who desirest that all people should dwell together in unity, let thy will be known and done among the nations; guide their feet into the way of peace. Remember us and all humanity in thy mercy. Deliver us from the sins which give rise to war and conflict, and strengthen within our hearts the will to establish righteousness and justice in the earth. Give unto us and to all who worship thee the sincere desire to live in peaceful and loving fellowship with all people. Fix our minds and hearts upon thine eternal purposes for your children on earth."

— *A Prayer for Peace*

THE *DAILY TEXTS* IN FAMILY WORSHIP

Almost from the very beginning the *Daily Texts* has been used as a guide for family worship as well as for private and personal devotions. The use of the *Daily Texts* in family worship will vary depending on the time available and the age of the children. One of the values of the *Daily Texts* is that it is adaptable to numerous patterns of use.

One pattern followed by many families is to begin the meal (usually breakfast or the evening meal) with the reading of the texts of the day and the accompanying hymn stanzas. After this, the family joins in the blessing or table grace. A suitable blessing may be chosen from among the following:

Come, Lord Jesus, our Guest to be,
and bless these gifts bestowed by thee.
Bless thy dear ones everywhere,
and keep them in thy loving care.

Be present at our table, Lord;
be here and everywhere adored;
from thine all-bounteous hand our food
may we receive with gratitude.

The worship of the family can then close with a prayer offered in the leader's own words or in those of the printed prayer offered in the *Daily Texts.* As a part of free prayer by the leader or in connection with the printed prayer, use can be made from day to day of the subjects of the Daily Topics for Prayer as given in the preceding pages.

HOW TO USE THE *DAILY TEXTS*

The strength of the *Daily Texts* lies in presenting the Scripture unhindered by illustration. The texts are left to stand alone and to speak to each reader in his or her life. This also allows the *Daily Texts* to be adaptable to different patterns of devotion and study.

Contents For Each Day

MARCH 83

1 **Monday, March 23** — Psalm 38:9–16
Exodus 29:1–30; Matthew 26:1–13

2 **You are the Lord, you alone; you have made heaven, the heaven of heavens, with all their host, the earth and all that is on it, the seas and all that is in them. Nehemiah 9:6**

3
God is love, let heav'n adore him; 463
God is love, let earth rejoice;
let creation sing before him
and exalt him with one voice.
God who laid the earth's foundation,
God who spread the heav'ns above,
God who breathes through all creation:
God is love, eternal love.

4 **God has not left himself without testimony: He has shown kindness by giving you rain from heaven and crops in their seasons; he provides you with plenty of food and fills your hearts with joy. Acts 14:17 NIV**

3
In the wild and in the city, 84s*
ev'ry living thing we find
demonstrates God's grace and power
to the hearts of humankind.
When we care for all the planet
then we truly do God's will.
When we seek to heal and nurture,
then our destiny's fulfilled.

5 Loving Creator, we give you thanks for your bountiful creation which you continue to form today. May the intricacies of the world remind us how much you care for it and all its creatures. Amen.

* © 2012 by June Edwards.

1. **SCRIPTURE LESSONS:** At the top of each page for ongoing study. Not related to the printed texts. Monday through Saturday are part of a plan to read through the Psalms in one year and the rest of the Bible in two. Sundays and special days are the assigned lessons for that day of the church year from the Moravian Revised Common Lectionary, also common to many denominations.

2. **WATCHWORD FOR THE DAY:** From the Old Testament, the first printed text. It is to be a "watchword" to accompany you throughout the day. Usually a promise, encouragement, admonition, or comfort.

3. **HYMN VERSES:** Broken down by meter and usually related to the watchword or theme for the day. It is a devotional response or commentary on the text. Can be used for prayers.

4. **DOCTRINAL TEXT:** From the New Testament. Usually contains some point of Christian doctrine to expand on the watchword.

5. **PRAYER:** A response to God of praise, confession, thanksgiving, or intercession in light of the texts and hymn verses.

- Every Sunday and some church holidays, the *Daily Texts* page will include the **WATCHWORD FOR THE WEEK/ HOLIDAY**. Like the daily watchword, the weekly/holiday text is to accompany the reader throughout the week or holiday and is related to the events of the church year. These differ every year based upon the lectionary cycle.

Devotions

The printed texts, hymn verses, and prayers are the heart of the devotional guide. Their purpose is to help the reader get more closely in touch with God and to meditate upon the Word of God. When reading the texts, hymns and prayers, feel the encouragement found in them. Hear any word or correction for your life; ponder the great message of faith; meditate upon the hymn verses and prayers; feel God's presence surrounding you in faith; and in silence, hear God's word speaking to you.

These texts can also be the center of a daily spiritual diary where you keep a journal of your daily meditations and their meaning in your life.

ACKNOWLEDGMENTS

Bible texts in this publication are quoted from the *New Revised Standard Version Bible,* © 1989 by the Division of Christian Education of the National Council of the Churches of Christ in the United States of America, and are used by permission. Verses marked NIV are taken from *The Holy Bible New International Version®,* NIV®, © 1973, 1978, 1984, 2011 by Biblica, Inc.® Used by permission. All rights reserved worldwide. Verses marked NASB are taken from the *New American Standard Bible®,* © 1960, 1962, 1963, 1968, 1971, 1972, 1973, 1975, 1977, 1995 by The Lockman Foundation. Used by permission. Verses marked NKJV are taken from the *New King James Version®* © 1982 by Thomas Nelson, Inc. Used by permission. All rights reserved. Verses marked GNT are taken from the *Good News Translation,* ©1992 by the American Bible Society.

Sunday readings are taken from the *Revised Common Lectionary,* © 1992 by the Consultation on Common Texts (CCT).

Unless otherwise noted, hymn stanzas found in the *Daily Texts* are taken from the *Moravian Book of Worship,* 1995. The number found to the right of each stanza designates the source of the stanza in that hymnal. If the number is preceded by a p the hymn used is from one of the liturgies and the p designates the page number. The letter b after a number denotes the Hymnal and Liturgies of the Moravian Church Unitas Fratrum, 1920. The letter r after a number denotes the Hymnal of the Moravian Church, 1969. The letter s after a number denotes a hymn or song from *Sing to the Lord A New Song, A New Moravian Songbook,* 2013. When hymns are copyrighted, information is given at the bottom of the page; we gratefully acknowledge permission to use copyrighted material.

Hymn stanzas are broken down by meter except when space would not allow.

The Scripture readings for Monday through Saturday are part of a plan to read through the Old and New Testaments in two years and the Psalms in one year.

Wednesday, January 1 — Psalm 1
Genesis 1:1–2:3; Matthew 1:1–17

You, O God, have tested us; you have tried us as silver is tried. Psalm 66:10

When through fiery trials your pathway shall lie, 709
my grace, all-sufficient, shall be your supply.
The flame shall not hurt you; I only design
your dross to consume and your gold to refine.

We know that suffering produces endurance, and endurance produces character, and character produces hope, and hope does not disappoint us, because God's love has been poured into our hearts through the Holy Spirit that has been given to us. Romans 5:3-5

Add to your believing 582*
deeds that prove it true—
knowing Christ as Savior,
make him Master too:
follow in his footsteps,
go where he has trod,
in the world's great trouble
risk yourself for God.

Dear Jesus, as we start another year, please guide us in ways we have yet to follow you. Even when tested, be the light on our paths and in our hearts to always remind us that you are near. Amen.

Thursday, January 2 — Psalm 2
Genesis 2:4–25; Matthew 1:18–25

The Lord God will wipe away the tears from all faces. Isaiah 25:8

Mighty God, we humbly pray, 586
let your pow'r now lead the way
that in all things we may show
that we in your likeness grow.

Rejoice in hope, be patient in suffering, persevere in prayer. Romans 12:12

The saints in prayer appear as one 749
in word, and deed, and mind,
while with the Father and the Son
sweet fellowship they find.

Gentle Comforter, you come to us when we are hurt, scared, or in distress. Remind us again and again that when we feel far from your presence, you will be with us again and we shall rejoice together. Amen.

Friday, January 3 — Psalm 3
Genesis 3,4; Matthew 2:1–12

Take delight in the Lord, and he will give you the desires of your heart. Psalm 37:4

Praise to the Lord, 530
who o'er all things is wondrously reigning,
shelt'ring you under his wings,
O, so gently sustaining.
Have you not seen
all you have needed has been
met by his gracious ordaining.

Whatever you ask for in prayer, believe that you have received it, and it will be yours. Mark 11:24

What a friend we have in Jesus, 743
all our sins and griefs to bear!
What a privilege to carry
ev'rything to God in prayer!
O what peace we often forfeit,
O what needless pain we bear,
all because we do not carry
ev'rything to God in prayer.

Dear Lord, we have faith that you are always there for us. It is with gratitude that we take comfort in knowing you answer our prayers. In Jesus' name, we pray. Amen.

Saturday, January 4 — Psalm 4
Genesis 5; Matthew 2:13–23

You shall not murder. Exodus 20:13

All that kills abundant living, 685*
let it from the earth be banned;
pride of status, race or schooling,
dogmas that obscure your plan.
In our common quest for justice
may we hallow life's brief span.

Love your enemies, do good to those who hate you, bless those who curse you, pray for those who abuse you. Luke 6:27-28

Always giving and forgiving, 544
ever blessing, ever blessed,
wellspring of the joy of living,
ocean depth of happy rest!
Loving Father, Christ our brother,
let your light upon us shine;
teach us how to love each other,
lift us to the joy divine.

Savior, like a shepherd, lead us to love one another. Teach us compassion to forgive and guide us to be a blessing to others in your name. Amen.

Second Sunday after Christmas

Watchword for the Week — Praise the name of the Lord, for his name alone is exalted; his glory is above earth and heaven. Psalm 148:13

Sunday, January 5 — Jeremiah 31:7-14; Psalm 147:12-20
Ephesians 1:3-14; John 1:(1-9),10-18

There are many who say, "O that we might see some good! Let the light of your face shine on us, O Lord!" Psalm 4:6

God gave us eyes to see them, 467
and lips that we might tell
how great is God Almighty,
who has made all things well.

Jesus said, "I am the light of the world. Whoever follows me will never walk in darkness but will have the light of life." John 8:12

Dark and cheerless is the morn 475
unaccompanied by you;
joyless is the day's return
till your mercy's beams I view;
till they inward light impart,
glad my eyes and warm my heart.

Guiding Light, shine in the dark places where we have yet to see your grace, mercy, and love. We will follow your light and see life. Amen.

Epiphany of the Lord

Watchword for Epiphany — Arise, shine; for your light has come, and the glory of the Lord has risen upon you. Isaiah 60:1

Epiphany of the Lord — Isaiah 60:1-6; Psalm 72:1-7,10-14
Ephesians 3:1-12; Matthew 2:1-12

Monday, January 6 — Psalm 5
Genesis 6:1–7:10; Matthew 3

Why do you say, O Jacob, and speak, O Israel, "My way is hidden from the Lord, and my right is disregarded by my God?" Isaiah 40:27

O bless the Lord, my soul! 546
His grace to all proclaim!
And all that is within me join
to bless his holy name.

God's firm foundation stands, bearing this inscription: "The Lord knows those who are his." 2 Timothy 2:19

"Fear not, I am with you; O be not dismayed, 709
for I am your God and will still give you aid;
I'll strengthen you, help you and cause you to stand
upheld by my righteous, omnipotent hand."

We pray, Lord, you will show us the way. Strengthen us and help us stand up for what is right, for we long to follow you with everything we are. Amen.

Tuesday, January 7 — Psalm 6
Genesis 7:11–8:22; Matthew 4:1–11

"For I," says the Lord, "will be a wall of fire all around Jerusalem." Zechariah 2:5 NKJV

Jerusalem the golden, 814
descending from above,
the city of God's presence,
the vision of God's love—
I know not, O I know not
what joys await us there,
what radiancy of glory,
what bliss beyond compare!

If God is for us, who is against us? Romans 8:31

We have received Christ Jesus, 434*
the Lord who sets us free
as sisters and as brothers
in one community,
a people deeply rooted
in Jesus' love and life.
We know who we are called to be:
Christ's body given melody
to sing God's praise resoundingly.
Alleluia!

We put our trust in you to protect us, O God. We need not build our own defenses. We are under your wing. You are for us, so let us live without walls and know that we are safe. Amen.

Wednesday, January 8 — Psalm 7:1–9
Genesis 9; Matthew 4:12–25

Let your steadfast love, O Lord, be upon us, even as we hope in you. Psalm 33:22

I need your presence every passing hour. 807
What but your grace can foil the tempter's pow'r?
Who like yourself my guide and strength can be?
Through cloud and sunshine, O abide with me.

Let us hold fast to the confession of our hope without wavering, for he who has promised is faithful. Hebrews 10:23

Now we our vow of faith renew, 410*
stretch wide our sights to global view,
and claim with Christians far and near
a larger family held dear.

Let us hold on, be strong, love faith. Trust. Walk with Christ. In the name of the Father, the Son, and the Holy Spirit. Amen.

Thursday, January 9 — Psalm 7:10–17
Genesis 10:1–11:9; Matthew 5:1–16

**It is God who arms me with strength.
Psalm 18:32 NIV**

When he shall come with trumpet sound, 771
O may I then in him be found
clothed in his righteousness alone,
redeemed to stand before the throne.

When I remember you in my prayers, I always thank my God. I pray that the sharing of your faith may become effective when you perceive all the good that we may do for Christ. Philemon 4,6

Sing praise and hallelujah! 435*
Long may our witness thrive,
for God still calls to service
and keeps our faith alive.
The future lies before us
with mission to increase.
All ages join the chorus
proclaiming joy and peace.

Lord, you breathed life into us; Christ, you have paid the price for our sins. Each day the Holy Spirit surrounds, encourages, and guides us. May our life be a window for others to see our faith in action and lead them to you. In Jesus' name, we pray. Amen.

Friday, January 10 — Psalm 8
Genesis 11:10–12:9; Matthew 5:17–26

The righteous has a refuge when he dies. Proverbs 14:32 NASB

How blessed are they who have not seen 369
and yet whose faith has constant been,
for they eternal life shall win!
Alleluia!

For I am convinced that neither death, nor life, nor angels, nor rulers, nor things present, nor things to come, nor powers, nor height, nor depth, nor anything else in all creation, will be able to separate us from the love of God in Christ Jesus our Lord. Romans 8:38-39

Great things he has taught us, 550
great things he has done,
and great our rejoicing through Jesus the Son:
but purer, and higher, and greater will be
our wonder, our transport when Jesus we see.

Remind us again today, O God, that there is nothing stronger than love; that not even death can overcome your love for us. Give us wisdom to fully understand how this can change the way we live. Amen.

Saturday, January 11 — Psalm 9:1–10
Genesis 12:10–13:18; Matthew 5:27–42

Let justice roll down like waters, and righteousness like an ever-flowing stream. Amos 5:24

Let justice roll on like the rivers of time, 56s*
and righteousness flow in continuous stream,
that we in God's wisdom and love may abide
and live in community, not selfish pride.

Jesus said, "You know that among the Gentiles those whom they recognize as their rulers lord it over them, and their great ones are tyrants over them. But it is not so among you; but whoever wishes to become great among you must be your servant." Mark 10:42-43

We must not be arrogant, boastful, unkind, 56s*
but practice compassion and be of one mind.
May we not be proud of our calling or place,
but treat all as members of one common race.

Lord, we ask your blessing on those who lead. May they be mindful of your advice to serve those they lead, just as Christ did. Amen.

First Sunday after the Epiphany

Watchword for the Week — A bruised reed he will not break, and a dimly burning wick he will not quench; he will faithfully bring forth justice. Isaiah 42:3

Sunday, January 12 — Isaiah 42:1-9; Psalm 29
Acts 10:34-43; Matthew 3:13-17

God reveals deep and hidden things. Daniel 2:22

Immortal, invisible, God only wise, 457
in light inaccessible hid from our eyes,
most blessed, most glorious, O Ancient of Days,
almighty, victorious, your great name we praise.

O the depth of the riches and wisdom and knowledge of God! How unsearchable are his judgments and how inscrutable his ways! Romans 11:33

Life-giving Creator of both great and small; 457
of all life the maker, the true life of all;
we blossom, then wither like leaves on the tree,
but you live forever who was and will be.

Mysterious God, we will never fully understand everything you know and see. In your merciful way, guide us through things seen and unseen. In Jesus' name, we pray. Amen.

Monday, January 13 — Psalm 9:11–20
Genesis 14,15; Matthew 5:43–6:4

All who forsake you shall be put to shame; for they have forsaken the fountain of living water, the Lord. Jeremiah 17:13

Living water, never ending, 767*
quench the thirst and flood the soul.
Wellspring, source of life eternal,
drench our dryness, make us whole.

Jesus said, "The time is fulfilled, and the kingdom of God has come near; repent, and believe in the good news." Mark 1:15

Come! Come, follow me. 49s**
Drop your nets beside the sea.
He said, come! Come, follow me.
I'll show you what you can be.
He said come! Come, follow me.
Will you be my devotee?
Jesus Christ said, hey! Come, follow me!

Lord, you call us to drink abundant, living water. We often look to other things to quench our thirst—money, popularity, fame—but they lead only to broken hearts. Teach us to pursue you and to have you as our first love. In the name of Jesus, we pray. Amen.

Tuesday, January 14 — Psalm 10:1–11
Genesis 16,17; Matthew 6:5–18

If you do well, will you not be accepted? And if you do not do well, sin is lurking at the door; its desire is for you, but you must master it. Genesis 4:7

O let me feel you near me; 603
the world is ever near:
I see the sights that dazzle,
the tempting sounds I hear.
My foes are ever near me,
around me and within;
but, Jesus, draw still nearer
and shield my soul from sin!

Pursue righteousness, godliness, faith, love, endurance, gentleness. 1 Timothy 6:11

We do not live by bread alone, 605
but by ev'ry word
that proceeds from the mouth of God.
Allelu, alleluia!

Living God, when our relationships in life break down, call us towards you—that we might turn away from the path we were on and head back into your loving embrace—for your way is difficult, but good. Amen.

Wednesday, January 15 — Psalm 10:12–18
Genesis 18; Matthew 6:19–34

The Lord said to Gideon, "Peace be to you; do not fear, you shall not die." Then Gideon built an altar there to the Lord, and called it, the Lord is peace. Judges 6:23-24

Lord, I did not freely choose you 612*
till by grace you set me free;
for my heart would still refuse you
had your love not chosen me.

Let us therefore approach the throne of grace with boldness, so that we may receive mercy and find grace to help in time of need. Hebrews 4:16

Now my heart sets none above you, 612*
for your grace alone I thirst,
knowing well that if I love you,
you, O Lord, have loved me first.

Dear Lord God, you are the God of grace and mercy. Please continue to bring peace into our lives. In Christ's name, we pray. Amen.

Thursday, January 16 — Psalm 11
Genesis 19:1–29; Matthew 7:1–12

The earth, O Lord, is full of your steadfast love; teach me your statutes. Psalm 119:64

O blessed Lord, teach me your law, 510
your righteous judgments I declare;
your testimonies make me glad,
for they are wealth beyond compare.

All scripture is inspired by God and is useful for teaching, for reproof, for correction, and for training in righteousness. 2 Timothy 3:16

To God who gave the scriptures 508*
we turn in faith to find
a taste of honeyed sweetness
to nourish heart and mind;
the promise of salvation,
the covenant restored,
the apostolic witness
that Jesus is the Lord.

Your word, O God, constantly recalls your truth and wisdom. Let us walk in the revelation of your love and the grace of your son, Jesus. Amen.

Friday, January 17 — Psalm 12
Genesis 19:30–20:18; Matthew 7:13–23

So Moses and Aaron went to Pharaoh, and said to him, "Thus says the Lord, 'Let my people go, so that they may worship me.'" Exodus 10:3

Take my love, my Lord, I pour 647
at your feet its treasure store;
take myself, and I will be
yours for all eternity.

See, I am sending you out like sheep into the midst of wolves; so be wise as serpents and innocent as doves. Matthew 10:16

Since, O Lord, you have demanded 401*
that our lives your love should show
so we wait to be commanded
forth into your world to go.
Kindle in us love's compassion
so that ev'ryone may see
in our faith and hope the promise
of a new humanity.

Lord, as your people—created, redeemed, and sustained—we seek to worship you in all we do, aware that true discipleship is no easy task. Give us simplicity of faith, courage to love, and the willingness to hope in all that we do. In Jesus' name, we pray. Amen.

Saturday, January 18 — Psalm 13
Genesis 21; Matthew 7:24–8:4

What god in heaven or on earth can perform deeds and mighty acts like yours! Deuteronomy 3:24

O Lord my God, when I in awesome wonder 465*
consider all the works thy hands have made,
I see the stars, I hear the mighty thunder,
thy pow'r throughout the universe displayed.

For from him and through him and to him are all things. To him be the glory forever. Romans 11:36

Christ, whose glory fills the skies, 475
Christ, the true and only light,
Sun of righteousness, arise,
triumph o'er the shades of night;
dayspring from on high, be near;
daystar, in my heart appear.

Lord, may we slow down the busy parts of our day so that we might take in more of the splendor of creation all around us, and that we might calibrate our eyes, ears, and hearts, to see the world is full of the good things of creation. In your holy name, we pray. Amen.

Second Sunday after the Epiphany

Watchword for the Week — God is faithful; by him you were called into the fellowship of his Son, Jesus Christ our Lord. 1 Corinthians 1:9

Sunday, January 19 — Isaiah 49:1-7; Psalm 40:1-11
1 Corinthians 1:1-9; John 1:29-42

When the wicked turn away from the wickedness they have committed and do what is lawful and right, they shall save their life. Ezekiel 18:27

I, the Lord of sea and sky, 641*
I have heard my people cry.
All who dwell in deepest sin
my hand will save.
I who made the stars of night,
I will make their darkness bright.
Who will bear my light to them?
Whom shall I send?

The saying is sure and worthy of full acceptance, that Christ Jesus came into the world to save sinners—of whom I am the foremost. 1 Timothy 1:15

Jesus, Master, will you use p42
one who owes you more than all?
As you will, I would not choose;
only let me hear your call.
Jesus, let me always be
in your service glad and free.

Gracious Lord, like a stormy sea, we often have times of turbulence in our lives. Help us to remember to turn to you for your guidance and calming love. Amen.

Monday, January 20 — Psalm 14
Genesis 22; Matthew 8:5–22

Happy are those to whom the Lord imputes no iniquity, and in whose spirit there is no deceit. Psalm 32:2

I am thine, O Lord—I have heard thy voice, 607
and it told thy love to me;
but I long to rise in the arms of faith
and be closer drawn to thee.

Everything old has passed away; see, everything has become new! All this is from God, who reconciled us to himself through Christ. 2 Corinthians 5:17-18

A new creation comes to life and grows 366
as Christ's new body takes on flesh and blood.
The universe restored and whole will sing:
Alleluia!

Loving God, although we try daily to live our lives full of love, caring, and acceptance as Jesus did, we fall short. Please forgive us and help us to live as true children of God. Amen.

Tuesday, January 21 — Psalm 15
Genesis 23:1–24:25; Matthew 8:23–34

I am the Lord your God who brought you out of the land of Egypt, to be their slaves no more; I have broken the bars of your yoke and made you walk erect. Leviticus 26:13

Then let us adore and give him his right, 565
all glory and pow'r and wisdom and might,
all honor and blessing, with angels above,
and thanks never ceasing for infinite love.

For freedom Christ has set us free. Stand firm, therefore, and do not submit again to a yoke of slavery. Galatians 5:1

New life for some means food and warmth, 481*
for some the right to speak,
for some the comfort of a friend
or loving God to meet.
So help us, Christ, as now we join
with Christians ev'rywhere
to touch and teach, to comfort, feed,
your love the world to share.

Remind us again and again, O God, that we have moved from being oppressed to being free, and that we are called to use our freedom to stand with those who want what we have. Let us share our freedom in Christ with all. In Jesus' name, we pray. Amen.

Wednesday, January 22 — Psalm 16:1–6
Genesis 24:26–66; Matthew 9:1–13

If you do not stand firm in faith, you shall not stand at all. Isaiah 7:9

Then grant us courage, Father God p221*
to choose again the pilgrim way,
and help us to accept with joy
the challenge of tomorrow's day.

Fight the good fight of the faith; take hold of the eternal life, to which you were called and for which you made the good confession in the presence of many witnesses. 1 Timothy 6:12

Stand up, stand up for Jesus, 752
stand in his strength alone;
the arm of flesh will fail you,
you dare not trust your own.
Put on the gospel armor,
each piece put on with prayer;
where duty calls, or danger,
be ever faithful there.

Lord, we stand firm and take hold, but we dare not trust in our own strength. Grant us this day, and every day, the strength to be firm in our belief and hold on to your promises. Amen.

Thursday, January 23 — Psalm 16:7–11
Genesis 25; Matthew 9:14–26

You have delivered my soul from death, my eyes from tears, my feet from stumbling. Psalm 116:8

Consecrate me now to thy service, Lord, 607
by the pow'r of grace divine;
let my soul look up with a steadfast hope
and my will be lost in thine.

Jesus might free those who all their lives were held in slavery by the fear of death. Hebrews 2:15

O Lamb of God, Lord Jesus Christ, 472*
whom God the Father gave us,
who for the world was sacrificed
upon the cross to save us,
at God's right hand you intercede
for those who for your mercy plead;
receive the prayer we offer.

Heavenly Father, we thank you for the gift of your son, Jesus. Help us to share this wonderful gift with others so that they may also share his everlasting love and grace. Amen.

Friday, January 24 — Psalm 17:1–7
Genesis 26; Matthew 9:27–38

The haughty eyes of people shall be brought low, and the pride of everyone shall be humbled; and the Lord alone will be exalted on that day. Isaiah 2:11

While we, deeply humbled, 746
own we're oft to blame,
this remains our comfort,
you are still the same.
In you all the needy
have a friend most dear,
whose love and forbearance
unexampled are.

Do not be deceived; God is not mocked. Galatians 6:7

O for the living flame, 531
from his own altar brought,
to touch our lips, our minds inspire,
and wing to heav'n our thought!

God, please help us to not be proud and to remember that all praise is owed to you. Your omnipotent power reigns over us, knowing our every triumph and downfall. Glory to God in the highest. Amen.

Saturday, January 25 — Psalm 17:8–15
Genesis 27:1–29; Matthew 10:1–16

Have you not known? Have you not heard? The Lord is the everlasting God, the Creator of the ends of the earth. He does not faint or grow weary; his understanding is unsearchable. Isaiah 40:28

If you but trust in God to guide you 712
and place your confidence in him,
you'll find him always there beside you
to give you hope and strength within;
for those who trust God's changeless love
build on the rock that will not move.

May the God of hope fill you with all joy and peace in believing, so that you may abound in hope by the power of the Holy Spirit. Romans 15:13

Only be still and wait his pleasure 712
in cheerful hope with heart content.
He fills your needs to fullest measure
with what discerning love has sent;
doubt not our inmost wants are known
to him who chose us for his own.

O God, creator of all things, blessed are we when we put our trust in you. Continue to fill us with your understanding and peace as we grow in our faith. In Jesus' name, we pray. Amen.

Third Sunday after the Epiphany

Watchword for the Week — The Lord is my light and my salvation; whom shall I fear? The Lord is the stronghold of my life; of whom shall I be afraid? Psalm 27:1

Sunday, January 26 — Isaiah 9:1-4; Psalm 27:1,4-9
1 Corinthians 1:10-18; Matthew 4:12-23

You rule the raging of the sea; when its waves rise, you still them. Psalm 89:9

Eternal Father, strong to save, 725
whose arm has bound the restless wave,
who bade the mighty ocean deep
its own appointed limits keep:
O hear us when we cry to thee
for those in peril on the sea.

Now may the Lord of peace himself give you peace at all times in all ways. 2 Thessalonians 3:16

From your house when I return, 553
may my heart within me burn,
and at evening let me say,
"I have walked with God today."

Lord, may we hold tightly to the peace which we share in Christ. May we also let it go to share it with others who need it. May our day be filled with acts of giving and receiving peace. In Christ's name, we pray. Amen.

Monday, January 27 — Psalm 18:1–6
Genesis 27:30–28:9; Matthew 10:17–25

Who is calling forth the generations from the beginning? I, the Lord—with the first of them and with the last—I am he. Isaiah 41:4 NIV

God has spoken by his prophets, 507*
spoken his unchanging word,
each from age to age proclaiming
God, the one, the righteous Lord.
In the world's despair and turmoil,
one firm anchor holds us fast:
God is king, his throne eternal;
God the first, and God the last.

You know the message God sent to the people of Israel, announcing the good news of peace through Jesus Christ, who is Lord of all. Acts 10:36 NIV

In Christ there is no east or west— 781
he breaks all barriers down:
by Christ redeemed, by Christ possessed,
in Christ we live as one.

God, you call us day by day to venture down the path that leads to love and peace. Uphold us in your peace and fill us with your love. From east to west, north to south, we stand united in you. Amen.

Tuesday, January 28 — Psalm 18:7–15
Genesis 28:10–29:14; Matthew 10:26–42

If God tears down, no one can rebuild; if he shuts someone in, no one can open up. Job 12:14

This is our Father's world: 456
O let us not forget
that though the wrong is often strong,
God is the ruler yet.
He trusts us with his world,
to keep it clean and fair—
all earth and trees, all skies and seas,
all creatures ev'rywhere.

These are the words of the holy one, the true one, who has the key of David, who opens and no one will shut, who shuts and no one opens: "I know your works. Look, I have set before you an open door, which no one is able to shut." Revelation 3:7-8

Open now the crystal fountain 790
where the healing waters flow;
let the fire and cloudy pillar
lead me all my journey through.
Strong deliv'rer, strong deliv'rer,
ever be my strength and shield;
ever be my strength and shield.

Lord, we thank you for holding open the way to you. May we embrace the grace you provide us daily. In Jesus' name, we pray. Amen.

Wednesday, January 29 — Psalm 18:16–24
Genesis 29:15–30:24; Matthew 11:1–10

A bruised reed he will not break, and a dimly burning wick he will not quench. Isaiah 42:3

Show'rs of blessing, show'rs of blessing 636
from the Lord proceed,
strength supplying, strength supplying
in the time of need;
for no servant of our King
ever lacked for anything.
He will never, he will never
break the bruised reed.

The Son of Man came to seek out and to save the lost. Luke 19:10

We praise the Christ who called the rich, 481*
the outcast, and the poor,
who said to them, "Come follow me,
my love for you is sure."
And Christ today invites us still
to follow and to live.
Christ calls us now to spread the news
that God new life does give.

Lord, lead us today to shine brightly, reflecting your light and love to the lost and helping those who are bruised. In Christ's name, we pray. Amen.

Thursday, January 30 — Psalm 18:25–29
Genesis 30:25–31:21; Matthew 11:11–24

You shall not be partial to the poor or defer to the great. Leviticus 19:15

Give me your courage, Lord, to speak 686*
whenever strong oppress the weak.
Should I myself as victim live,
rememb'ring you, may I forgive.

My brothers and sisters, believers in our glorious Lord Jesus Christ must not show favoritism. James 2:1 NIV

Let your heart be tender 582**
and your vision clear—
rouse yourself to action,
serve God far and near.
Let your heart be broken
by another's pain,
share your rich resources—
give and give again.

Loving God, help us to see everyone we encounter as you see them—precious and loved. Challenge us in our prejudices and favoritism. We shall rejoice in how your love is changing us and helping us to see others through your eyes. Amen.

Friday, January 31 — Psalm 18:30–36
Genesis 31:22–55; Matthew 11:25–12:8

I have been pouring out my soul before the Lord. 1 Samuel 1:15

My soul he doth restore again, 720
and me to walk doth make
within the paths of righteousness,
e'en for his own name's sake;
within the paths of righteousness,
e'en for his own name's sake.

Cast all your anxiety on him, because he cares for you. 1 Peter 5:7

Remember, Lord, though frail we be, 339*
in your own image were we made;
help us, lest in anxiety,
we cause your name to be betrayed.

Lord, empty us of self so that we can be filled with you. Empty us of every vain ambition and poison of pride, every foolishness our hearts hold onto, so that we may be filled with you. In Jesus' name, we pray. Amen.

Saturday, February 1 — Psalm 18:37–45
Genesis 32:1–21; Matthew 12:9–21

If only you had paid attention to my commands, your peace would have been like a river, your well-being like the waves of the sea. Isaiah 48:18 NIV

When peace, like a river, attendeth my way, 754
when sorrows like sea billows roll;
whatever my lot, you have taught me to say,
it is well, it is well with my soul.

Christ Jesus became for us wisdom from God, and righteousness and sanctification and redemption. 1 Corinthians 1:30

The name of Jesus charms our fears, 548
and bids our sorrows cease—
'tis music in the sinner's ears,
'tis life, and health, and peace.

God, we turn to you to lighten our way; to help us see that you are there, not only to guide, but to bring us peace. May we always turn to your wisdom when we struggle, knowing that you will not steer us wrong. In Christ Jesus, we pray. Amen.

Fourth Sunday after the Epiphany

Watchword for the Week — For the message about the cross is foolishness to those who are perishing, but to us who are being saved it is the power of God. 1 Corinthians 1:18

Sunday, February 2 — Micah 6:1-8; Psalm 15
1 Corinthians 1:18-31; Matthew 5:1-12

The Lord God helps me; therefore I have not been disgraced. Isaiah 50:7

O use me, Lord, use even me, 646
just as you will, and when, and where,
until your blessed face I see,
your rest, your joy, your glory share.

To this day I have had help from God, and so I stand here, testifying. Acts 26:22

Help me walk in the paths of righteousness; 728*
be my aid when Satan and sin oppress.
I am trusting you whate'er may be.
Lead me, O Lord, lead me.

Dear God, let us walk beside you. May we listen for your voice and allow it to guide us to do your will. Although we may stumble and fall, we know you will be there to pick us up and brush us off. Thank you, Lord, our guide and comforter. Amen.

Monday, February 3 — Psalm 18:46–50
Genesis 32:22–33:20; Matthew 12:22–32

All who were incensed against the Lord shall come to him and be ashamed. Isaiah 45:24

Father, now your sinful child 779
through your love is reconciled.
By your pard'ning grace I live;
daily still I cry, forgive.

Every tongue should confess that Jesus Christ is Lord, to the glory of God the Father. Philippians 2:11

Praise to the Lord! 530
O, let all that is in me adore him!
All that has life and breath,
come now with praises before him!
Let the amen
sound from his people again.
Gladly forever adore him!

Oh, gentle Jesus, forgive our sins, our negative thoughts, and the pain we have caused others. It is through your love and grace that we can have a new start. May our hearts and souls praise you and speak of your glory. Amen.

Tuesday, February 4 — Psalm 19:1–6
Genesis 34; Matthew 12:33–45

When the poor and needy seek water, and there is none, and their tongue is parched with thirst, I the Lord will answer them. Isaiah 41:17

He leadeth me: O blessed thought! 787
O words with heav'nly comfort fraught!
Whate'er I do, where'er I be,
still 'tis God's hand that leadeth me.

To the thirsty I will give water as a gift from the spring of the water of life. Revelation 21:6

I heard the voice of Jesus say, 606
"Behold, I freely give
the living water; thirsty one,
stoop down and drink and live."
I came to Jesus, and I drank
of that life-giving stream;
my thirst was quenched, my soul revived,
and now I live in him.

Lord, it is your comfort that we seek when we are in need. May we allow you to quench our thirst and revive our souls when we are most in need. In Jesus' name, we pray. Amen.

Wednesday, February 5 — Psalm 19:7–14
Genesis 35:1–36:8; Matthew 12:46–13:9

The Lord will save me, and we will sing to stringed instruments at the house of the Lord. Isaiah 38:20

Sing praise to God who reigns above, 537
the God of all creation,
the God of pow'r, the God of love,
the God of our salvation.
My soul with comfort rich he fills,
and ev'ry grief he gently stills:
to God all praise and glory!

Jumping up, he stood and began to walk, and he entered the temple with them, walking and leaping and praising God. Acts 3:8

How good the name of Jesus sounds 487
to all believing ears!
It soothes our sorrows, heals our wounds,
and drives away our fears.
It makes the wounded spirit whole,
and calms the troubled mind;
his manna for each hungry soul,
the lost and weary find.

Great is our faithfulness, Lord, as we turn to you in our times of need. May we rejoice and sing your praise to all who can hear, knowing that you are the healer of all our hurts. In Jesus' name, we pray. Amen.

Thursday, February 6 — Psalm 20
Genesis 36:9–43; Matthew 13:10–23

He is mindful of his covenant forever, of the word that he commanded, for a thousand generations. Psalm 105:8

We come to you, our Father, 433
with thoughts of thanks and praise,
for your abundant mercy,
and all your love and grace;
we praise you for your goodness
and for your loving care,
for daily show'rs of blessing,
for answers to our prayers.

Jesus said, "Heaven and earth will pass away, but my words will not pass away." Mark 13:31

When we've been there ten thousand years, 783
bright shining as the sun,
we've no less days to sing God's praise
than when we'd first begun.

O faithful One, you are the beginning and the end. When we are in need, let us quiet our souls and remember how almighty you are and the promise of eternal life with you. Amen.

Friday, February 7 — Psalm 21
Genesis 37; Matthew 13:24–35

Keep these words that I am commanding you today in your heart. Recite them to your children and talk about them. Deuteronomy 6:6-7

O tell of his might, O sing of his grace, 566
whose robe is the light, whose canopy space.
His chariots of wrath the deep thunderclouds form,
and dark is his path on the wings of the storm.

The aim of such instruction is love that comes from a pure heart, a good conscience, and sincere faith. 1 Timothy 1:5

Ev'ry God-given day 53s*
offers chances to grow,
to challenge our faith
and to strengthen it so
to increase our knowledge,
and therefore we pray
to God in thanksgiving
for ev'ry new day.

Loving Creator, you have shaped us from the very beginning. Open our hearts so that we might know you more each day. May we live authentically in your love as we share your ways with the world. Amen.

Saturday, February 8 — Psalm 22:1–8
Genesis 38; Matthew 13:36–46

Sing to the Lord; praise the Lord! He has delivered the life of the needy from the hands of evildoers. Jeremiah 20:13

The right hand of God is lifting in our land, 690*
lifting the fallen one by one,
each one is known by name
and rescued now from shame
by the lifting of the right hand of God.

He has brought down the powerful from their thrones and lifted up the lowly. Luke 1:52

He comes with rescue speedy 263
to those who suffer wrong,
to help the poor and needy,
and bid the weak be strong,
to give them songs for sighing,
their darkness turn to light,
whose souls, condemned and dying,
were precious in his sight.

Gracious Savior, as your followers, may we humbly lift up the lowly and serve the needy, just as you did. In doing so, may we be reminded of the kinship we all have in you. Amen.

Fifth Sunday after the Epiphany

Watchword for the Week — For I decided to know nothing among you except Jesus Christ, and him crucified. 1 Corinthians 2:2

Sunday, February 9 — Isaiah 58:1-9a,(9b-12); Psalm 112:1-9,(10) 1 Corinthians 2:1-12,(13-16); Matthew 5:13-20

Blessed is the one who comes in the name of the Lord. Psalm 118:26

Rejoice, rejoice, the kingdom comes; 260*
be glad, for it is near.
It comes with joy surprising us;
it triumphs o'er our fears.
Give thanks, for as the kingdom comes
it brings God's own shalom,
a state of peace and justice
where all with God are one.

Jesus Christ came and proclaimed peace to you. Ephesians 2:17

O come, Desire of Nations, bind 274
all peoples in one heart and mind;
bid envy, strife and quarrels cease;
fill the whole world with heaven's peace.

Dearest Jesus, you came proclaiming peace in these times of geopolitical tension, war, and disaster. Help us to promote peace in all we say and do. Hasten the day when your peace will reign supreme and all strife and suffering ceases. In your name, we pray. Amen.

Monday, February 10 — Psalm 22:9–21
Genesis 39; Matthew 13:47–58

The Lord will send his angel with you and make your way successful. Genesis 24:40

Great Father of glory, pure Father of light, 457
your angels adore you, all veiling their sight;
all praise we would render, O lead us to see
the light of your splendor, your love's majesty.

The disciples, with wives and children, escorted us until we were out of the city. After kneeling down on the beach and praying, we said farewell to one another. Acts 21:5 NASB

We are disciples of our day, 46s*
we journey with our Lord.
Let's help each other on the way,
we journey with our Lord.
And with his love he took our shame,
he even dared to take the blame.
He lives for me and you the same.
We journey with our Lord.

Lord, as your disciples, help us to discern the paths that you have set before us, searching for others who need support or who will support us on our journey. In Christ's name, we pray. Amen.

* By Rick Beck (2010).

Tuesday, February 11 — Psalm 22:22–28
Genesis 40:1–41:16; Matthew 14:1–14

He leads me in right paths for his name's sake. Psalm 23:3

The Lord's my shepherd; I'll not want. 720
He makes me down to lie
in pastures green; he leadeth me
the quiet waters by;
he leadeth me, he leadeth me
the quiet waters by.

Jesus said, "I am the good shepherd. I know my own and my own know me." John 10:14

I am Jesus' little lamb; 723
ever glad at heart I am;
for my Shepherd gently guides me,
knows my need and well provides me,
loves me ev'ry day the same,
even calls me by my name.

Good Shepherd, you know us completely. We ask that you continue to lead us in right paths so that we may grow to know you more deeply. Amen.

Wednesday, February 12 — Psalm 22:29–31
Genesis 41:17–57; Matthew 14:15–24

I will remember my covenant with you in the days of your youth, and I will establish with you an everlasting covenant. Ezekiel 16:60

Remembering what our fathers told 399
you did in their young day,
this solemn jubilee we hold.
May we, as then did they,
ourselves in covenant now bind
with soul and strength, with heart and mind,
through life, in death, on land, o'er sea
to you disciples be.

After you have suffered for a little while, the God of all grace, who has called you to his eternal glory in Christ, will himself restore, support, strengthen, and establish you. 1 Peter 5:10

Are we weak and heavy laden, 743
cumbered with a load of care?
Precious Savior, still our refuge,
take it to the Lord in prayer!
Do your friends despise, forsake you?
Take it to the Lord in prayer!
In his arms he'll take and shield you;
you will find a solace there.

God, we thank you for sending Jesus to strengthen and renew the promised covenant. We rejoice in your abundant grace and look to you for support in our daily travels. We praise you in Jesus' name. Amen.

Thursday, February 13 — Psalm 23
Genesis 42; Matthew 14:25–15:9

It is the Lord who goes before you. He will be with you; he will not fail you or forsake you. Do not fear or be dismayed. Deuteronomy 31:8

Wherever he may guide me, 732
no want shall turn me back;
my Shepherd is beside me,
and nothing can I lack.
His wisdom ever waking,
his sight is never dim,
he knows the way he's taking,
and I will walk with him.

Jesus said, "My sheep hear my voice. I know them, and they follow me. I give them eternal life, and they will never perish. No one will snatch them out of my hand." John 10:27-28

Those who are by Christ directed, 717
trusting the Good Shepherd's care,
from all harm will be protected,
and no danger need to fear.

Dear Lord, thank you for being our shepherd; for watching over us no matter where we are in our life's journey. You are ever-faithful, never forsaking us even in our darkest hours. Be with us and watch over us—ensuring no harm comes to those under your care. Amen.

Friday, February 14 — Psalm 24
Genesis 43; Matthew 15:10–20

Why have you despised the word of the Lord, to do what is evil in his sight? 2 Samuel 12:9

Restrain me lest I harbor pride, 733
lest I in my own strength confide;
though I am weak, show me anew
I have my pow'r, my strength from you.

Let us also lay aside every weight and the sin that clings so closely, and let us run with perseverance the race that is set before us, looking to Jesus the pioneer and perfecter of our faith. Hebrews 12:1-2

May I run the race before me, 585
strong and brave to face the foe,
looking only unto Jesus
as I onward go.

Loving God, may we always remember to turn to you when we are weak, fearful, or self-righteous. Remind us of your presence, even when we are clinging to sin, that our strength comes from you. May we put you first and follow the guidance and direction you provide. In Jesus' name, we pray. Amen.

Saturday, February 15 — Psalm 25:1–7
Genesis 44; Matthew 15:21–28

Come, let us walk in the light of the Lord! Isaiah 2:5

Light of the world, come near and bless p68
your children here below,
who in your house your name confess,
on us your grace bestow.

You know what time it is, how it is now the moment for you to wake from sleep. For salvation is nearer to us now than when we became believers; the night is far gone, the day is near. Romans 13:11-12

Zion hears the watchmen singing, 258
and in her heart new joy is springing.
She wakes, she rises from her gloom.
For her Lord comes down all glorious,
the strong in grace, in truth victorious.
Her star's arising light has come!
"Now come, O blessed one,
Lord Jesus, God's own Son.
Hail, hosanna!
We answer all in joy your call,
we follow to the wedding hall."

Oh Lord, show us the path to salvation and help us by guiding us in a world of darkness. Let us be your light bearers to the wider world and brighten our communities with your love. Amen.

Sixth Sunday after the Epiphany

Watchword for the Week — Choose life so that you and your descendants may live, loving the Lord your God, obeying him, and holding fast to him. Deuteronomy 30:19,20

Sunday, February 16 — Deuteronomy 30:15-20; Psalm 119:1-8
1 Corinthians 3:1-9; Matthew 5:21-37

You gave me room when I was in distress. Be gracious to me, and hear my prayer. Psalm 4:1

My soul before you prostrate lies; 721
to you, its Source, my spirit flies;
O turn to me your cheering face;
I'm poor, enrich me with your grace.

Blessed are those who mourn, for they will be comforted. Matthew 5:4

From tender childhood's helplessness, 581
from human grief and burdened toil,
from famished souls, from sorrow's stress
your heart has never known recoil.

O Lord, deliver us from our despair. Hear our cries and comfort us. You know the troubles we face; be the balm our souls need in our times of trial. In your name, we pray. Amen.

Monday, February 17 — Psalm 25:8–22
Genesis 45; Matthew 15:29–16:4

All the ends of the earth shall turn to the Lord. Psalm 22:27

Worship, honor, glory, blessing, 454
Lord, we offer as our gift;
young and old, your praise expressing,
our glad songs to you we lift.
All the saints in heav'n adore you;
we would join their glad acclaim;
as your angels serve before you,
so on earth we praise your name.

God desires everyone to be saved and to come to the knowledge of the truth. 1 Timothy 2:4

O word of God incarnate, 505
O wisdom from on high,
O truth unchanged, unchanging,
O light of our dark sky:
we praise you for the radiance
that from the scripture's page,
a lantern to our footsteps,
shines on from age to age.

God, you are the light of our dark sky. We pray that you shine your light into every corner of our being so that we follow your path clearly until we meet face to face. Amen.

Tuesday, February 18 — Psalm 26
Genesis 46:1–27; Matthew 16:5–20

Do not fear, O soil; be glad and rejoice, for the Lord has done great things! Joel 2:21

For the herald's voice is crying 264
in the desert far and near,
calling us to true repentance,
since the Kingdom now is here.
O, that warning cry obey!
Now prepare for God a way!
Let the valleys rise to meet him,
and the hills bow down to greet him!

Without any doubt, the mystery of our religion is great: He was revealed in flesh, vindicated in spirit, seen by angels, proclaimed among Gentiles, believed in throughout the world, taken up in glory. 1 Timothy 3:16

Church, rejoice! Raise your voice, 631
sing Jehovah's worthy praise;
extol his name forever;
laud him, our God and Savior;
proclaim to ev'ry nation
the tidings of salvation;
bear the witness to his greatness;
spread the story of his glory
to the earth's remotest bounds.

God of creation, we rejoice in your faithfulness. Though unworthy, we trust that you heal, forgive, and save. In that knowledge, we find joy and peace and give thanks. Amen.

Wednesday, February 19 — Psalm 27:1–6
Genesis 46:28–47:31; Matthew 16:21–28

The mighty one, God the Lord, speaks and summons the earth from the rising of the sun to its setting. Psalm 50:1

This is my Father's world: 456
he shines in all that's fair;
in rustling grass I hear him pass—
he speaks to me ev'rywhere.
This is my Father's world:
why should my heart be sad?
The Lord is King, let heaven ring!
God reigns; let earth be glad.

God was reconciling the world to himself in Christ, not counting people's sins against them. And he has committed to us the message of reconciliation. 2 Corinthians 5:19 NIV

Much forgiven, may I learn 779
love for hatred to return;
then my heart assured shall be
you, my God, have pardoned me.

Lord, as we rise to a new day of creation, lead us in thought, word, and deed, we pray. We recognize our imperfection and find hope in your patience and forgiveness. With gratitude, we pray. Amen.

Thursday, February 20 — Psalm 27:7–14
Genesis 48; Matthew 17:1–13

Thus says the Lord, I myself have spoken to you persistently, and you have not obeyed me. Jeremiah 35:14

We have sinned against your law. 760*
We have failed to do your will,
disobeyed your holy word.
Lord, have mercy on us still.

Blessed are those who hear the word of God and obey it! Luke 11:28

Lord, obediently we go, 789
gladly leaving all below;
lead us now in all we do
and we still will follow you.

Lord, how stubborn we are in stopping our ears! How graciously you continue to speak to us, that we may hear you at last! Bring us from disobedience into obedience, that we may find our way to your joy. We pray in Jesus' name. Amen.

Friday, February 21 — Psalm 28
Genesis 49; Matthew 17:14–27

Out of the ground the Lord God formed every animal of the field and every bird of the air, and brought them to the man. The man gave names to all. Genesis 2:19,20

> Each little flow'r that opens, 467
> each little bird that sings—
> God made their glowing colors,
> God made their tiny wings.

Look at the birds of the air; they neither sow nor reap nor gather into barns, and yet your heavenly Father feeds them. Are you not of more value than they? Matthew 6:26

> We thank you, our Creator, 453
> for all things bright and good,
> the seedtime and the harvest,
> our life, our health, our food;
> accept the gifts we offer
> for all your love imparts,
> and what you most would treasure—
> our humble, thankful hearts.

Loving Creator of all things—we give you thanks for everything we can see, hear, touch, smell, and taste. May our faith be strong knowing that although you created all things, that our worth is greater than the birds, and that our needs will always be met. May we be able to distinguish between a need and a want. In Jesus' name, we pray. Amen.

Saturday, February 22 — Psalm 29
Genesis 50; Matthew 18:1–14

You say, 'The way of the Lord is unfair.' Hear now, O house of Israel: Is my way unfair? Is it not your ways that are unfair? Ezekiel 18:25

Dear Lord and Father of mankind, 739
forgive our foolish ways;
reclothe us in our rightful mind;
in purer lives thy service find,
in deeper rev'rence, praise.

If we say that we have no sin, we deceive ourselves, and the truth is not in us. If we confess our sins, he who is faithful and just will forgive us our sins and cleanse us from all unrighteousness. 1 John 1:8-9

Pardon, Lord, and are there those 779
who my debtors are, or foes?
I, who by forgiveness live,
here their trespasses forgive.

Teach us to examine our ways, Lord. Show us how our steps may lead to harm for ourselves and others. Help us to confess our sins, redirect our steps, and walk in your way of justice. Amen.

Last Sunday after the Epiphany

Watchword for the Week — God said, "This is my Son, the Beloved; with him I am well pleased; listen to him!" Matthew 17:5

Sunday, February 23 — Exodus 24:12-18; Psalm 2
2 Peter 1:16-21; Matthew 17:1-9

Their congregation shall be established before me. Jeremiah 30:20

O be not thou dismayed, 247r
believing little band.
God, in his might arrayed,
to help thee is at hand.
Upon his palm engraven
thy name is ever found.
He knows, who dwells in heaven;
the ills that thee surround.

In Jesus Christ the whole structure is joined together and grows into a holy temple in the Lord. Ephesians 2:21

Jesus, great High Priest of our profession, 400
we in confidence draw near;
grant us, then, in mercy, the confession
of our grateful hearts to hear;
you we gladly own in ev'ry nation,
Head and Master of your congregation,
conscious that in ev'ry place
you are giving life and grace.

O Head and Savior of your church, let us always be grateful for the privilege of living as your body! Let us always show our gratitude in loving action. In your name, we pray. Amen.

Monday, February 24 — Psalm 30:1–5
Exodus 1:1–2:10; Matthew 18:15–35

Let us test and examine our ways, and return to the Lord. Lamentations 3:40

But examine first your case, 416
whether you be in the faith;
do you long for pard'ning grace?
Is your only hope his death?
Then howe'er your soul's oppressed,
come, you are a worthy guest.

Whoever is united with the Lord is one with him in spirit. 1 Corinthians 6:17 NIV

Spirit of God, who dwells within my heart, 490
wean it from sin, through all its pulses move.
Stoop to my weakness, mighty as you are,
and make me love you as I ought to love.

Guiding Spirit, though this world may challenge us with diversion and distraction, we will always find a home in you. Surround us with your inviting spirit and bring us back into your loving arms. Amen.

Tuesday, February 25 — Psalm 30:6–12
Exodus 2:11–3:22; Matthew 19:1–12

I will do more good to you than ever before. Then you shall know that I am the Lord. Ezekiel 36:11

Breathe on me, breath of God, 494
my will to yours incline,
until this selfish part of me
glows with your fire divine.

God is able to provide you with every blessing in abundance, so that by always having enough of everything, you may share abundantly in every good work. 2 Corinthians 9:8

Lord, grant that we impelled by love 643
in smallest things may faithful prove;
till we depart, our lives be true,
devoted wholly unto you.

Provider God, you have gifted us with blessings of faith, love, hope, and goodness. Help us to put these blessings to work in service to those most in need of your grace. In the name of Jesus. Amen.

Ash Wednesday — Joel 2:1-2,12-17; Psalm 51:1-17
2 Corinthians 5:20b-6:10; Matthew 6:1-6,16-21

Wednesday, February 26 — Psalm 31:1–5
Exodus 4:1–5:9; Matthew 19:13–22

O that my ways may be steadfast in keeping your statutes! Psalm 119:5

Unto such as keep God's cov'nant 458
and are steadfast in his way,
unto those who still remember
the commandments and obey.

As the time approached for him to be taken up to heaven, Jesus resolutely set out for Jerusalem. Luke 9:51 NIV

When Jesus wept, the falling tear 335
in mercy flowed beyond all bound;
when Jesus groaned, a trembling fear
seized all the guilty world around.

Holy Redeemer, your strength and determination is the face of your sacrifice: a lesson and encouragement to us all. Help us to follow your example, living lives of compassion, hope, love, and devotion to you and our brothers and sisters. In your name, we pray. Amen.

Thursday, February 27 — Psalm 31:6–9
Exodus 5:10–6:12; Matthew 19:23–30

My salvation and my honor depend on God. Psalm 62:7 NIV

Am I of my salvation 795
assured through thy great love?
May I on each occasion
to thee more faithful prove.
Hast thou my sins forgiven?
Then, leaving things behind,
may I press on to heaven
and bear the prize in mind.

Blessed are you when people insult you, persecute you and falsely say all kinds of evil against you because of me. Matthew 5:11 NIV

Blessed are the brave and peaceful, 595
bringing peace where'er they live,
God shall own them as his children
and through them his peace will give.
All for love and truth who suffer,
in your God rejoice and sing;
he, the end of all your striving,
he, your Father, Lord, and King.

Lord, only you can save us. Help us to more closely follow Jesus' example so that we may live our lives according to your will. When we face hatred or discrimination, grant us the strength to stand firm in our faith, trusting in you. In Jesus' name, we pray. Amen.

Friday, February 28 — Psalm 31:10–20
Exodus 6:13–7:24; Matthew 20:1–16

My God, my God, why have you forsaken me? Why are you so far from helping me, from the words of my groaning? Psalm 22:1

Lord, we cry to you for help. 760*
Only you can heal our pain.
Out of deep distress we call.
Help us, Lord; send peace again.

While Peter was kept in prison, the church prayed fervently to God for him. Acts 12:5

When we seem in vain to pray 352
and our hope seems far away,
in the darkness be our stay:
hear us, holy Jesus.

Hear us, holy Jesus—we are so often afraid. We feel so often alone. May your spirit give us the words to cry out to you, and may we find comfort, knowing you are near. We pray in your name. Amen.

Saturday, February 29 — Psalm 31:21–24
Exodus 8; Matthew 20:17–28

I will save you that you may become a blessing. Zechariah 8:13 NASB

Be present with your servants, Lord; 734
we look to you with one accord;
refresh and strengthen us anew,
and bless what in your name we do.

I am grateful to Christ Jesus our Lord, who has strengthened me, because he judged me faithful and appointed me to his service, even though I was formerly a blasphemer, a persecutor, and a man of violence. But I received mercy. 1 Timothy 1:12-13

Through many dangers, toils, and snares, 783
I have already come;
'tis grace has brought me safe thus far,
and grace will lead me home.

Forgiving God, thank you for the blessings you have bestowed upon us. Your mercy and forgiveness saved us, and we are eternally grateful. May our service to you be worthy of your love. In Jesus' name, we pray. Amen.

First Sunday in Lent

March 1, 1457:
Beginning of the Unity of the Brethren in Bohemia

Watchword for the Week — Be glad in the Lord and rejoice, O righteous, and shout for joy, all you upright in heart. Psalm 32:11

Sunday, March 1 — Genesis 2:15-17;3:1-7; Psalm 32
Romans 5:12-19; Matthew 4:1-11

Lord, I thank you that you have answered me and have become my salvation. Psalm 118:21

God is my strong salvation, 769
no enemy I fear;
he hears my supplication,
dispelling all my care;
if he, my head and master,
defend me from above,
what pain or what disaster
can part me from his love?

Jesus said to the woman, "Daughter, your faith has made you well; go in peace, and be healed of your disease." Mark 5:34

O be our mighty healer still, 736*
O Lord of life and death;
restore and strengthen, soothe and bless,
with your almighty breath:
on hands that work and eyes that see,
your healing wisdom pour,
that whole and sick, and weak and strong,
may praise you evermore.

God of salvation, may your goodness to us and others in the past remind us to have faith in you today. Fill us with your assurance that you will guide us, strengthen us, and hear our prayers. In Jesus' name, we pray. Amen.

Monday, March 2 — Psalm 32
Exodus 9; Matthew 20:29–21:11

Judgment will again be righteous, and all the upright in heart will follow it. Psalm 94:15 NASB

Grant by guidance from above 586
that obedience, faith, and love
show our hearts to you are giv'n,
that our treasure is in heav'n.

Jesus said, "In the same way, let your light shine before others, so that they may see your good works and give glory to your Father in heaven." Matthew 5:16

Heart with loving heart united, 401*
met to know God's holy will.
Let his love in us ignited
more and more our spirits fill.
He the head, we are his members;
we reflect the light he is.
He the master, we disciples,
he is ours and we are his.

O great Light of the world, come shine in our lives and reignite our hearts. Make us beacons of faith, love, and hope for all who find themselves surrounded by darkness. Amen.

Tuesday, March 3 — Psalm 33:1–5
Exodus 10; Matthew 21:12–22

O Lord, do not rebuke me in your anger, or discipline me in your wrath. Psalm 6:1

He pardons all our sins, 546
prolongs our feeble breath;
he heals all our infirmities
and ransoms us from death.

God has destined us not for wrath but for obtaining salvation through our Lord Jesus Christ. 1 Thessalonians 5:9

They who Jesus' mercy know 416
are from wrath and envy freed;
love unto our neighbor shows
that we are his flock indeed;
thus we may in all our ways
show forth our Redeemer's praise.

Gracious Redeemer, we humbly thank you for the gift of your mercy. May your forgiveness of our sins rid us from all shame, guilt, and fear so that we may live freely in your name. Amen.

Wednesday, March 4 — Psalm 33:6–11
Exodus 11:1–12:20; Matthew 21:23–32

You who fear the Lord, trust in the Lord!
Psalm 115:11

Frail children of dust, and feeble as frail, 566
in you do we trust, nor find you to fail;
your mercies how tender, how firm to the end,
our maker, defender, redeemer, and friend.

I pray that the eyes of your heart may be enlightened in order that you may know the hope to which he has called you, the riches of his glorious inheritance in his holy people.
Ephesians 1:18 NIV

My faith looks trustingly 705
to Christ of Calvary,
my Savior true!
Lord, hear me while I pray,
take all my guilt away,
strengthen in ev'ry way
my love for you!

Abiding Lord, often when we pray, we look for you outside of ourselves. Today, help us to look inward to see just how much you have shaped our hearts. May we trust in your continuing love and guidance. Amen.

Thursday, March 5 — Psalm 33:12–22
Exodus 12:21–51; Matthew 21:33–46

Therefore keep the commandments of the Lord your God, by walking in his ways and by fearing him. Deuteronomy 8:6

Thus may we, as your anointed, 716
walk with you in truth and grace
in the path you have appointed,
till we reach your dwelling-place.

But as for you, continue in what you have learned and firmly believed, knowing from whom you learned it. 2 Timothy 3:14

O teach me, Lord, that I may teach 646
the precious truths which you impart.
And wing my words that they may reach
the hidden depths of many a heart.

Divine Teacher, help us to make our ways like your ways. Give us strength to continue following you and enrich us with your wisdom from on high. In Jesus' name, we pray. Amen.

Friday, March 6 — Psalm 34:1–7
Exodus 13:1–14:18; Matthew 22:1–14

Then the eyes of the blind shall be opened, and the ears of the deaf unstopped. Isaiah 35:5

Your hands, O Lord, in days of old 736*
were strong to heal and save;
they triumphed over pain and death,
fought darkness and the grave.
To you they went, the blind, the mute,
the palsied and the lame,
the leper set apart and shunned,
the sick and those in shame.

The poor have the gospel preached to them. Matthew 11:5 NKJV

I heard the voice of Jesus say, 606
"Come unto me and rest;
lay down, O weary one, lay down
your head upon my breast."
I came to Jesus as I was,
so weary, worn and sad,
I found in him a resting-place,
and he has made me glad.

Wonderful Savior, you came into the world to be with those who needed you. May we follow your calling to be with those who need you today, and as we follow, remind us how we need you too. In your holy name, we pray. Amen.

Saturday, March 7 — Psalm 34:8–18
Exodus 14:19–15:21; Matthew 22:15–22

Speak the truth to one another, render in your gates judgments that are true and make for peace. Zechariah 8:16

Thanks we give and adoration 559
for your gospel's joyful sound.
May the fruits of your salvation
in our hearts and lives abound.
Ever faithful, ever faithful
to your truth may we be found.

Love does not rejoice in wrongdoing, but rejoices in the truth. 1 Corinthians 13:6

Let us each for others care, 672
each another's burden bear,
to your church a pattern give,
showing how believers live.

Holy God, your truth prevails in all things. Grant us the courage to seek your truth in our relationships, our homes, our churches, our communities, our world, and our lives. Amen.

Second Sunday in Lent

Watchword for the Week — For God so loved the world that he gave his only Son, so that everyone who believes in him may not perish but may have eternal life. John 3:16

Sunday, March 8 — Genesis 12:1-4a; Psalm 121
Romans 4:1-5,13-17; John 3:1-17

You shall not hate in your heart anyone of your kin; you shall reprove your neighbor, or you will incur guilt yourself. Leviticus 19:17

Grant, Lord, that with thy direction, 673
"Love each other," we comply,
aiming with unfeigned affection
thy love to exemplify;
let our mutual love be glowing;
thus the world will plainly see
that we, as on one stem growing,
living branches are in thee.

Love your enemies and pray for those who persecute you, so that you may be children of your Father in heaven. Matthew 5:44-45

'Tis a pleasant thing to see 670
brothers in the Lord agree,
sisters of a God of love
live as they shall live above,
acting each a Christian part,
one in word and one in heart.

Gracious God, you remind us that we are loved, and we are forever grateful. You also remind us that your love is not just for one, but for all. Send us to share your love today. Amen.

Monday, March 9 — Psalm 34:19–22
Exodus 15:22–16:36; Matthew 22:23–40

Your sins have deprived you of good. Jeremiah 5:25

Amazing grace, how can it be 77s*
that God to us is true,
that we are precious in God's sight,
despite the things we do?
Creator, former, shaper, making real
what we have known,
that God's love is dependable,
and names us as God's own.

For I do not do the good I want, but the evil I do not want is what I do. Romans 7:19

Savior, now with contrite hearts 741
we approach your throne of love,
asking pardon for our sins,
peace and comfort from above.
You once suffered on the cross
to atone for sinners' guilt;
may we never, Lord, forget
that for us your blood was spilled.

Merciful Lord, forgive us our sins, we pray. Because of your redeeming power and grace, may we go forth renewed to live for you without guilt or shame. In Jesus' name, we pray. Amen.

Tuesday, March 10 — Psalm 35:1–10
Exodus 17:1–18:6; Matthew 22:41–23:12

The Lord is the stronghold of my life; of whom shall I be afraid? Psalm 27:1

God is our refuge, strength, and home, 20s*
our help and peace today.
Though pow'rs may fail and sorrows come,
God's light will show the way.

God did not give us a spirit of cowardice, but rather a spirit of power and of love and of self-discipline. 2 Timothy 1:7

God of grace and God of glory, 751**
on your people pour your power;
crown your ancient Church's story;
bring its bud to glorious flower.
Grant us wisdom, grant us courage
for the facing of this hour,
for the facing of this hour.

Almighty God, in a world of uncertanties, you are the source of our hope. Strengthen us to stand for what is right and encourage us to face any challenges that today may bring. Amen.

* By Willie Israel (2010). © 2013 by IBOC and MMF.

** Used by permission of Elinor Fosdick Downs.

Wednesday, March 11 — Psalm 35:11–18
Exodus 18:7–19:9; Matthew 23:13–22

All his works are truth, and his ways are justice; and he is able to bring low those who walk in pride. Daniel 4:37

Still your children wander homeless; 688*
still the hungry cry for bread;
still the captives long for freedom;
still in grief we mourn our dead.
As you, Lord, in deep compassion
healed the sick and freed the soul,
by your Spirit send your power
to our world to make it whole.

Jesus said, "Take my yoke upon you, and learn from me; for I am gentle and humble in heart, and you will find rest for your souls." Matthew 11:29

Take my hands, Lord Jesus, 578**
let them work for you,
make them strong and gentle, kind in all I do;
let me watch you, Jesus, till I'm gentle too,
till my hands are kind hands, quick to work for you.

God of justice, your love and peace overcomes hatred and violence. As your children made in your image, soften our hearts so that we may be kind and gentle with each other. In Jesus' name, we pray. Amen.

Thursday, March 12 — Psalm 35:19–28
Exodus 19:10–20:21; Matthew 23:23–32

Lord, plead my cause and redeem me; revive me according to your word. Psalm 119:154 NKJV

Renew us, as of old; 674*
restore the joy of youth,
so soon we'll spread your great, good news,
your ancient, timeless truth.

So Philip ran up to it and heard an Ethiopian reading the prophet Isaiah. He asked, "Do you understand what you are reading?" He replied, "How can I, unless someone guides me?" And he invited Philip to get in and sit beside him. Acts 8:30-31

Into the world Christ Jesus sends us 74s**
to make disciples wherever we go:
teaching his truth, seeking commitment,
welcoming strangers and watching them grow.
Warming cold hearts with the flames of God's love—
this is the challenge of our mission.

Savior of the world, we are grateful that you bring us close to teach, comfort, and revive us. May we trust that you will abide in us as you send us out to share your love. In Jesus' name, we pray. Amen.

Friday, March 13 — Psalm 36
Exodus 20:22–21:27; Matthew 23:33–39

You shall not revile the deaf or put a stumbling-block before the blind; you shall fear your God. Leviticus 19:14

Father, in gratitude for homes and loved ones, 671*
we open now our hearts to humankind.
Grant us your spirit—love for one another—
so in your peace may we our concord find.

Bear one another's burdens, and in this way you will fulfill the law of Christ. Galatians 6:2

We bear another's burdens, Lord, 93s**
forgiving and forgiv'n.
You clothe us in your perfect love,
as pure as harmony above.
In the name of Jesus live:
our love to others give.

Savior and loving friend, help us to live in community with our sisters and brothers. Inspire us to be good neighbors and may we love them just as you have loved us. Amen.

Saturday, March 14 — Psalm 37:1–6
Exodus 21:28–22:24; Matthew 24:1–25

With you is the fountain of life; in your light we see light. Psalm 36:9

Plenteous grace with thee is found, 724
grace to cover all my sin;
let the healing streams abound;
make and keep me pure within.
Thou of life the fountain art,
freely let me take of thee;
spring thou up within my heart,
rise to all eternity.

Whoever has the Son has life. 1 John 5:12

You only are true life— 486*
to know you is to live
the more abundant life
that earth can never give.
O risen Lord! we live in you:
in us each day your life renew!

Gracious Lord, you are the source of all life and blessings. Just as you did in the beginning of creation, breathe new life into us today. Restore us and help us to recognize the abundance you provide. In Jesus' name, we pray. Amen.

Third Sunday in Lent

Watchword for the Week — O come, let us worship and bow down, let us kneel before the Lord, our Maker! Psalm 95:6

Sunday, March 15 — Exodus 17:1-7; Psalm 95
Romans 5:1-11; John 4:5-42

God said to Solomon, "Because you have not asked for yourself long life or riches, or for the life of your enemies, but have asked for yourself understanding to discern what is right, I now do according to your word." 1 Kings 3:11-12

Grant us your truth, your freedom give, 464
that hearts for you might solely live
till all your living altars claim
one holy light, one heav'nly flame!

Strive first for the kingdom of God and his righteousness, and all these things will be given to you as well. Matthew 6:33

Seek ye first the kingdom of God 605
and his righteousness,
and all these things shall be added unto you—
Allelu, alleluia!

God of righteousness, forgive us when we conform to the ways of this world instead of following your commands. Give us wisdom and courage that we may live according to your kingdom. Amen.

Monday, March 16 — Psalm 37:7–15
Exodus 22:25–23:26; Matthew 24:26–35

I cry to God Most High, to God who fulfills his purpose for me. Psalm 57:2

Sing praise to God, who reigns above, p15
the God of all creation,
the God of power, the God of love,
the God of our salvation;
with healing balm my soul he fills,
and ev'ry faithless murmur stills.
To God all praise and glory!

The one who endures to the end will be saved. Mark 13:13

O Jesus, you have promised 603
to all who follow you
that where you are in glory
your servants shall be too.
And Jesus, I have promised
to serve you to the end;
O give me grace to follow,
my master and my friend.

Omnipresent Lord, we give you thanks for your listening ear. When we grow tired running the race set before us, bless us with your presence to rejuvenate us to live a life of love and service. Amen.

Tuesday, March 17 — Psalm 37:16–22
Exodus 23:27–25:9; Matthew 24:36–44

By the ordinances of the Lord is your servant warned. Psalm 19:11

O God, in whom our trust we place, 509
we thank you for your word of grace;
help us its precepts to obey
till we shall live in endless day.

Train yourself in godliness. 1 Timothy 4:7

In the crowds that came to Jesus, p130*
teaching up and down the land,
there were some who scorned and mocked him,
some who did not understand.
But the ones who listened humbly
learned to trust him and obey,
learned to love and be forgiving,
and believe in Jesus' way.

God of wisdom, we long to be trustworthy and obedient disciples. May we never outgrow your guidance or become complacent with our knowledge of you. Instill in us a desire to seek your wisdom for all our days. Amen.

Wednesday, March 18 — Psalm 37:23–26
Exodus 25:10–40; Matthew 24:45–51

All look to you to give them their food in due season; when you give to them, they gather it up; when you open your hand, they are filled with good things. Psalm 104:27-28

This food is good for my heart and my body. 71s*
This food is so good for ev'ryone, a party!
Come eat! Come be fit!
Complete! So be it!
Come eat! Come be fit!
Complete! So be it!
This food.

You have tasted that the Lord is good. 1 Peter 2:3

God sent out the invitation 70s**
to the banquet, to the feast.
God calls us to search the byways,
gathering both great and least.
For God's bounty knows no limits.
At God's table all are fed.
Eat the bread, his body broken;
drink the wine, the blood he shed.

Holy Provider, today we are grateful for your provisions, your love for the hungry and your sacramental holy meal. Thank you for continuing to bless us with your grace. Amen.

* By David Melby-Gibbons (2012). © 2013 IBOC and MMF.

** © 2011 by June Edwards.

Thursday, March 19 — Psalm 37:27–33
Exodus 26; Matthew 25:1–13

The Lord turned toward Israel, because of his covenant with Abraham, Isaac, and Jacob, and would not destroy them; nor has he banished them from his presence until now. 2 Kings 13:23

O gracious God, whose love upholds 66s*
your people ev'rywhere,
infuse us now with eagerness
your selfless way to share.

The gifts and the calling of God are irrevocable. Romans 11:29

Christian workers, give your talents 75s**
to the holy plan.
Feed the hungry, house the homeless,
lend a helping hand.
Heal the sick, console the weak;
act through love, God's message speak.
Christian workers, be committed
to God's ministry.

Lord Almighty, you made a covenant to be our God. May your steadfast faithfulness toward us inspire us to love and care for others just as you do for us. Amen.

Friday, March 20 — Psalm 37:34–40
Exodus 27:1–28:14; Matthew 25:14–30

The Lord will hide me in his shelter in the day of trouble; he will conceal me under the cover of his tent. Psalm 27:5

When foes without and fears within 17s*
and cares upon us weigh,
God, who our strength and shield has been,
will help us still today.

Therefore I am content with weaknesses, insults, hardships, persecutions, and calamities for the sake of Christ; for whenever I am weak, then I am strong. 2 Corinthians 12:10

Lead on, O King eternal; 753
we follow, not with fears,
for gladness breaks like morning
where'er your face appears:
your cross is lifted o'er us;
we journey in its light;
the crown awaits the conquest;
lead on, O God of might!

Lamb of God, protect us through our hardships, steady us in the midst of our anxieties, and remind us that we need not fear, for you have already conquered for us. Amen.

* By Carl Helmich, Jr. (2012). © 2013 by IBOC and MMF.

Saturday, March 21 — Psalm 38:1–8
Exodus 28:15–43; Matthew 25:31–46

The Lord said, "I will grant peace in the land, and you shall lie down, and no one shall make you afraid." Leviticus 26:6

O may this gracious God 533
through all our life be near us,
with ever joyful hearts
and blessed peace to cheer us,
and keep us in his grace,
and guide us when perplexed,
and free us from all ills
in this world and the next.

And the peace of God, which surpasses all understanding, will guard your hearts and your minds in Christ Jesus. Philippians 4:7

O the pure delight of a single hour 607
that before thy throne I spend,
when I kneel in prayer and with thee, my God,
I commune as friend with friend.

Prince of peace, fill our hearts and souls with your heavenly peace. May it lead to comfort, healing, and reconciliation as your peace permeates our lives, our relationships, and our communities. Amen.

Fourth Sunday in Lent

Watchword for the Week — Surely goodness and mercy shall follow me all the days of my life, and I shall dwell in the house of the Lord my whole life long. Psalm 23:6

Sunday, March 22 — 1 Samuel 16:1-13; Psalm 23
Ephesians 5:8-14; John 9:1-41

There is a God in heaven who reveals mysteries. Daniel 2:28

Great God of all wisdom, of science and art, p128*
O grant us the wisdom that comes from the heart.
Technology, learning, philosophy, youth—
all leave us still yearning for your word of truth.

In Christ are hidden all the treasures of wisdom and knowledge. Colossians 2:3

O come, O wisdom from on high, 274
and order all things far and nigh;
to us the path of knowledge show,
and teach us in her ways to go.

God of the universe, there is far more of you that has yet to be seen by us. Increase our faith so that the unknown does not frighten us but instead causes us to marvel at your grandeur. Amen.

Monday, March 23 — Psalm 38:9–16
Exodus 29:1–30; Matthew 26:1–13

You are the Lord, you alone; you have made heaven, the heaven of heavens, with all their host, the earth and all that is on it, the seas and all that is in them. Nehemiah 9:6

God is love, let heav'n adore him; 463
God is love, let earth rejoice;
let creation sing before him
and exalt him with one voice.
God who laid the earth's foundation,
God who spread the heav'ns above,
God who breathes through all creation:
God is love, eternal love.

God has not left himself without testimony: He has shown kindness by giving you rain from heaven and crops in their seasons; he provides you with plenty of food and fills your hearts with joy. Acts 14:17 NIV

In the wild and in the city, 84s*
ev'ry living thing we find
demonstrates God's grace and power
to the hearts of humankind.
When we care for all the planet
then we truly do God's will.
When we seek to heal and nurture,
then our destiny's fulfilled.

Loving Creator, we give you thanks for your bountiful creation which you continue to form today. May the intricacies of the world remind us how much you care for it and all its creatures. Amen.

Tuesday, March 24 — Psalm 38:17–22
Exodus 29:31–30:16; Matthew 26:14–30

The Lord is just in all his ways, and kind in all his doings. Psalm 145:17

Whatever God ordains is right; 718*
his will is just and holy.
He holds us in his perfect might;
in him, our lives are godly.
He is our God and all we need,
the Father who preserves us still;
to him we bend each heart and will.

We have not ceased praying for you and asking that you may be filled with the knowledge of God's will in all spiritual wisdom and understanding. Colossians 1:9

Spirit of the living God, fall afresh on me. p96**
Spirit of the living God, fall afresh on me.
Melt me, mold me, fill me, use me:
spirit of the living God, fall afresh on me.

Holy Spirit, we have faith that you are at work in the world, yet sometimes we have trouble recognizing that. Fill us with wisdom and insight so that we might see your movements around us. Amen.

Wednesday, March 25 — Psalm 39:1–6
Exodus 30:17–31:11; Matthew 26:31–35

You turn things upside down! Shall the potter be regarded as the clay? Shall the thing made say of its maker, 'He did not make me'; or the thing formed say of the one who formed it, 'He has no understanding'? Isaiah 29:16

O wind of God, come bend us, break us, p47
till humbly we confess our need;
then in your tenderness remake us,
revive, restore, for this we plead.

All of you must clothe yourselves with humility. 1 Peter 5:5

O Jesus, my Lord, 608
forever adored,
my portion, my all,
at your holy feet humbly pleading I fall.

Humble Master, there is nothing we can do to earn salvation. Therefore, take away our pride and false securities so that we may humbly trust in your guidance and care. Shape us into who you would have us be. Amen.

Thursday, March 26 — Psalm 39:7–13
Exodus 31:12–32:29; Matthew 26:36–46

I confess my iniquity; I am sorry for my sin. Psalm 38:18

Forgive our sins, our souls repair 17s*
by your redeeming grace;
by faith we'll walk and work and share
until we see your face.

Godly grief produces a repentance that leads to salvation and brings no regret. 2 Corinthians 7:10

Just as I am, and waiting not 762
to rid my soul of one dark blot,
to thee, whose blood can cleanse each spot,
O Lamb of God, I come, I come!

Merciful God, forgive us, we pray. As far as the east is from the west, remove our sins from us. Cleanse our hearts and free us from the weight of guilt and regret. Amen.

Friday, March 27 — Psalm 40:1–8
Exodus 32:30–33:23; Matthew 26:47–58

The heart is devious above all else; it is perverse—who can understand it? I the Lord test the mind and search the heart, to give to all according to their ways. Jeremiah 17:9-10

Breathe on me, breath of God, 494
until my heart is pure,
until with you I will one will
to do or to endure.

By this we will know that we are from the truth and will reassure our hearts before him whenever our hearts condemn us; for God is greater than our hearts, and he knows everything. 1 John 3:19-20

Fling wide the portals of your heart; p51
make it a temple set apart
from earthly use for heaven's employ,
adorned with prayer and love and joy.

Forgiving God, we confess that at times, we rely more on our own abilities than your grace. May we open our hearts to you again so that we may follow where your Spirit leads. Amen.

Saturday, March 28 — Psalm 40:9–17
Exodus 34; Matthew 26:59–75

The Lord takes pleasure in those who fear him, in those who hope in his steadfast love. Psalm 147:11

Praise to the Lord, 530
who will prosper your work and defend you;
surely his goodness and mercy shall daily attend you.
Ponder anew
what the almighty can do
if with his love he befriend you.

Jesus said, "Whoever does the will of God is my brother and sister and mother." Mark 3:35

By love's closest bonds united, 515
as the Lord's own family,
be to serve his name excited,
be to him a fruitful tree.

Blessed Jesus, your love for us runs so deep that you call us children, sisters, brothers, and friends. May we be known by others as members of your family through the ways we follow your will. Amen.

Fifth Sunday in Lent

Watchword for the Week — I wait for the Lord, my soul waits, and in his word I hope. Psalm 130:5

Sunday, March 29 — Ezekiel 37:1-14; Psalm 130
Romans 8:6-11; John 11:1-45

When my spirit grows faint within me, it is you who watch over my way. Psalm 142:3 NIV

O God, our help in ages past, 461
our hope for years to come,
our shelter from the stormy blast,
and our eternal home!

Blessed be the God and Father of our Lord Jesus Christ, the Father of mercies and the God of all consolation, who consoles us in all our affliction. 2 Corinthians 1:3-4

As you once calmed a storm on the sea, 88s*
and you spoke words of "Peace! Let it be!"
In my raging and doubt,
fears within and without,
as you once calmed that storm, calm me.

Gracious and almighty God, as we weather the storms of life, may we look to you as our shelter and source of strength. Bless and comfort all who may be experiencing difficult times. We pray in the name of Jesus. Amen.

* By David M. Henkelmann (1981).

Monday, March 30 — Psalm 41
Exodus 35; Matthew 27:1–10

When people fall, do they not get up again? If they go astray, do they not turn back? Jeremiah 8:4

Come, you weary, heavy laden, 765
lost and ruined by the fall;
if you tarry till you're better,
you will never come at all.

Jesus said, "Anyone who comes to me I will never drive away." John 6:37

Jesus, your arms are open 54s*
to children filled with grace,
who trust you without question,
who know your warm embrace.
We look to their example,
their simple faith, so true;
Jesus, your arms are open
for us to live in you.

Gracious Savior, in the times when we go astray, fall short, or lack faith, you are there. In the times when we are heart-broken, grieving, or discouraged, you are there. Thank you for always welcoming us with open arms. Amen.

* By John D. Rights (2000). © 2000 by Mary White Rights.

Tuesday, March 31 — Psalm 42
Exodus 36; Matthew 27:11–31

Those who are far off shall come and help to build the temple of the Lord. Zechariah 6:15

Not in a temple made with hands 512
God the Almighty is dwelling;
high in the heav'ns his temple stands,
all earthly temples excelling.
Yet he who dwells in heav'n above
chooses to live with us in love,
making our bodies his temple.

In Jesus Christ you also are built together spiritually into a dwelling place for God. Ephesians 2:22

We are God's house of living stones, 512
built for his own habitation;
he fills our hearts, his humble thrones,
granting us life and salvation.
Yet to this place, an earthly frame,
we come with thanks to praise his name;
God grants his people true blessing.

Abiding God, we give you thanks for filling us with your spirit. Enable us to see the holy in others and inspire us to encourage and build up one another. Amen.

Wednesday, April 1 — Psalm 43
Exodus 37; Matthew 27:32–44

I will delight in my people; no more shall the sound of weeping be heard in [Jerusalem], or the cry of distress. Isaiah 65:19

Be still, my soul: the hour is hast'ning on 757
when we shall be forever with the Lord,
when disappointment, grief, and fear are gone,
sorrow forgot, love's purest joys restored.
Be still, my soul: when change and tears are past,
all safe and blessed we shall meet at last.

Jesus said to the disciples, "So you have pain now; but I will see you again, and your hearts will rejoice, and no one will take your joy from you." John 16:22

Praise the Lord, God our salvation, 298
praise him who retrieved our loss;
sing, with awe and love's sensation,
hallelujah, God with us.

Comforting and restoring God, in the pain of our mortality we pray to keep our eyes fixed on your divinity. Let us be joyful for the coming reconciliation and let us share that joy with all. Amen.

Thursday, April 2 — Psalm 44:1–8
Exodus 38; Matthew 27:45–56

O God, from my youth you have taught me, and I still proclaim your wondrous deeds. Psalm 71:17

Lord of our growing years, 800*
with us from infancy,
laughter and quick-dried tears,
freshness and energy:
your grace surrounds us all our days—
for all your gifts we bring our praise.

Simeon took the child Jesus in his arms and praised God, saying, "Master, now you are dismissing your servant in peace, according to your word; for my eyes have seen your salvation." Luke 2:28-30

Lord of our closing years, 800*
always your promise stands;
hold us when death appears
safely within your hands:
your grace surrounds us all our days—
for all your gifts we bring our praise.

Creator God, you form us, know us, and carry us through this life. Help us to trust you at every stage and to praise you always. Amen.

Friday, April 3 — Psalm 44:9–16
Exodus 39:1–31; Matthew 27:57–66

Blessed are the people who know the joyful sound! They walk, O Lord, in the light of your countenance. Psalm 89:15 NKJV

Lord of all life, below, above, 464
whose light is truth, whose warmth is love,
before your ever-blazing throne
we ask no luster of our own.

Live as children of light—for the fruit of the light is found in all that is good and right and true. Ephesians 5:8-9

Love, and joy, and peace, and patience, 496*
kindness, caring, self-control;
these the fruits for which we hunger
as your gifts for all unfold.

Lord of light, illuminate our lives. Draw us out of our dark and lonely places into community that reflects your light for the world. Amen.

Saturday, April 4 — Psalm 44:17–26
Exodus 39:32–40:23; Matthew 28:1–20

Why should the nations say, "Where is their God?" Our God is in the heavens; he does whatever he pleases. Psalm 115:2-3

Praise to the Lord, who o'er all things 530
is wondrously reigning,
shelt'ring you under his wings,
O, so gently sustaining.
Have you not seen
all you have needed has been
met by his gracious ordaining.

Ever since the creation of the world God's eternal power and divine nature, invisible though they are, have been understood and seen through the things he has made. Romans 1:20

The purple-headed mountain, 467
the river running by,
the sunset, and the morning
that brightens up the sky.

All-present and all-powerful God, keep our eyes open, that we may see you everywhere; and keep us grateful for all we see. Amen.

Palm Sunday

Watchword for the Week — And being found in human form, Jesus humbled himself and became obedient to the point of death—even death on a cross. Philippians 2:7,8

Sunday, April 5 — Isaiah 50:4-9a; Psalm 31:9-16
Philippians 2:5-11; Matthew 21:1-11

Bless God in the great congregation. Psalm 68:26

The company of angels 342
is praising you on high;
and we with all creation
in chorus make reply.
The people of the Hebrews
with palms before you went;
our praise and prayer and anthems
before you we present.

The great crowd that had come to the festival heard that Jesus was coming to Jerusalem. So they took branches of palm trees and went out to meet him, shouting, "Hosanna! Blessed is the one who comes in the name of the Lord—the King of Israel!" John 12:12-13

Ride on! Ride on in majesty! 343
Hear all the tribes hosanna cry;
O Savior meek, your road pursue,
with palms and scattered garments strewed.

Lord Jesus, the time comes again for us to journey with you to the cross. As we move this week from triumph to unimaginable loss, let us hold in our hearts the end of the story: hope beyond all expectation. Through your name, we pray. Amen.

Monday, April 6 — Psalm 45:1–9
Exodus 40:24–Leviticus 1:17; Mark 1:1–8

Though I write the multitude of my instructions, they are regarded as a strange thing. Hosea 8:12

Isaiah the prophet has written of old 682*
how God's earthly kingdom shall come.
Instead of the thorn tree the fir tree shall grow;
the wolf shall lie down with the lamb.
The mountains and hills shall break forth into song,
the peoples be led forth in peace;
for the earth shall be filled with the knowledge of God
as the waters cover the seas.

Jesus said, "For this I was born, and for this I came into the world, to testify to the truth. Everyone who belongs to the truth listens to my voice." John 18:37

You are the truth; your word alone 661
true wisdom can impart;
you only can inform the mind
and purify the heart.

Lord Jesus, the sound of your truth cuts through the noise of this world. Especially during this Holy Week, tune our ears to hear it and teach our tongues to speak it. Amen.

Tuesday, April 7 — Psalm 45:10–17
Leviticus 2,3; Mark 1:9–20

The king of Israel, the Lord, is in your midst; you shall fear disaster no more. Zephaniah 3:15

See the Lord, your keeper, 729
stand omnipotently near.
Now he holds you by the hand,
and banishes your fear;
shadows with his wings your head,
guards from all impending harms;
round you and beneath are spread
the everlasting arms.

Jesus said to the disciples, "Why are you afraid? Have you still no faith?" Mark 4:40

Lord Jesus, think on me, 764
by anxious thoughts oppressed;
let me your loving servant be
and taste your promised rest.

Help us, Lord, for we are so often afraid. Take away the fear that robs us of our best selves and robs you of our service. Make us brave to live for you. Amen.

Wednesday, April 8 — Psalm 46
Leviticus 4; Mark 1:21–34

Restore to me the joy of your salvation, and sustain in me a willing spirit. Psalm 51:12

Create in me a clean heart, O God, p79
and renew a right spirit within me;
cast me not away from your presence,
and take not your Holy Spirit from me.
Restore unto me the joy of salvation;
anoint me with your spirit free.
Create in me a clean heart, O God,
and renew a right spirit within me.

You will grieve, but your grief will turn to joy. John 16:20 NIV

People in sorrow are yearning to sing, 266*
come, come, come Jesus Christ;
people in misery want bells to ring,
come, Lord Jesus Christ.
These days of adventure when all people wait
are days for the advent of joy.

Great Encourager, we pray that all who are sad or discouraged will find you especially close today. Make each of us an encourager, and let us all walk together into your joy. In Jesus' name, we pray. Amen.

Maundy Thursday

Watchword for Maundy Thursday — He has gained renown by his wonderful deeds; the Lord is gracious and merciful. Psalm 111:4

Thursday, April 9 — Psalm 47
Leviticus 5:1–6:13; Mark 1:35–45

Come, let us go to entreat the favor of the Lord, and to seek the Lord of hosts; I myself am going. Zechariah 8:21

Gracious God, I come before thee; 12r
come thou also down to me;
where we find thee and adore thee,
there a heaven on earth must be.
To my heart, O enter thou;
Let it be thy temple now.

When they had sung the hymn, they went out to the Mount of Olives. Mark 14:26

It's midnight; and on Olive's brow 119r
the star is dimmed that lately shone;
It's midnight; in the garden now
the suffering Savior prays alone.

For the privilege of walking through this Holy Week with you, we thank you, Lord Jesus. As we approach this time of darkness, keep us by your side in Gethsemane—awake and praying in your name. Amen.

Good Friday

Watchword for Good Friday — For God so loved the world that he gave his only Son, so that everyone who believes in him may not perish but may have eternal life. John 3:16

Friday, April 10 — Psalm 48
Leviticus 6:14–7:21; Mark 2:1–12

Happy are those who fear the Lord, who greatly delight in his commandments. Psalm 112:1

Upon your precepts and your ways 510
my heart will meditate with awe;
your word shall be my chief delight,
and I will not forget your law.

By his wounds you have been healed. For you were going astray like sheep, but now you have returned to the shepherd and guardian of your souls. 1 Peter 2:24-25

To avert from us God's wrath, 416
Jesus suffered in our stead;
by an ignominious death
he a full atonement made;
and by his most precious blood
brought us, sinners, nigh to God.

Jesus, call us in from the many paths onto which we have strayed, and gather us around your cross. Seeing your wounds, may we never look away from the wounds of the world. Amen.

Saturday, April 11 — Psalm 49:1–12
Leviticus 7:22–8:17; Mark 2:13–28

Although our sins testify against us, do something, Lord, for the sake of your name. Jeremiah 14:7 NIV

Father, in your mysterious presence kneeling, 446r
fain would our souls feel all your kindling love;
for we are weak and need some deep revealing
of trust and strength and calmness from above.

Christ himself bore our sins in his body on the cross, so that, free from sins, we might live for righteousness. 1 Peter 2:24

Bane and blessing, pain and pleasure, p76
by the cross are sanctified;
peace is there that knows no measure,
joys that through all time abide.

Lord, when in desperation we cry, "Do something," restore us with the truth of what you have already done. May we spend this day of Sabbath vigil remembering, and may we be grateful. Amen.

Easter

Watchword for the Week — So if you have been raised with Christ, seek the things that are above, where Christ is, seated at the right hand of God. Colossians 3:1

Sunday, April 12 — Acts 10:34-43; Psalm 118:1-2,14-24 Colossians 3:1-4; John 20:1-18

For darkness shall cover the earth, and thick darkness the peoples; but the Lord will arise upon you, and his glory will appear over you. Isaiah 60:2

Holy, holy, holy! 381
Though the darkness hides thee,
though the eye made blind by sin
thy glory may not see,
only thee art holy; there is none beside thee,
perfect in pow'r, in love, and purity.

Very early on the first day of the week, when the sun had risen, Mary Magdalene, and Mary the mother of James and Salome, went to the tomb. They had been saying to one another, "Who will roll away the stone for us from the entrance to the tomb?" When they looked up, they saw that the stone had already been rolled back. Mark 16:2-4

Vain the stone, the watch, the seal; alleluia! 359
Christ has burst the gates of hell! Alleluia!
Death in vain forbids his rise; alleluia!
Christ has opened paradise. Alleluia!

Oh, holy and risen Lord, the stone is rolled away and the light breaks upon us. May we bear the brightness and may we live as people rescued from the grave! Amen and amen!

Monday, April 13 — Psalm 49:13–20
Leviticus 8:18–9:11; Mark 3:1–12

Jacob went on his way and the angels of God met him. Genesis 32:1

Blessed be the day when I must roam 794
far from my country, friends, and home,
an exile, poor and mean;
my fathers' God will be my guide,
will angel guards for me provide,
my soul, my soul in danger screen.

The angel said to the women, "Go quickly and tell his disciples, 'He has been raised from the dead, and indeed he is going ahead of you to Galilee; there you will see him.'" Matthew 28:5,7

Go spread the news, he's not in the grave. 357*
He has arisen, the world to save.
Jesus' redeeming labors are done.
Even the battle with sin is won.

Risen Savior, we go forth to wherever you call us. Meet us there and give us the words to speak in your name. Amen.

Tuesday, April 14 — Psalm 50:1–6
Leviticus 9:12–10:20; Mark 3:13–19

My righteousness is near, my salvation has gone forth, and my arms will judge the peoples. Isaiah 51:5 NASB

"Comfort, comfort now my people; 264
tell of peace!" So says our God.
Comfort those who sit in darkness
bowed beneath oppression's load.
To God's people now proclaim
that God's pardon waits for them!
Tell them that their war is over;
God will reign in peace forever!

Blessed be the God and Father of our Lord Jesus Christ! By his great mercy he has given us a new birth into a living hope through the resurrection of Jesus Christ from the dead. 1 Peter 1:3

So let us keep the festival 367
to which the Lord invites us;
Christ is himself the joy of all,
the sun that warms and lights us.
Now his grace to us imparts
eternal sunshine to our hearts;
the night of sin is ended.
Alleluia!

God and father of our Lord Jesus Christ, we thank you for the hope of resurrection. We pray to bear that hope into a hurting world. In the name of Jesus, we pray. Amen.

Wednesday, April 15 — Psalm 50:7–15
Leviticus 11:1–28; Mark 3:20–35

The Lord your God has been with you; you have lacked nothing. Deuteronomy 2:7

Show'rs of blessing, show'rs of blessing 636
from the Lord proceed,
strength supplying, strength supplying
in the time of need;
for no servant of our King
ever lacked for anything.
He will never, he will never
break the bruised reed.

As servants of God we have commended ourselves in every way: through great endurance, in afflictions, hardships, calamities; as sorrowful, yet always rejoicing; as poor, yet making many rich; as having nothing, and yet possessing everything. 2 Corinthians 6:4,10

Only be still and wait his pleasure 712
in cheerful hope with heart content.
He fills your needs to fullest measure
with what discerning love has sent;
doubt not our inmost wants are known
to him who chose us for his own.

We are often tired and discouraged, Lord. Like the saints before us, may we be strengthened and supplied by the beloved community. In your name, we pray. Amen.

Thursday, April 16 — Psalm 50:16–23
Leviticus 11:29–13:8; Mark 4:1–20

Woe to those who are wise in their own eyes and clever in their own sight. Isaiah 5:21 NIV

Let us never claim your blessings 496*
come as trophies we deserve;
make the goal of all our striving
not to glory, but to serve.

We have received not the spirit of the world, but the Spirit that is from God, so that we may understand the gifts bestowed on us by God. 1 Corinthians 2:12

Gifts may differ, as may service, 496*
yet we follow one true Lord,
manifested in your presence,
for the common good outpoured.

Holy Spirit, open our eyes and our minds to see ourselves as God sees us: beautiful and beloved, equipped with God's gifts for service in God's kingdom. Amen.

Friday, April 17 — Psalm 51:1–6
Leviticus 13:9–46; Mark 4:21–29

Be my strong refuge, to which I may resort continually; you have given the commandment to save me. Psalm 71:3 NKJV

In heav'nly love abiding, 732
no change my heart shall fear;
and safe is such confiding,
for nothing changes here.
The storm may roar around me,
my heart may low be laid,
but God is round about me,
and can I be dismayed?

The Lord will rescue me from every evil attack and save me for his heavenly kingdom. 2 Timothy 4:18

In your arms I rest me; 722
foes who would molest me
cannot reach me here.
Though the earth be shaking,
ev'ry heart be quaking,
Jesus calms my fear.
Sin and hell in conflict fell
with their bitter storms assail me.
Jesus will not fail me.

Lord, we pray today for all who are in peril, who live with violence, and those who work for good among people bent on harm. Protect them and make us their protectors, too. Amen.

Saturday, April 18 — Psalm 51:7–12
Leviticus 13:47–14:18; Mark 4:30–41

Even the stork in the heavens knows its times; and the turtle-dove, swallow, and crane observe the time of their coming; but my people do not know the ordinance of the Lord. Jeremiah 8:7

I need thee ev'ry hour; 740
teach me thy will,
and thy rich promises
in me fulfill.

Jesus Christ gave himself for us that he might redeem us from all iniquity and purify for himself a people of his own who are zealous for good deeds. Titus 2:14

He conquered death and the grave, 639*
and our foe is defeated;
now ev'rywhere must the story of hope be repeated;
so he sends you—
daily his conquest renew:
live in the strength of his Spirit!

Lord Jesus, remind us that the commandments are pure and simple: Love God, love neighbor. Inflame us with zeal to show that love in action. Amen.

Second Sunday of Easter

Watchword for the Week — Blessed be the God and Father of our Lord Jesus Christ! By his great mercy he has given us a new birth into a living hope through the resurrection of Jesus Christ from the dead. 1 Peter 1:3

Sunday, April 19 — Acts 2:14a,22-32; Psalm 16
1 Peter 1:3-9; John 20:19-31

He guarded his people as the apple of his eye. Deuteronomy 32:10

I love your church, O God! 513
Her walls before you stand,
dear as the apple of your eye,
and graven on your hand.

Do not be afraid, little flock, for it is your Father's good pleasure to give you the kingdom. Luke 12:32

Whoe'er would spend their days 593
in lasting pleasure
must come to Christ and join his flock with speed;
here is a feast prepared, rich beyond measure,
the world meanwhile on empty husks must feed.
Those souls may share in ev'ry good
whose Shepherd does possess the treasuries of God.

Lord, keeper of mysteries, shepherd of souls, why do we mean so much to you? Let us spend this day pondering how much you love us and striving to love others in response. Amen.

Monday, April 20 — Psalm 51:13–19
Leviticus 14:19–57; Mark 5:1–20

The Lord said, "I have chosen Abraham, that he may charge his children and his household after him to keep the way of the Lord by doing righteousness and justice." Genesis 18:19

Let justice roll on like the rivers of time, 56s*
and righteousness flow in continuous stream,
that we in God's wisdom and love may abide
and live in community, not selfish pride.

Now you have been set free from sin and are the slaves of God. Your gain is a life fully dedicated to him, and the result is eternal life. Romans 6:22 GNT

My heart is weak and poor 604
until it master find;
it has no spring of action sure,
it varies with the wind.
It cannot freely move
till you have wrought its chain;
enslave it with your matchless love,
and deathless it shall reign.

Help us to better understand what it means to be chosen by you, God. May we live accordingly: doing justice, loving kindness, and walking humbly with you. In Jesus' name, we pray. Amen.

* By E. Artis W. Weber (2002).

Tuesday, April 21 — Psalm 52
Leviticus 15:1–24; Mark 5:21–43

Daniel was taken up out of the den, and no kind of harm was found on him, because he had trusted in his God. Daniel 6:23

If you but trust in God to guide you 712
and place your confidence in him,
you'll find him always there beside you
to give you hope and strength within;
for those who trust God's changeless love
build on the rock that will not move.

Keep alert, stand firm in your faith, be courageous, be strong. 1 Corinthians 16:13

Jesus, my Redeemer, lives! p215
I, too, unto life must waken;
he will have me where he is.
Shall my courage then be shaken?
Shall I fear? Or could the Head
rise and leave his members dead?

Alert, firm in faith, courageous, strong: all these things we pray to be, today and always, through you, risen Savior. In the face of all hardship, all grief, all fear, keep us strong for your service. Amen.

Wednesday, April 22 — Psalm 53
Leviticus 15:25–16:25; Mark 6:1–6

"I pledged myself to you and entered into a covenant with you," says the Lord God, "and you became mine." Ezekiel 16:8

He by his name has sworn, 468
on this we shall depend,
and as on eagles' wings upborne
to heav'n ascend.
There we shall see his face,
his pow'r we shall adore
and sing the wonders of his grace
forevermore.

In Christ Jesus you are all children of God through faith. Galatians 3:26

O dear Jesus, you have called us 420*
with your gentle voice;
as your children we receive you
and rejoice.

Great God, as we remember our covenant with you, let us covenant with one another to love and serve you. Bless your followers wherever they gather today in fellowship and faith. Amen.

Thursday, April 23 — Psalm 54
Leviticus 16:26–18:5; Mark 6:7–13

I formed you, you are my servant; O Israel, you will not be forgotten by me. Isaiah 44:21

Make me your abode, 608
a temple of God,
a vessel of grace,
prepared for your service and formed to your praise.

Do not, therefore, abandon that confidence of yours; it brings a great reward. Hebrews 10:35

Be still, my soul: your God will undertake 757
to guide the future, as in ages past.
Your hope, your confidence, let nothing shake;
all now mysterious shall be bright at last.
Be still, my soul: the waves and winds still know
the Christ who ruled them while he dwelt below.

Great Creator, you formed us for your service, and you will not abandon us. We pray never to abandon our confidence in you. Guide us forward to your future. We pray in the name of Jesus. Amen.

Friday, April 24 — Psalm 55:1–8
Leviticus 18:6–19:11; Mark 6:14–29

Lord, remember and do not break your covenant with us. Jeremiah 14:21

Remember, Lord, though frail we be, 339*
in your own image were we made;
help us, lest in anxiety,
we cause your name to be betrayed.

God is faithful; by him you were called into the fellowship of his Son, Jesus Christ our Lord. 1 Corinthians 1:9

Ye who called, ye who called 636
to Christ's service are,
join together, join together
both in work and prayer;
venture all on him, our Lord,
who assures us in his word,
we are always, we are always
objects of his care.

Faithful God, keep us true to the covenant you have made with us, and to the Christian fellowship into which you have called us. May we show our faithfulness each day in love and service. In the name of Jesus. Amen.

Saturday, April 25 — Psalm 55:9–15
Leviticus 19:12–20:8; Mark 6:30–44

The Lord will again rejoice over you for good as He rejoiced over your fathers. Deuteronomy 30:9 NKJV

Lord, you have been our dwelling place p147
in ev'ry generation.
Your people still have known your grace
and your blessed consolation.
Through ev'ry age you heard our cry,
through ev'ry age we found you nigh,
our strength and our salvation.

Jesus said, "If you keep my commandments, you will abide in my love, just as I have kept my Father's commandments and abide in his love. I have said these things to you so that my joy may be in you, and that your joy may be complete." John 15:10-11

Jesus is my joy, 594
therefore blessed am I;
O his mercy is unbounded,
all my hope on him is grounded;
Jesus is my joy,
therefore blessed am I.

Creator God, rejoice over us. Redeemer God, may your joy be in us. Blessing God, complete our joy, through Jesus Christ our Lord. Amen.

Third Sunday of Easter

Watchword for the Week — You have been born anew, not of perishable but of imperishable seed, through the living and enduring word of God. 1 Peter 1:23

Sunday, April 26 — Acts 2:14a,36-41; Psalm 116:1-4,12-19
1 Peter 1:17-23; Luke 24:13-35

I called to the Lord out of my distress, and he answered me. Jonah 2:2

When foes without and fears within 17s*
and cares upon us weigh,
God, who our strength and shield has been,
will help us still today.

Then one of the leaders of the synagogue named Jairus came and, when he saw him, fell at his feet and begged him repeatedly, "My little daughter is at the point of death. Come and lay your hands on her, so that she may be made well, and live." So he went with him. Mark 5:22-24

Yea, though I walk in death's dark vale, 720
yet will I fear no ill;
for thou art with me, and thy rod
and staff me comfort still;
for thou art with me, and thy rod
and staff me comfort still.

Heavenly Father, you are a comforting presence. Let us feel you ever beside us, going with us into situations that cause us pain and fear. In darkness, let us find your light; in death, let us find your life. Amen.

* By Carl Helmich, Jr. (2010).

Monday, April 27 — Psalm 55:16–19
Leviticus 20:9–21:12; Mark 6:45–56

The man and his wife hid themselves from the presence of the Lord God. Genesis 3:8

O Lord of all the living, 763*
both banished and restored,
compassionate, forgiving
and ever caring Lord,
grant now that my transgressing,
my faithlessness may cease.
Stretch out your hand in blessing,
in pardon and in peace.

You did not receive the spirit of bondage again to fear, but you received the Spirit of adoption by whom we cry out, "Abba, Father." Romans 8:15 NKJV

And now at length discerning 763*
the evil that I do,
behold me, Lord, returning
with hope and trust to you.
In haste you come to meet me
and home rejoicing bring,
in gladness there to greet me
with calf and robe and ring.

Abba, Father, help us to lay down our pride. Help us to repent our errors. Help us to acknowledge our dependence on you. Forgive us and welcome us home. Amen.

Tuesday, April 28 — Psalm 55:20–23
Leviticus 21:13–22:16; Mark 7:1–8

Now set your mind and heart to seek the Lord your God. 1 Chronicles 22:19

I search for you, Lord, 90s*
in the washing and churning of ocean's tide.
I look for your presence
in all of the brightness of morning's sky.
I wander in fields of clover and flowers
that smell so sweet.
I feel the brown earth and soft grass under my feet.
Lord, I know you're not far away.
God, I reach for you each day.
You are my life, you are my way.

Run in such a way that you may win the prize. 1 Corinthians 9:24

Then with delight may I employ 638
all that your bounteous grace has giv'n,
and run my earthly course with joy,
and closely walk with you to heav'n.

Dear God, it is delightful to seek you in all that is beautiful. It is delightful to serve you by using the gifts you have given us. It is delightful to be alive with you, here and in the life to come. Thank you! In Jesus' name, we pray. Amen.

* By Rick Sides and Jim Newsom, Jr. (1974). © 2013 IBOC and MMF.

Wednesday, April 29 — Psalm 56:1–8
Leviticus 22:17–23:22; Mark 7:9–23

Whatever your hand finds to do, do with your might. Ecclesiastes 9:10

The task your wisdom has assigned 638
here let me cheerfully fulfill,
in all my work your presence find
and prove your good and perfect will.

Do not lag in zeal, be ardent in spirit, serve the Lord. Romans 12:11

Kindle within us and preserve that fire, 377
which will with holy love our hearts inspire,
and with an active zeal our soul inflame
to do your will and glorify your name.

We stretch out our hands, Lord Jesus, seeking the work that will serve and please you. Place that work within our reach and inspire and strengthen us in our labor. In your name, we pray. Amen.

Thursday, April 30 — Psalm 56:9–13
Leviticus 23:23–24:9; Mark 7:24–37

Surely God is good to Israel, to those who are pure in heart. Psalm 73:1 NIV

Lord, we your presence seek; 584
we ask this blessing true:
give us a pure and lowly heart,
a temple fit for you.

Beloved, if our hearts do not condemn us, we have boldness before God; and we receive from him whatever we ask, because we obey his commandments and do what pleases him. 1 John 3:21-22

Approach, my soul, the mercy-seat, 447r
where Jesus answers prayer;
there humbly fall before his feet,
for none can perish there.

God, surely you are good to us, for you know our weakness and our disobedience, and love us anyway. May your love make us bold to approach you in prayer. May we be grateful for how you respond. Amen.

Friday, May 1 — Psalm 57:1–6
Leviticus 24:10–25:17; Mark 8:1–13

Is the Lord's arm too short? Numbers 11:23 NIV

I fully am persuaded 769
and joyfully declare
I'm never left unaided,
my Father hears my prayer;
his comforts never fail me,
he stands at my right hand;
when tempests fierce assail me,
they're calm at his command.

Consider the lilies of the field, how they grow; they neither toil nor spin, yet I tell you, even Solomon in all his glory was not clothed like one of these. Therefore do not worry, saying, 'What will we eat?' or 'What will we drink?' or 'What will we wear?' Matthew 6:28-29,31

Ask and it shall be given unto you, 605
seek and you shall find,
knock and the door shall be opened unto you—
Allelu, alleluia!

Great Provider, forgive us when our worries and our desires get the best of us and we lose sight of your generosity. We are truly grateful for all that you bless us with. Amen.

Saturday, May 2 — Psalm 57:7–11
Leviticus 25:18–55; Mark 8:14–21

Do not cast me away from your presence, and do not take your holy spirit from me. Psalm 51:11

Sometimes I feel discouraged, 500
and think my work's in vain,
but then the Holy Spirit
revives my soul again.

We always thank God, the Father of our Lord Jesus Christ. He has rescued us from the power of darkness and transferred us into the kingdom of his beloved Son. Colossians 1:3,13

For the darkness shall turn to dawning, 621
and the dawning to noonday bright;
and Christ's great kingdom shall come on earth,
the kingdom of love and light.

Holy One, be with us as we experience the trials and tribulations of life. Remain steadfast and help us to see that you are our light in darkness. Amen.

Fourth Sunday of Easter

Watchword for the Week — Jesus says, "I am the gate. Whoever enters by me will be saved, and will come in and go out and find pasture." John 10:9

Sunday, May 3 — Acts 2:42-47; Psalm 23
1 Peter 2:19-25; John 10:1-10

Abner called to Joab, "Is the sword to keep devouring forever? Do you not know that the end will be bitter?" 2 Samuel 2:26

O God of ev'ry nation, 683*
of ev'ry race and land,
redeem your whole creation
with your almighty hand;
where hate and fear divide us,
and bitter threats are hurled,
in love and mercy guide us,
and heal our strife-torn world.

God has called us to live in peace. 1 Corinthians 7:15 NIV

Sing alleluia, Christ does live, 364
and peace on earth restore;
come, ransomed souls, and glory give,
sing, worship and adore:
to him our heartfelt thanks we pay
in deep humility.
It's God alone whose saving way
has set believers free.

Giver of all good, help us to walk in your path as peacemakers. Fill our relationships with love, mercy, and forgiveness. Grant us patience and help us be slow to anger when disagreements arise. Amen.

Monday, May 4 — Psalm 58
Leviticus 26:1–35; Mark 8:22–38

Those he gathered from the east and from the west, from the north and from the south: Let them thank the Lord for his steadfast love, for his wonderful works to humankind. Psalm 107:3,8

Now thank we all our God 533
with heart and hands and voices,
who wondrous things has done,
in whom his world rejoices;
who, from our mother's arms,
has blessed us on our way
with countless gifts of love,
and still is ours today.

And the slave said, 'Sir, what you ordered has been done, and there is still room.' Then the master said to the slave, 'Go out into the roads and lanes, and compel people to come in, so that my house may be filled.' Luke 14:22-23

Jesus calls us; o'er the tumult 600
of our life's wild, restless sea,
day by day his voice is sounding,
saying, "Christian, follow me."

Heavenly Father, we thank you for your unconditional love and grace. Inspire us to share your word with those around us through our actions and provide us the words when needed. In your holy name, we pray. Amen.

Tuesday, May 5 — Psalm 59:1–9
Leviticus 26:36–27:15; Mark 9:1–10

God stretches out the heavens and treads on the waves of the sea. He is the Maker of the Bear and Orion, the Pleiades and the constellations of the south. Job 9:8-9 NIV

This is my Father's world, 456
and to my list'ning ears
all nature sings and round me rings
the music of the spheres.
This is my Father's world;
I rest me in the thought
of rocks and trees, of skies and seas—
his hand the wonders wrought.

Christ is the image of the invisible God, the firstborn of all creation; for in him all things in heaven and on earth were created, things visible and invisible. Colossians 1:15-16

For the beauty of the earth, 538
for the glory of the skies,
for the love which from our birth
over and around us lies,
Lord of all, to you we raise
this our hymn of grateful praise.

God, creator of heaven and earth, thank you for the beautiful architecture of your creation. We know you are in every twinkling star and technicolor sunset; the calming rhythm of the ocean waves and grandeur of the mountain peaks. Amen.

Wednesday, May 6 — Psalm 59:10–17
Leviticus 27:16–Numbers 1:16; Mark 9:11–29

I will turn the darkness before them into light, the rough places into level ground. Isaiah 42:16

While life's dark maze I tread, 705
and griefs around me spread,
O, be my guide;
make darkness turn to day,
wipe sorrow's tears away,
nor let me ever stray
from you aside.

By the tender mercy of our God, the dawn from on high will break upon us, to give light to those who sit in darkness and in the shadow of death, to guide our feet into the way of peace. Luke 1:78-79

Dark and cheerless is the morn 475
unaccompanied by you;
joyless is the day's return
till your mercy's beams I view;
till they inward light impart,
glad my eyes and warm my heart.

Merciful Lord, be the lamp unto our feet and the light in the dark spaces of our lives. Your unending love is a comfort in times of trial. Amen.

Thursday, May 7 — Psalm 60
Numbers 1:17–54; Mark 9:30–37

You are a God ready to forgive, gracious and merciful, slow to anger and abounding in steadfast love. Nehemiah 9:17

Come, Almighty to deliver, 474
let us all your life receive;
suddenly return, and never,
never more your temple leave.
You we would be always blessing,
serve you as your hosts above,
pray, and praise you without ceasing,
glory in your perfect love.

If we are faithless, he remains faithful—for he cannot deny himself. 2 Timothy 2:13

O God, my faithful God, 615
O fountain ever flowing,
without whom nothing is,
all perfect gifts bestowing,
grant me a faithful life,
and give me, Lord, within,
commitment free from strife,
a soul unhurt by sin.

Compassionate Lord, thank you for your mercy and love when we stray from your word. Help us to remain faithful to your path even when straying seems easier and more satisfying in the moment. Amen.

Friday, May 8 — Psalm 61
Numbers 2; Mark 9:38–50

Lord, let your mercy come to me, that I may live. Psalm 119:77

Sincerely I have sought you, Lord, 510
O let me not from you depart;
to know your will and keep from sin,
your word I cherish in my heart.

Simon's mother-in-law was in bed with a fever, and they told Jesus about her at once. He came and took her by the hand and lifted her up. Then the fever left her. Mark 1:30-31

Manifest in making whole 313
palsied limbs and fainting soul;
manifest in valiant fight,
quelling all the devil's might;
manifest in gracious will,
ever bringing good from ill;
anthems be to you addressed,
God in flesh made manifest.

Savior God, offer your loving touch in times of illness and pain. Be with those whose mind, body, or spirit suffer, and give strength to caretakers of the weak and vulnerable. Amen.

Saturday, May 9 — Psalm 62
Numbers 3:1–32; Mark 10:1–12

The Lord your God has blessed you in all your undertakings. Deuteronomy 2:7

May we faithful, may we faithful 636
in our service be,
truly careful, truly careful
in our ministry;
keep us to your church fast bound,
in the faith preserve us sound,
often weeping, often weeping
grateful tears of joy.

It is required of stewards that they be found trustworthy. 1 Corinthians 4:2

We give you but your own 657
in any gifts we bring;
all that we have is yours alone,
a trust from you, our King.

Loving Jesus, empower us to be trustworthy stewards of your church. We pray for all who answer your call to serve as lay leaders and ordained clergy. Bless them with patience, courage, and understanding. Amen.

Fifth Sunday of Easter

Watchword for the Week — Jesus says, "I am the way, and the truth, and the life. No one comes to the Father except through me." John 14:6

Sunday, May 10 — Acts 7:55-60; Psalm 31:1-5,15-16
1 Peter 2:2-10; John 14:1-14

Do as the occasion demands; for God is with you. 1 Samuel 10:7 NKJV

Am I of my salvation 795
assured through thy great love?
May I on each occasion
to thee more faithful prove.
Hast thou my sins forgiven?
Then, leaving things behind,
may I press on to heaven
and bear the prize in mind.

The Lord will give you understanding in all things. 2 Timothy 2:7

If dangers gather round, 615
still keep me calm and fearless;
help me to bear the cross
when life is bleak and cheerless,
to overcome my foes
with words and actions kind;
O God, your will disclose,
your counsel let me find.

Life-giving Spirit, help us to act in accordance to your will. Let us live with confidence and assurance that you have carefully set our path. Amen.

Monday, May 11 — Psalm 63
Numbers 3:33–4:14; Mark 10:13–31

We have heard with our ears, O God, our ancestors have told us, what deeds you performed in their days, in the days of old. Psalm 44:1

Come now, O Lord, and as in days of old 742
to us your Spirit gracefully unfold;
pour forth your love and all-abounding grace
till we in spirit see you face to face.

Mary sat at the Lord's feet and listened to what he was saying. Luke 10:39

O let me hear you speaking 603
in accents clear and still,
above the storms of passion,
the murmurs of self-will.
O speak to reassure me,
to hasten or control;
and speak to make me listen,
O guardian of my soul.

Great Teacher, grant us the patience to hear you amidst the noise in our all-too-busy lives. Give us an understanding to apply your message to our words and actions. Amen.

Tuesday, May 12 — Psalm 64
Numbers 4:15–49; Mark 10:32–45

The Lord said to Solomon, "Ask for whatever you want me to give you." Solomon answered, "So give your servant a discerning heart to govern your people and to distinguish between right and wrong." 1 Kings 3:5,9 NIV

Teach us to use our lives 801*
with purpose and with power
for visions of a better world
and for decision's hour;
to choose the way of life,
reject the way of death,
until the radiant force of God
fills mind and strength and breath.

This is my prayer, that your love may overflow more and more with knowledge and full insight to help you to determine what is best. Philippians 1:9-10

The task your wisdom has assigned 638
here let me cheerfully fulfill,
in all my work your presence find
and prove your good and perfect will.

Triune God, we pray for the leaders in our community, our country, and the world. Grant all who lead a discerning heart, love for their brothers and sisters, and wisdom in all decisions they make. Amen.

Wednesday, May 13 — Psalm 65:1–8
Numbers 5; Mark 10:46–52

Only you know what is in every human heart. 1 Kings 8:39

Take full possession of my heart; 721
to me your lowly mind impart;
break nature's bonds, and let me see,
he whom you free indeed is free.

Now may our Lord Jesus Christ himself and God our Father, who loved us and through grace gave us eternal comfort and good hope, comfort your hearts and strengthen them in every good work and word. 2 Thessalonians 2:16-17

O could we but love that Savior, 589
who loves us so ardently,
as we ought, our souls would ever
full of joy and comfort be;
if we, by his love incited,
could ourselves and all forget,
then, with Jesus Christ united,
we should heav'n anticipate.

Holy One, you know our human hearts. Thank you for loving us unconditionally and for giving us grace, mercy, and eternal life. May we respond today and each day with faithfulness, hope, and love. Amen.

Thursday, May 14 — Psalm 65:9–13
Numbers 6; Mark 11:1–11

Can you deceive God, as one person deceives another? Job 13:9

My Father, I have wandered 763*
and hidden from your face;
in foolishness have squandered
your legacy of grace.
But now, in exile dwelling,
I rise with fear and shame,
as distant but compelling,
I hear you call my name.

Examine yourselves to see whether you are living in the faith. Test yourselves. Do you not realize that Jesus Christ is in you? 2 Corinthians 13:5

But examine first your case, 416
whether you be in the faith;
do you long for pard'ning grace?
Is your only hope his death?
Then, how e'er your soul's oppressed,
come, you are a worthy guest.

Omnipotent God, give us the strength to see inside ourselves and to acknowledge when we fall short of your expectations. Forgive us of our shortcomings and failures—empower us to be worthy of your love. Amen.

Friday, May 15 — Psalm 66:1–7
Numbers 7:1–35; Mark 11:12–26

The Lord heard our voice and saw our affliction, our toil, and our oppression. Deuteronomy 26:7

Take us under your protection, 716
grant us to obey your voice,
simply follow your direction,
to your will resign our choice.

Will not God grant justice to his chosen ones who cry to him day and night? Will he delay long in helping them? Luke 18:7

Light of light, we humbly pray, 276*
shine upon your world today;
break the gloom of our dark night,
fill our souls with love and light,
give your blessed word rebirth,
"Peace, good will to all on earth."

Gracious Lord, hear those who cry in the night. Be with your people who suffer at the hands of others. Bring justice and mercy to your world. In your name, we pray. Amen.

Saturday, May 16 — Psalm 66:8–15
Numbers 7:36–71; Mark 11:27–12:12

The heavens will vanish like smoke, the earth will wear out like a garment, and those who live on it will die like gnats; but my salvation will be forever. Isaiah 51:6

God is my strong salvation, 769
no enemy I fear;
he hears my supplication,
dispelling all my care;
if he, my head and master,
defend me from above,
what pain or what disaster
can part me from his love?

Jesus said, "Heaven and earth will pass away, but my words will not pass away." Luke 21:33

Swift to its close ebbs out life's little day; 807
earth's joys grow dim, its glories pass away.
Change and decay in all around I see.
O Lord who changes not, abide with me.

Great Provider, so much of our days are spent trying to receive material things that lack permanence. May we have the courage to refocus our lives on receiving the gift of everlasting life that you grant us. Amen.

Sixth Sunday of Easter

Watchword for the Week — Make a joyful noise to God, all the earth; sing the glory of his name; give to him glorious praise. Psalm 66:1,2

Sunday, May 17 — Acts 17:22-31; Psalm 66:8-20
1 Peter 3:13-22; John 14:15-21

May the Lord our God incline our hearts to him, to walk in all his ways. 1 Kings 8:58

Lead me, guide me, along the way, 728*
for if you lead me, I cannot stray.
Lord, let me walk each day with you,
lead me my whole life through.

As you therefore have received Christ Jesus the Lord, continue to live your lives in him, rooted and built up in him and established in the faith, just as you were taught, abounding in thanksgiving. Colossians 2:6-7

As we are taught of Jesus 434**
we celebrate the faith
built up by those before us
and passed through us today.
Thus our lives are established
in time and history.
We know who we are called to be:
The church, empow'red in ministry
to serve all people lovingly.
Alleluia!

Christ Jesus, thank you for your presence in our lives. Continue to lead and guide us to live a life rooted in faith, love, and hope. In your name, we pray. Amen.

Monday, May 18 — Psalm 66:16–20
Numbers 7:72–8:4; Mark 12:13–17

Lord, you gave your good spirit to instruct our ancestors. Nehemiah 9:20

Long ago apostles heard it 600
by the Galilean lake,
turned from home and work and fam'ly,
leaving all for his dear sake.

Jesus said, "The Advocate, the Holy Spirit, whom the Father will send in my name, will teach you everything, and remind you of all that I have said to you." John 14:26

Holy Spirit, mighty God, 497*
move our will, despite our sin,
into new deeds of truth, not lies;
teach us love, peace; make us wise.

Giver of all good, thank you for those saints who walked in faith before us, who have taught us about your love, and prayed for us. In your name, we pray. Amen.

Tuesday, May 19 — Psalm 67
Numbers 8:5–9:14; Mark 12:18–34

Turn back from your evil ways; for why will you die? Ezekiel 33:11

Lord, forgive me, day by day, 779
debts I cannot hope to pay,
duties I have left undone,
evils I have failed to shun.

Zacchaeus stood there and said to the Lord, "Look, half of my possessions, Lord, I will give to the poor; and if I have defrauded anyone of anything, I will pay back four times as much." Luke 19:8

Take my wealth, all I possess, 647
make me rich in faithfulness.
Take my mind that I may use
ev'ry pow'r as you should choose.

Lord, giver of life, let us reflect today on the pure unbridled joy that our relationship with you brings us when we truly commit our lives to your will. Amen.

Wednesday, May 20 — Psalm 68:1–6
Numbers 9:15–10:36; Mark 12:35–44

The righteous know the rights of the poor. Proverbs 29:7

You have promised to receive us, 731
poor and sinful though we be;
you have mercy to relieve us,
grace to cleanse and pow'r to free.
Blessed Jesus, blessed Jesus,
early let us turn to you.
Blessed Jesus, blessed Jesus,
early let us turn to you.

God is not unjust; he will not overlook your work and the love that you showed for his sake in serving the saints, as you still do. Hebrews 6:10

God's word alive and active 503*
is offered free to all,
in ev'ry tribe and nation
so all will hear God's call
to feed the hungry children,
give drink to those who thirst,
and serve the human fam'ly
by putting God's will first.

Compassionate Lord, there is great need in your world. Be with the poor, the homeless, the orphaned, and the forgotten in our midst. Ease their burden and give them hope. Amen.

Ascension Day

Watchword for the Ascension — Christ said, "I, when I am lifted up from the earth, will draw all people to myself." John 12:32

Ascension of the Lord — Acts 1:1-11; Psalm 47
Ephesians 1:15-23; Luke 24:44-53

Thursday, May 21 — Psalm 68:7–18
Numbers 11; Mark 13:1–13

You who love the Lord, hate evil! Psalm 97:10 NKJV

Seek the Lord, whose willing presence 780*
moves your heart to make appeal.
Turn from wickedness and evil;
God will pardon, cleanse, and heal.

But speaking the truth in love, we must grow up in every way into him who is the head, into Christ. Ephesians 4:15

May we all so love each other 401**
and all selfish claims deny,
so that each one for the other
will not hesitate to die.
Even so our Lord has loved us;
for our lives he gave his life.
Still he grieves and still he suffers,
for our selfishness and strife.

Great Teacher, we know that our faith as Christians is a journey. Help us to grow closer to you each day through practices of prayer, worship, and acts of love for one another and you. In your name, we pray. Amen.

Friday, May 22 — Psalm 68:19–27
Numbers 12:1–13:16; Mark 13:14–27

Is Ephraim my dear son? Is he the child I delight in? As often as I speak against him, I still remember him. Therefore I am deeply moved for him; I will surely have mercy on him, says the Lord. Jeremiah 31:20

Father, now your sinful child 779
through your love is reconciled.
By your pard'ning grace I live;
daily still I cry, forgive.

But while the son was still far off, his father saw him and was filled with compassion; he ran and put his arms around him and kissed him. Luke 15:20

As a parent's love is endless, 534*
so God's mercy follows us;
for the Lord who framed our being
well recalls that we are dust!

Holy One, thank you for embracing us as parents embrace their children. We are truly grateful for your unconditional love and mercy. In your name, we pray. Amen.

Saturday, May 23 — Psalm 68:28–35
Numbers 13:17–33; Mark 13:28–37

Moses said, "See, I am setting before you today a blessing and a curse: the blessing, if you obey the commandments of the Lord your God that I am commanding you today; and the curse, if you do not obey the commandments of the Lord your God." Deuteronomy 11:26-28

Unto such as keep God's cov'nant 458
and are steadfast in his way,
unto those who still remember
the commandments and obey.

Serve the Lord Christ. For the wrongdoer will be paid back for whatever wrong has been done, and there is no partiality. Colossians 3:24-25

While we, deeply humbled, 746
own we're oft to blame,
this remains our comfort,
you are still the same.
In you all the needy
have a friend most dear,
whose love and forbearance
unexampled are.

Risen Lord, help us to strip away the many things in our lives that distract us from being truly faithful, so we can find peace in simply loving and serving you. Amen.

Ascension Sunday
Seventh Sunday of Easter

Watchword for the Week — Cast all your anxiety on him, because he cares for you. 1 Peter 5:7

Sunday, May 24 — Acts 1:6-14; Psalm 68:1-10,32-35
1 Peter 4:12-14;5:6-11; John 17:1-11

There is forgiveness with you, so that you may be revered. Psalm 130:4

Lord, make us servants of our peace: 693*
where there is hate, may we sow love;
where there is hurt, may we forgive;
where there is strife, may we make one.

Just as the Lord has forgiven you, so you also must forgive. Colossians 3:13

Lord, cleanse the depths within our souls, 777**
and bid resentment cease;
then, bound to all in bonds of love,
our lives will spread your peace,
our lives will spread your peace.

Gracious God, your greatest commandment to love one another is often the hardest to follow. Give us strength to follow your example and forgive those who have hurt us. Amen.

Monday, May 25 — Psalm 69:1–12
Numbers 14; Mark 14:1–11

In the morning, O Lord, you will hear my voice; in the morning I will order my prayer to you and eagerly watch. Psalm 5:3 NASB

Joyful, joyful, we adore you, 544
God of glory, Lord of love;
hearts unfold like flow'rs before you,
op'ning to the sun above.
Melt the clouds of sin and sadness;
drive the dark of doubt away;
giver of immortal gladness,
fill us with the light of day!

Pray in the Spirit at all times in every prayer and supplication. To that end keep alert and always persevere in supplication for all the saints. Ephesians 6:18

Prayer is the Christian's vital breath, 749
the Christian's native air,
his watchword at the gates of death;
he enters heaven with prayer.

Dear Jesus, you are the focus of our lives. May all of our thoughts, words, and deeds, today and everyday, be an act of prayer to you. In your name, we pray. Amen.

Tuesday, May 26 — Psalm 69:13–21
Numbers 15:1–31; Mark 14:12–31

The Lord looks down from heaven on humankind to see if there are any who are wise, who seek after God. Psalm 14:2

O, send your Spirit, Lord, 502
now unto me,
that he may touch my eyes
and make me see.
Show me the truth concealed
within your Word,
and in your book revealed
I see my Lord.

Do not be conformed to this world, but be transformed by the renewing of your minds, so that you may discern what is the will of God—what is good and acceptable and perfect. Romans 12:2

Spirit of Love, transform our ways, 491*
fill with new feeling all of our days;
replace our hatred, our anger, our fear
with new compassion, new struggle to care.

Heavenly Lord, it is all too easy to choose our own path instead of following you. Grant us the wisdom to see past the temptations of this world in order to walk more closely with you. Amen.

Wednesday, May 27 — Psalm 69:22–29
Numbers 15:32–16:27; Mark 14:32–42

The Lord will fulfill his purpose for me. Psalm 138:8

Take my motives and my will, 647
all your purpose to fulfill.
Take my heart–it is your own;
it shall be your royal throne.

I am confident of this, that the one who began a good work among you will bring it to completion by the day of Jesus Christ. Philippians 1:6

Good news! Our Christ has come! 630*
His mission is proclaimed.
He wants for all a life
that's free of want and pain.
God's Spirit calls for us to work,
for us to serve 'til love prevails.

Compassionate Lord, help us to identify our gifts and to answer your call to service. Let our hands, our voices, and our hearts do good works in your honor. Amen.

Thursday, May 28 — Psalm 69:30–36
Numbers 16:28–17:13; Mark 14:43–52

Turn to me and be gracious to me, for I am lonely and afflicted. Psalm 25:16

For food in a world where many walk in hunger, 829
for friends in a world where many walk alone,
for faith in a world where many walk in fear,
we give you thanks, O God.

The sick man answered Jesus, "Sir, I have no one to put me into the pool when the water is stirred up; and while I am making my way, someone else steps down ahead of me." Jesus said to him, "Stand up, take your mat and walk." John 5:7-8

Renew us all, O Lord; 674*
renew us, heart and soul.
Now heal our anger, hurt and pain;
now make the wounded whole.

Loving God, grant peace and healing to those who suffer from illness of mind, body, and spirit. We know that pain can often cause isolation and loneliness. Let us not forget those who are separated from us because of their burdens. Amen.

Friday, May 29 — Psalm 70
Numbers 18:1–24; Mark 14:53–65

My tongue shall tell of your righteousness and of your praise all day long. Psalm 35:28

My gracious master and my God, 548
assist me to proclaim,
to spread through all the earth abroad
the honors of your name.

The disciples returned to Jerusalem with great joy; and they were continually in the temple blessing God. Luke 24:52-53

All praise to you, ascended Lord, 374
all glory ever be
to Father, Son, and Spirit now
and through eternity,
and through eternity.

Risen Lord, thank you for the many blessings you bestow on us daily. May we be reminded of your greatest gift—your triumph over death that leads us to our own eternal life. Amen.

Saturday, May 30 — Psalm 71:1–8
Numbers 18:25–19:22; Mark 14:66–72

Balaam replied, "Although Balak were to give me his house full of silver and gold, I could not go beyond the command of the Lord my God." Numbers 22:18

So may I prove true, 608
devoted to you,
and cheerfully stand,
prepared to comply with your ev'ry command.

For we are not peddlers of God's word like so many; but in Christ we speak as persons of sincerity, as persons sent from God and standing in his presence. 2 Corinthians 2:17

Not your merit brings God near, 275*
but God's great compassion
for the creature he fashioned.
He will prove his faithfulness to you
and in holy ways he will lead you.
So to God give praise which is his due.

Redeeming Lord, you call us to be true and faithful followers; help us to remain steadfast in our sincere devotion to you rather than turn to hollow acts of vanity. In your name. Amen.

Day of Pentecost

Watchword for the Week — Now there are varieties of gifts, but the same Spirit; and there are varieties of services, but the same Lord. 1 Corinthians 12:4,5

Sunday, May 31 — Acts 2:1-21; Psalm 104:24-34,35b
1 Corinthians 12:3b-13; John 20:19-23

Woe to you who add house to house and join field to field till no space is left and you live alone in the land. Isaiah 5:8 NIV

We turn to you, God, 678*
with our thanks and our tears
for all of the fam'lies we've known through the years,
the intimate networks on whom we depend
of parent and partner and roommate and friend.

For we were all baptized by one Spirit so as to form one body—whether Jews or Gentiles, slave or free—and we were all given the one Spirit to drink. 1 Corinthians 12:13 NIV

What brought us together, 675
what joined our hearts?
The pardon which Jesus, our High Priest, imparts;
'Tis this which cements the disciples of Christ,
who are into one by the Spirit baptized.

Holy Spirit, fill our hearts on this day of Pentecost. Let us remember that we are all children of God. Help us to interact with compassion and love. Amen.

Monday, June 1 — Psalm 71:9–18a
Numbers 20:1–21:9; Mark 15:1–20

Do not fear, or be afraid; have I not told you from of old and declared it? You are my witnesses! Isaiah 44:8

Be still my soul: the Lord is on your side. 757
Bear patiently the cross of grief or pain;
leave to your God to order and provide;
in ev'ry change God faithful will remain.
Be still, my soul: your best, your heav'nly friend
through thorny ways leads to a joyful end.

What is whispered in your ear, proclaim from the roofs. Matthew 10:27 NIV

Ready, Lord, I'm ready, Lord, 601*
to follow where you lead.
Show me, Lord, just show me, Lord,
the service you will need.
Ready, Lord, I'm ready, Lord,
I'm ready, come what may,
so call me, Lord, just call me, Lord,
and I'll be on your way.

Patient and loving God, we praise your name for your continued presence and power with us this day. Continue to speak your words to us so that we may be your witnesses throughout this day and forevermore. Amen.

Tuesday, June 2 — Psalm 71:18b–24
Numbers 21:10–22:6; Mark 15:21–32

My heart exults in the Lord. 1 Samuel 2:1

545*

Joyfully, heartily resounding,
let ev'ry instrument and voice
peal out the praise of grace abounding,
calling the whole world to rejoice.
Trumpets and organs set in motion
such sounds as make the heavens ring:
all things that live in earth and ocean,
make music for your mighty King.

Although you have not seen him, you love him; and even though you do not see him now, you believe in him and rejoice with an indescribable and glorious joy. 1 Peter 1:8

372

Rejoice, the Lord is King!
Your Lord and King adore.
Rejoice, give thanks and sing
and triumph evermore.
Lift up your heart, lift up your voice,
rejoice, again I say, rejoice!

King of kings, and Lord of lords, our hearts sing praises to you for who you are. Our words are so inadequate to describe your majesty and glory. May your presence continue to sustain us this day as we magnify your holy name. Amen.

Wednesday, June 3 — Psalm 72:1–11
Numbers 22:7–41; Mark 15:33–47

The eyes of the Lord are on the righteous, and his ears are open to their cry. Psalm 34:15

Frail children of dust, and feeble as frail, 566
in you do we trust, nor find you to fail;
your mercies how tender, how firm to the end,
our maker, defender, redeemer, and friend.

Ask, and it will be given you; search, and you will find; knock, and the door will be opened for you. Matthew 7:7

Seek ye first the kingdom of God 605
and his righteousness,
and all these things shall be added unto you—
Allelu, alleluia!

Supportive God, we know that you are a loving and constant presence in our hearts; however, there are days when we feel overwhelmed by the darkness all around us. Help us to experience your light and powerful presence as we seek to do your will this day. In Jesus' name, we pray. Amen.

Thursday, June 4 — Psalm 72:12–20
Numbers 23; Mark 16:1–13

David said to the Philistine, "You come to me with sword and spear and javelin; but I come to you in the name of the Lord of hosts." 1 Samuel 17:45

Triumphant hosts on high 468
give thanks to God and sing,
and "Holy, holy, holy," cry,
"Almighty King!"
Hail, Abraham's God and ours!
One mighty hymn we raise.
All pow'r and majesty be yours
and endless praise!

Stand therefore, and fasten the belt of truth around your waist, and put on the breastplate of righteousness. As shoes for your feet put whatever will make you ready to proclaim the gospel of peace. Ephesians 6:14-15

Save us from weak resignation 751*
to the evils we deplore;
let the gift of your salvation
be our glory evermore.
Grant us wisdom, grant us courage
serving you whom we adore,
serving you whom we adore.

Loving Savior, how we depend on your presence and guidance. Open our hearts to opportunities to proclaim the gospel of peace through the power of your Holy Spirit. In the precious name of Jesus. Amen.

* Used by permission of Elinor Fosdick Downs.

Friday, June 5 — Psalm 73:1–12
Numbers 24,25; Mark 16:14–Luke 1:4

My tears have been my food day and night, while people say to me continually, "Where is your God?" Psalm 42:3

Breath of God, O life-giving Spirit, 499*
yours the truth that we seek this day.
Yours the wisdom, yours the understanding,
yours the guidance on life's dark way.
Source of courage when hearts are weary,
source of strength for the day's long journey,
spirit God, our hope and our faith,
breathe now within us your holy breath.

My grace is sufficient for you, for power is made, perfect in weakness. 2 Corinthians 12:9

May your rich grace impart 705
strength to my fainting heart,
my zeal inspire;
as you have died for me,
my love, adoringly,
pure, warm and changeless be,
a living fire!

Source of courage, we acknowledge your grace and mercy. Send your loving comfort to strengthen us in these times of weakness and powerlessness. Thank you for your divine presence and refreshing power. In the name of Emanuel. Amen.

Saturday, June 6 — Psalm 73:13–20
Numbers 26:1–24; Luke 1:5–25

How great are God's signs, how mighty his wonders! His kingdom is an eternal kingdom; his dominion endures from generation to generation. Daniel 4:3 NIV

Immortal, invisible, God only wise, 457
in light inaccessible hid from our eyes,
most blessed, most glorious, O Ancient of Days,
almighty, victorious, your great name we praise.

Since we are receiving a kingdom that cannot be shaken, let us give thanks, by which we offer to God an acceptable worship. Hebrews 12:28

While your glorious praise is sung, 553
touch my lips, unloose my tongue
that my joyful soul may bless
Christ the Lord, my righteousness.

Source of joy, we come this day to exalt your holy and righteous name; you are worthy of all adoration and praise. Your grace and mercies abound each day, for which we are grateful. May we share our joyous praise with those we meet this day. In Jesus' name, we pray. Amen.

Trinity Sunday

Watchword for the Week — O Lord, our Sovereign, how majestic is your name in all the earth! Psalm 8:9

Sunday, June 7 — Genesis 1:1-2:4a; Psalm 8
2 Corinthians 13:11-13; Matthew 28:16-20

The Lord is coming to judge the earth. He will judge the world with righteousness, and the peoples with equity. Psalm 98:9

He rules the world with truth and grace, 294
and makes the nations prove
the glories of his righteousness
and wonders of his love,
and wonders of his love,
and wonders, wonders of his love.

This good news of the kingdom will be proclaimed throughout the world, as a testimony to all the nations; and then the end will come. Matthew 24:14

"Go forth in all the earth,"— 633
your word to us is given:
"Proclaim salvation's worth
to people under heaven."
This holy task, O Lord,
your church must quite fulfill;
to us your grace afford,
and mold us to your will.

Loving and merciful God, we are grateful to be called your children and reminded of our call to be faithful disciples. Help us to share your love and mercy with all whom we meet in these troubled times, where greed, deceit, and self-centeredness have a stronger hold than generosity, honesty, and selflessness. We ask for your guidance as we seek to manifest your presence in this dark world. In Jesus' name, we pray. Amen.

Monday, June 8 — Psalm 73:21–28
Numbers 26:25–56; Luke 1:26–38

Speak tenderly to Jerusalem, and proclaim to her that her hard service has been completed, that her sin has been paid for. Isaiah 40:2 NIV

Straight shall be what long was crooked 264
and the rougher places plain!
Let your hearts be true and humble,
as befits his holy reign!
For the glory of the Lord
now on earth is shed abroad,
and all flesh shall see the token
that God's word is never broken.

The creation itself will be set free from its bondage to decay and will obtain the freedom of the glory of the children of God. Romans 8:21

His oath, his covenant, his blood 771
sustain me in the raging flood;
when all supports are washed away,
he then is all my hope and stay.

Forgiving Savior, so often we find ourselves wandering away from you, caught up in the ways of the world. We are so grateful for your cleansing blood and forgiveness. Create in us a clean heart and renew within us a new spirit. Amen.

Tuesday, June 9 — Psalm 74:1–9
Numbers 26:57–27:23; Luke 1:39–45

You shall not steal. Exodus 20:15

Out of the depths I cry to you; 761*
O Father, hear me calling.
Incline your ear to my distress
in spite of my rebelling.
Do not regard my sinful deeds.
Send me the grace my spirit needs;
without it I am nothing.

Do not seek your own advantage, but that of the other. 1 Corinthians 10:24

Lo! The hosts of evil round us 751
scorn the Christ, assail his ways!
From the fears that long have bound us,
free our hearts to faith and praise.
Grant us wisdom, grant us courage,
for the living of these days,
for the living of these days.

O God of grace and mercy, our souls sing hallelujah, praise, and thanksgiving for your greatness. Your grace continually abounds even in the midst of our darkest moments. Thank you for your prevailing spirit indwelling and comforting us. In the name of our lamb who has conquered. Amen.

Wednesday, June 10 — Psalm 74:10–17
Numbers 28:1–29:6; Luke 1:46–56

The jar of meal was not emptied, neither did the jug of oil fail, according to the word of the Lord that he spoke by Elijah. 1 Kings 17:16

All the world is God's own field, 450
fruit unto his praise to yield,
wheat and weeds together sown,
unto joy or sorrow grown;
first the blade, and then the ear,
then the full corn shall appear;
Lord of harvest, grant that we
wholesome grain and pure may be.

Jesus, taking the five loaves and the two fish and looking up to heaven, gave thanks and broke the loaves. Then he gave them to his disciples to distribute to the people. He also divided the two fish among them all. They all ate and were satisfied. Mark 6:41-42 NIV

Day by day, at home, away, 723
Jesus is my staff and stay.
When I hunger, Jesus feeds me,
into pleasant pastures leads me;
when I thirst, he bids me go
where the quiet waters flow.

God our provider, our hearts praise and sing with gratitude for your merciful provision in our depths of need. Hallelujah, praise the Lord, for his excellent greatness! In Jesus' name, we pray. Amen.

Thursday, June 11 — Psalm 74:18–23
Numbers 29:7–40; Luke 1:57–66

We have escaped like a bird from the snare of the fowlers; the snare is broken, and we have escaped. Psalm 124:7

The right hand of God is pointing in our land, 690*
pointing the way we must go.
So clouded is the way, so easily we stray,
but we're guided by the right hand of God.

Suddenly an angel of the Lord appeared, and a light shone in the cell. He tapped Peter on the side and woke him, saying, "Get up quickly." And the chains fell off his wrists. Acts 12:7

Long my imprisoned spirit lay 773
fast bound in sin and nature's night.
Your sunrise turned that night to day;
I woke—the dungeon flamed with light!
My chains fell off, your voice I knew;
was freed, I rose, and followed you.
My chains fell off, your voice I knew;
was freed, I rose, and followed you.

O God, our rock—we long for your deliverance from the injustices and oppression we face in a nation permeated with arrogance and self-centeredness. Your people suffer hunger, homelessness, illness, and death; deliver us O Lord! Hear our cry and answer our prayers. Amen.

Friday, June 12 — Psalm 75
Numbers 30:1–31:12; Luke 1:67–80

You know me, O Lord; you see me; and you examine my heart's attitude toward you. Jeremiah 12:3 NASB

Riches I heed not nor man's empty praise, 719
thou mine inheritance now and always;
thou and thou only first in my heart,
high King of heaven, my treasure thou art.

Jesus said, "As the Father has loved me, so I have loved you; abide in my love." John 15:9

I am lost if you take your hand from me, 728*
I am blind without your light to see.
Lord, forever may I your servant be.
Lead me, O Lord, lead me.

Loving God, we are lost without you; lead and guide us this day as we seek to do your will. In Jesus' name, we pray. Amen.

Saturday, June 13 — Psalm 76
Numbers 31:13–47; Luke 2:1–20

I will pour out on the house of David and on the inhabitants of Jerusalem the Spirit of grace and of supplication. Zechariah 12:10 NASB

Move in our midst, O Spirit of God. 489
Go with us down from your holy hill.
Walk with us through the storm and the calm.
Spirit of God, now go with us still.

The Spirit helps us in our weakness; for we do not know how to pray as we ought. Romans 8:26

Come now, O Lord, and teach us how to pray. 742
Teach us to ask ourselves from day to day
if we are yours and yours alone will be
through earthly days and through eternity.

Lord God Almighty, we long to pray as you taught your disciples: hallowed be your holy name. May your kingdom come in us this day. Help us to forgive others as you have forgiven us; deliver us from evil. Yours is the kingdom, now and forever. Amen.

Second Sunday after Pentecost

Watchword for the Week — The Lord is good; his steadfast love endures forever, and his faithfulness to all generations. Psalm 100:5

Sunday, June 14 — Exodus 19:2-8a; Psalm 100
Romans 5:1-8; Matthew 9:35-10:8,(9-23)

You have given human beings dominion over the works of your hands; you have put all things under their feet. Psalm 8:6

We would be stewards true 653*
holding in trust from you
all that you give;
help us in love to share;
teach us like you to care,
that earth may all be fair
and all may live.

Therefore be imitators of God, as beloved children, and live in love, as Christ loved us. Ephesians 5:1-2

Great God, in Christ you set us free 579**
your life to live, your joy to share.
Give us your Spirit's liberty
to turn from guilt and dull despair
and offer all that faith can do
while love is making all things new.

Redeemer—source of love—you set us free to live abundantly; grant that we may be good stewards of the earth and kind neighbors to her peoples. Bigotry, hatred, and oppression threaten to overwhelm us; help us, O God, to stay strong and work towards peace. Amen.

Monday, June 15 — Psalm 77:1–9
Numbers 31:48–32:27; Luke 2:21–32

Your dead shall live. Isaiah 26:19

It was a strange and dreadful strife 367
when life and death contended;
the victory remained with life:
the reign of death was ended.
Stripped of pow'r, no more it reigns,
an empty form alone remains;
death's sting is lost forever!
Alleluia!

We know that the one who raised the Lord Jesus will raise us also with Jesus. 2 Corinthians 4:14

When ends life's transient dream, 705
when death's cold, sullen stream
rolls over me,
blessed Savior, then, in love,
fear and distrust remove;
O bear me safe above,
redeemed and free!

O Lord, we thank you for your resurrection power and your promise of eternal life. Our hearts rejoice in your majesty and we lift up our voices in praise, for you are worthy of honor and glory. In Jesus' name, we pray. Amen.

Tuesday, June 16 — Psalm 77:10–15
Numbers 32:28–33:9; Luke 2:33–40

Have you not brought this upon yourself by forsaking the Lord your God, while he led you in the way? Jeremiah 2:17

Lord, have mercy upon my soul; 48s*
the war within seems out of control.
Take this bitterness and turn it into gratefulness
Lord, have mercy upon my soul.

Jesus said, "If you continue in my word, you are truly my disciples." John 8:31

God's word alive and active, 503**
proclaimed throughout the years,
still comforts us when hurting
and calms our hidden fears.
God's word of truth and justice
sets weary captives free,
and joins God's holy people
in new community.

Source of wisdom, our souls cry praise and thanksgiving to you for your divine guidance through your word. Help us to continue to abide in your word through the power of your indwelling spirit. We long to manifest your light to those in darkness this day. Glory be to God. Amen.

Wednesday, June 17 — Psalm 77:16–20
Numbers 33:10–56; Luke 2:41–52

Worship the Lord with gladness; come into his presence with singing. Psalm 100:2

Praise to the Lord, the almighty, 530
the King of creation!
O my soul, praise him,
for he is your health and salvation!
Let all who hear
now to his temple draw near,
joining in glad adoration.

Give thanks to the Father, who has enabled you to share in the inheritance of the saints in the light. Colossians 1:12

To God whose mercy knows no bounds, 541
we gratefully direct our sounds,
O praise him, alleluia!
Within this space and then beyond
his presence stirs us to respond.

Holy, Holy, Holy Lord, we offer praise unto you and sing, "Glory Alleluia." May our praise be a sweet incense to you. We know that you inhabit the praise of your people and we are strengthened by our praises. Help us to remember that the joy of the Lord is our strength. Amen.

Thursday, June 18 — Psalm 78:1–8
Numbers 34; Luke 3:1–20

Noah did all that God commanded him. Genesis 6:22

"When through the deep waters I call you to go, 709
the rivers of sorrow shall not overflow;
for I will be with you in trouble to bless,
and sanctify to you your deepest distress."

Faith is the assurance of things hoped for, the conviction of things not seen. Hebrews 11:1

My faith looks trustingly 705
to Christ of Calvary,
my Savior true!
Lord, hear me while I pray,
take all my guilt away,
strengthen in ev'ry way
my love for you!

Gracious and loving God, we offer ourselves to you this day, and look faithfully for opportunities to witness to your love, mercy, and grace. Open our hearts and our minds to be receptive to the guidance of your spirit. In Jesus' name, we pray. Amen.

Friday, June 19 — Psalm 78:9–16
Numbers 35:1–30; Luke 3:21–38

The Lord said, "I will instruct you and teach you the way you should go." Psalm 32:8

Teach us to love in truth, 801*
to give and to receive
with joyful and with open hearts,
with all that we believe;
to seek another's good,
to honor what is right,
to let our will and our desire
be held in holy light.

Understand what the will of the Lord is. Ephesians 5:17

Take my life, O Lord, renew, 610
consecrate my heart to you.
Take my self, and I will be
yours for all eternity,
yours for all eternity.

God of wisdom and power, our prayers are lifted this day for your divine guidance to help those who make decisions concerning the welfare of our country. Magnify your divine light in our homes, and help us to love one another as you have loved us. Thy will be done. In Jesus' name, we pray. Amen.

Saturday, June 20 — Psalm 78:17–31
Numbers 35:31–Deuteronomy 1:18; Luke 4:1–13

Full of honor and majesty is the Lord's work, and his righteousness endures forever. Psalm 111:3

"Fear not, I am with you; O be not dismayed, 709
for I am your God and will still give you aid;
I'll strengthen you, help you and cause you to stand
upheld by my righteous, omnipotent hand."

Let everyone who calls on the name of the Lord turn away from wickedness. 2 Timothy 2:19

And now at length discerning 763*
the evil that I do,
behold me, Lord, returning
with hope and trust to you.
In haste you come to meet me
and home rejoicing bring,
in gladness there to greet me
with calf and robe and ring.

Holy Redeemer, we acknowledge we have often strayed from you and your word. We thank you for your cleansing blood and redemption as we start a new day renewed with faith and hope. Help us to walk in the paths you have chosen for us. Amen.

Third Sunday after Pentecost

Watchword for the Week — Jesus said, "Those who find their life will lose it, and those who lose their life for my sake will find it." Matthew 10:39

Sunday, June 21 — Jeremiah 20:7-13; Psalm 69:7-10,(11-15),16-18 Romans 6:1b-11; Matthew 10:24-39

It is good to give thanks to the Lord, to sing praises to your name, O Most High; to declare your steadfast love in the morning, and your faithfulness by night. Psalm 92:1-2

We thank you with uplifted voice, 541
this word of praise our joyful choice:
Alleluia, alleluia!
O gracious Spirit, may our song
to you eternally belong!

May the God of steadfastness and encouragement grant you to live in harmony with one another, in accordance with Christ Jesus, so that together you may with one voice glorify the God and Father of our Lord Jesus Christ. Romans 15:5-6

There we to all eternity 543
shall join th'angelic lays
and sing in perfect harmony
to God our Savior's praise;
he has redeemed us by his blood,
and made us kings and priests to God;
for us, for us, the Lamb was slain!
Praise ye the Lord! Amen.

Spirit of the living God, fall afresh on us with revival. Speak to us with your tongues of fire, empowering us to show forth the joy and light which draws others to hear our witness of your abiding love, grace, and mercy. Alleluia! Amen!

Monday, June 22 — Psalm 78:32–39
Deuteronomy 1:19–46; Luke 4:14–21

You crown the year with your bounty. Psalm 65:11

We come to you, our Father, 433
with thoughts of thanks and praise,
for your abundant mercy,
and all your love and grace;
we praise you for your goodness
and for your loving care,
for daily show'rs of blessing,
for answers to our prayers.

Every generous act of giving, with every perfect gift, is from above, coming down from the Father of lights. James 1:17

He only is the Maker 453
of all things near and far;
he paints the wayside flower,
he lights the evening star;
the winds and waves obey him,
by him the birds are fed;
much more to us, his children,
he gives our daily bread.

Divine Friend and Provider, in this world filled with materialism and temptation to leave the paths of righteous living—forgive us when we fall prey to those temptations and help us to walk in your new mercies daily. In Jesus' name, we pray. Amen.

Tuesday, June 23 — Psalm 78:40–55
Deuteronomy 2; Luke 4:22–30

He sends out his command to the earth; his word runs swiftly. Psalm 147:15

His law he enforces; 448*
the stars in their courses
and sun in its orbit obediently shine;
the hills and the mountains,
the rivers and fountains,
the deeps of the ocean proclaim him divine.
We too should be voicing
our love and rejoicing;
with glad adoration a song let us raise,
till all things now living
unite in thanksgiving:
to God in the highest,
hosanna and praise!

The word of God is not chained. 2 Timothy 2:9

Bless your own truth, dear Lord, 502
to me, to me,
as when you blessed the bread
by Galilee.
Then shall all bondage cease,
all fetters fall;
and I shall find my peace,
my All in All!

O Word incarnate, how we long for you to continually burn within our hearts—that others may see your light shining through us and be drawn to you. Help us to strive for truth and justice in a world of brokenness. We long to live righteous lives of love, justice, mercy, and grace. In Jesus' name, we pray for your divine wisdom and guidance. Amen.

Wednesday, June 24 — Psalm 78:56–64
Deuteronomy 3; Luke 4:31–44

For as the earth brings forth its shoots, so the Lord God will cause righteousness and praise to spring up before all the nations. Isaiah 61:11

What God's almighty pow'r has made, 537
in mercy he is keeping;
by morning glow or evening shade
his eye is never sleeping.
And where he rules in kingly might,
there all is just and all is right:
to God all praise and glory!

A harvest of righteousness is sown in peace for those who make peace. James 3:18

God, teach us peacemaking, justice and love. 687*
Blessed by Christ's teaching, we're lifted above
all thought of vengeance or envy or hate.
Help us, your children, shalom to create.

Patient God, we need the presence and power of the Holy Spirit to help us be agents of peace, justice, and love, and to lead us to serve those who are treated unjustly or are oppressed. We seek to follow the teaching of our Lord: to love one another as sisters and brothers this day and forever more. Amen.

Thursday, June 25 — Psalm 78:65–72
Deuteronomy 4:1–31; Luke 5:1–11

I, the Lord, am your Savior and your Redeemer, the Mighty One. Isaiah 60:16

In his temple now behold him, 314
see the long-expected Lord;
ancient prophets had foretold him,
God has now fulfilled his word.
Now to praise him, his redeemed
shall break forth with one accord.

Who will separate us from the love of Christ? Romans 8:35

Neither life nor death shall ever 667*
from the Lord his children sever;
for to them his grace revealing,
he turns sorrow into healing.

O Lord our redeemer, we praise your holy and righteous name. Our voices sing, "Halleluiah, Halleluiah, praise the Lord," for you are worthy of glory and adoration. Thank you for your unending love and your ever-abiding presence. May our hearts continually lift your holy name in praise this day. Amen.

Friday, June 26 — Psalm 79:1–8
Deuteronomy 4:32–5:21; Luke 5:12–26

Blessed are they who maintain justice, who constantly do what is right. Psalm 106:3 NIV

God, teach us peacemaking in church and home, 687*
in school and hall beneath Capitol dome,
in shop and industry, city and farm—
show us the pathways that cause no one harm.

The world and its desire are passing away, but those who do the will of God live forever. 1 John 2:17

Be with me, Lord, where'er I go; 733
teach me what you would have me do;
suggest whate'er I think or say;
direct me in the narrow way.

Loving God, we thank you for this day and ask for your divine guidance as we seek to do your will. Amen.

Saturday, June 27 — Psalm 79:9–13
Deuteronomy 5:22–6:25; Luke 5:27–39

God, remember your congregation, which you acquired long ago, which you redeemed to be the tribe of your heritage. Psalm 74:2

Glorious things of you are spoken, 522
Zion, city of our God;
he whose word cannot be broken
formed you for his own abode;
on the rock of ages founded,
what can shake your sure repose?
With salvation's walls surrounded
you may smile at all your foes.

You know the grace of our Lord Jesus Christ, that though he was rich, yet for your sake he became poor, so that you through his poverty might become rich. 2 Corinthians 8:9 NIV

Chosen flock, your faithful Shepherd follow, 444
who laid down his life for you;
all your days unto his service hallow,
each to be disciples true;
evermore rejoice to do his pleasure,
be the fullness of his grace your treasure;
should success your labor crown,
give the praise to him alone.

Holy Redeemer, savior and friend, we confess we have often fallen short of loving those that are less fortunate. Forgive us and lead us on the paths of righteousness, grace, and mercy. Help us to be more compassionate and manifest your loving service to others. Amen.

Fourth Sunday after Pentecost

Watchword for the Week — Happy are the people who know the festal shout, who walk, O Lord, in the light of your countenance. Psalm 89:15

Sunday, June 28 — Jeremiah 28:5-9; Psalm 89:1-4,15-18 Romans 6:12-23; Matthew 10:40-42

I keep my eyes always on the Lord. Psalm 16:8 NIV

More than words, yes, more than words, 601*
I know you want from me.
Moving, Lord, I'm moving, Lord,
I'm moving eagerly.
Take my heart, and take my hands,
my feet, my life, my all.
I'm ready, Lord, so ready, Lord,
to follow till I fall.

No one who puts a hand to the plow and looks back is fit for the kingdom of God. Luke 9:62

O Jesus, I have promised 603
to serve you to the end;
be now and ever near me,
my master and my friend.
I shall not fear the battle
if you are by my side,
nor wander from the pathway
if you will be my guide.

Source of joy, we sing praises and thanksgiving for all your blessings. Help us to be faithful in our service according to your divine command to follow you. Thank you for your love and faithfulness. In your holy name, we pray. Amen, Amen, Amen.

Monday, June 29 — Psalm 80:1–7
Deuteronomy 7; Luke 6:1–11

Daniel said, "My God sent his angel and shut the lions' mouths so that they would not hurt me." Daniel 6:22

Under the shadow of your throne 461
your saints have dwelt secure;
sufficient is your arm alone,
and our defense is sure.

We are persecuted, but not forsaken; struck down, but not destroyed. 2 Corinthians 4:9

In your arms I rest me; 722
foes who would molest me
cannot reach me here.
Though the earth be shaking,
ev'ry heart be quaking,
Jesus calms my fear.
Sin and hell in conflict fell
with their bitter storms assail me.
Jesus will not fail me.

Divine Parent, we marvel at your unfailing grace and provisions. Thank you for your presence and protection on this new day. Grant us wisdom and courage to stand firm in our resolve to continue in service to others, loving as you have loved us. In Jesus' name, we pray. Amen.

Tuesday, June 30 — Psalm 80:8–11
Deuteronomy 8:1–9:6; Luke 6:12–26

When you said, "Seek my face," my heart said to you, "Your face, O Lord, I shall seek." Psalm 27:8 NASB

Lord, I would clasp thy hand in mine, 787
nor ever murmur nor repine,
content, whatever lot I see,
since 'tis my God that leadeth me.

Do not worry about anything, but in everything by prayer and supplication with thanksgiving let your requests be made known to God. Philippians 4:6

Have we trials and temptations? 743
Is there trouble anywhere?
We should never be discouraged;
take it to the Lord in prayer!
Can we find a friend so faithful
who will all our sorrows share?
Jesus knows our ev'ry weakness;
take it to the Lord in prayer!

Merciful Savior, thank you for another day to rejoice and praise your holy name. Help us to let go of all our insecurities and lean on your strength and power. God, we know that all things are possible through you, so we vow to let go and wholly depend on you through the power of the Holy Spirit. We thank you for this blessed assurance and comfort. Amen.

Wednesday, July 1 — Psalm 80:12–19
Deuteronomy 9:7–10:22; Luke 6:27–38

Who can hide in secret places so that I cannot see them? says the Lord. Do I not fill heaven and earth? says the Lord. Jeremiah 23:24

My Father, I have wandered 763*
and hidden from your face;
in foolishness have squandered
your legacy of grace.
But now, in exile dwelling,
I rise with fear and shame,
as distant but compelling,
I hear you call my name.

Anyone who loves God is known by him. 1 Corinthians 8:3

The Lord is never far away, 537
but through all grief distressing,
an everpresent help and stay,
our peace, and joy, and blessing.
As with a mother's tender hand,
he leads his own, his chosen band.
To God all praise and glory!

Merciful God, even when we feel that you are far away, help us to always remember your love and mercy. Forgive us when our worries in this life overcome our reliance on you. May we always hear you when you call our names. Amen.

Thursday, July 2 — Psalm 81:1–5
Deuteronomy 11; Luke 6:39–49

O Lord, our Sovereign, how majestic is your name in all the earth! Psalm 8:1

Praise the Lord! You heav'ns, adore him, 454
praise him, angels in the height;
sun and moon, rejoice before him;
praise him, all you stars and light.
Praise the Lord! For he has spoken;
worlds his mighty voice obeyed;
laws which never shall be broken
for their guidance he has made.

Mary said, "The Mighty One has done great things for me, and holy is his name." Luke 1:49

To God be the glory—great things he has done! 550
So loved he the world that he gave us his Son,
who yielded his life an atonement for sin,
and opened the lifegate that all may go in.

Our sovereign Lord, our mighty God, fill us with joy as we lift your name on high! Let our voices fill the earth and the heavens as we sing our admiration to you. All our praises to you! Amen.

Friday, July 3 — Psalm 81:6–10
Deuteronomy 12; Luke 7:1–17

Your hands have made and fashioned me; give me understanding that I may learn your commandments. Psalm 119:73

Upon your precepts and your ways 510
my heart will meditate with awe;
your word shall be my chief delight,
and I will not forget your law.

And this is his commandment, that we should believe in the name of his son Jesus Christ and love one another. 1 John 3:23

Grant, Lord, that with thy direction, 673
"Love each other," we comply,
aiming with unfeigned affection
thy love to exemplify;
let our mutual love be glowing;
thus the world will plainly see
that we, as on one stem growing,
living branches are in thee.

Loving Creator and Teacher, help us grow together as your congregation of students. Teach us your love and give us opportunities to show that love to each other. May we never stop learning from you. Amen.

Saturday, July 4 — Psalm 81:11–16
Deuteronomy 13:1–14:21; Luke 7:18–30

The Lord said, "I will look with favor upon you and make you fruitful and multiply you; and I will maintain my covenant with you." Leviticus 26:9

Praise to the Father for his loving kindness, 383
tenderly caring for his erring children;
praise him, all angels; praise him in the heavens;
praise to the Father!

In Jesus Christ every one of God's promises is a "Yes." For this reason it is through him that we say the "Amen," to the glory of God. 2 Corinthians 1:20

Standing on the promises of Christ my king, *
through eternal ages let his praises ring;
glory in the highest, I will shout and sing,
standing on the promises of God.

Heavenly Father, as we consider the promises you so graciously give us, may we remember that you are always faithful, giving us hope and mercy. Help us to be ever faithful to you as well. Amen.

* *Standing on the Promises*, verse 1 by Author Russel Kelso Carter. Public Domain.

Fifth Sunday after Pentecost

Watchword for the Week — The Lord is gracious and merciful, slow to anger and abounding in steadfast love. Psalm 145:8

Sunday, July 5 — Zechariah 9:9-12; Psalm 145:8-14
Romans 7:15-25a; Matthew 11:16-19,25-30

Be glad and rejoice in the Lord your God. Joel 2:23

Your hallelujahs loud, 786
your clear hosannas raise!
Send forth your sturdy hymns of old,
the psalms of ancient days.

In Christ Jesus our Lord we have access to God in boldness and confidence through faith in him. Ephesians 3:12

Blessed name! The rock on which we build, 487
our shield and resting place,
our never-failing comfort, filled
with blessings of his grace.
O Jesus, Shepherd, Guardian, Friend,
our Prophet, Priest, and King,
our Lord, our Life, our Way, our End,
accept the praise we bring.

God, you are the rock we stand upon as we sing hallelujah! Praise you Lord, for you are everything. May our hosannas be heard to the ends of the earth! With joyful hearts we sing. Amen!

John Hus Festival† — Isaiah 49:1-7; Psalm 135:1-13
1 Corinthians 1:18-24; Mark 8:34-38

Monday, July 6 — Psalm 82:1–4
Deuteronomy 14:22–15:18; Luke 7:31–38

As far as the east is from the west, so far he removes our transgressions from us. Psalm 103:12

Far as east from west is distant, 458
God has put away our sin;
like the pity of a father
has the Lord's compassion been.

Where sin increased, grace abounded all the more. Romans 5:20

O most wholesome balm of healing, 419*
all our debt to sins repealing,
feed us; set us free from evil;
lead us in your light primeval.

Father, give us courage, like the courage of John Hus, to call out the wrong in our world and fight for what is right and good and God-given. Give us strength in our quest to be more like you. Amen.

† On July 6, 1415, John Hus was martyred at the Council of Constance.

Tuesday, July 7 — Psalm 82:5–8
Deuteronomy 15:19–17:7; Luke 7:39–50

I had said in my alarm, 'I am driven far from your sight.' But you heard my supplications when I cried out to you for help. Psalm 31:22

Enrich me always with your love; 733
my kind protector ever prove;
Lord, put your seal upon my heart,
that I from you may not depart.

Bartimaeus son of Timaeus, a blind beggar, was sitting by the roadside. When he heard that it was Jesus of Nazareth, he began to shout out and say, "Jesus, Son of David, have mercy on me!" Many sternly ordered him to be quiet. Jesus stood still and said, "Call him here." Mark 10:46-48,49

Just as I am, poor, wretched, blind; 762
sight, riches, healing of the mind,
yea, all I need, in thee to find,
O Lamb of God, I come, I come!

O great Healer, let us always reach for you in times of trouble and sickness. Heal our hearts, bodies, and minds. Thank you for your great mercy and everlasting love. In Jesus' name, we pray. Amen.

Wednesday, July 8 — Psalm 83:1–8
Deuteronomy 17:8–18:22; Luke 8:1–15

Once more I will astound these people with wonder upon wonder; the wisdom of the wise will perish. Isaiah 29:14 NIV

Praise we all our God eternal 637*
who created land and sea
bringing forth the human story
life and love that's true and free.
Alleluia! Through this journey
let our lives inspired be.

Many who heard Jesus were astounded. They said, "Where did this man get all this? What is this wisdom that has been given to him? What deeds of power are being done by his hands!" Mark 6:2

Holy is your name! 473
Who can make this claim?
Source of rest and consolation,
life, and light, and full salvation;
Son of God your name,
none can make this claim.

Beautiful Savior, even though you have the power of the heavens, you live as a servant to others. May we follow your example of humbleness as we serve those around us and spread your love to the world. Amen.

Thursday, July 9 — Psalm 83:9–12
Deuteronomy 19:1–20:9; Luke 8:16–25

You have made the Lord your refuge. Psalm 91:9

God is my strong salvation, 769
no enemy I fear;
he hears my supplication,
dispelling all my care;
if he, my head and master,
defend me from above,
what pain or what disaster
can part me from his love?

Since, then, we have such a hope, we act with great boldness. 2 Corinthians 3:12

Our hope and expectation, 256
O Jesus, now appear;
arise, O Sun so longed for,
o'er this benighted sphere.
With hearts and hands uplifted,
we look, O Lord, to you
for all the earth's redemption,
creation made anew.

Like an oasis in the desert, gracious Lord, you protect and shelter us, and give us courage so that we may boldly go into the world to proclaim your love and mercy for all. In the name of Jesus, we pray. Amen.

Friday, July 10 — Psalm 83:13–18
Deuteronomy 20:10–21:23; Luke 8:26–39

One generation shall laud your works to another, and shall declare your mighty acts. Psalm 145:4

Worship, honor, glory, blessing, 454
Lord, we offer as our gift;
young and old, your praise expressing,
our glad songs to you we lift.
All the saints in heav'n adore you;
we would join their glad acclaim;
as your angels serve before you,
so on earth we praise your name.

Grace, as it extends to more and more people, may increase thanksgiving, to the glory of God. 2 Corinthians 4:15

All glory, honor, thanks, and praise 518*
to Christ our Lord and Savior,
that still his church in these our days
may know his boundless favor:
for brothers and sisters united by love
stand firm o'er the earth far extended,
as countless more legions in heaven above
extol how his grace them attended.

Thank you, glorious God, for the generations of ancestors who have served you before us. May we continue this tradition, extending our love to all, praising your great name to the ends of the earth. In Jesus' name, we pray. Amen.

Saturday, July 11 — Psalm 84:1–7
Deuteronomy 22; Luke 8:40–56

The Lord will give strength to his people. Psalm 29:11 NKJV

Lord, who throughout these forty days 341
for us did fast and pray,
teach us with you to mourn our sins,
and close by you to stay.

Now when they saw the boldness of Peter and John and realized that they were uneducated and ordinary men, they were amazed and recognized them as companions of Jesus. Acts 4:13

Today we all are called to be 696*
disciples of the Lord,
to help to set the captive free,
make plowshare out of sword,
to feed the hungry, quench their thirst,
make love and peace our fast,
to serve the poor and homeless first,
our ease and comfort last.

Great Creator, help us realize that you can use us just the way we are, just as you picked your disciples from among the common people. Please give us the strength and wisdom we need to continue your work. Amen.

Sixth Sunday after Pentecost

Watchword for the Week — There is therefore now no condemnation for those who are in Christ Jesus. Romans 8:1

Sunday, July 12 — Isaiah 55:10-13; Psalm 65:(1-8),9-13 Romans 8:1-11; Matthew 13:1-9,18-23

Lord, you are righteous, but this day we are covered with shame. Daniel 9:7 NIV

Lord, we cry to you for help. 760*
Only you can heal our pain.
Out of deep distress we call.
Help us, Lord; send peace again.

By grace you have been saved through faith, and this is not your own doing; it is the gift of God. Ephesians 2:8

What brought us together, 675
what joined our hearts?
The pardon which Jesus, our High Priest, imparts;
'tis this which cements the disciples of Christ,
who are into one by the Spirit baptized.

Amazing Father, you give us such great gifts; gifts we feel we don't deserve. But you hold us in your hands, love us, and save us. Help us appreciate your amazing grace. Amen.

Monday, July 13 — Psalm 84:8–12
Deuteronomy 23:1–24:13; Luke 9:1–11

Break up your fallow ground; for it is time to seek the Lord, that he may come and rain righteousness upon you. Hosea 10:12

God of the fertile fields, 653*
Lord of the earth that yields
our daily bread,
forth from your bounteous hand
come gifts your love has planned,
that all in ev'ry land
be clothed and fed.

Clothe yourselves with the new self, created according to the likeness of God in true righteousness and holiness. Ephesians 4:24

O that such may be our union 673
as thine with the Father is,
and not one of our communion
e'er forsake the path of bliss;
may our light break forth with brightness,
from thy light reflected shine;
thus the world will bear us witness
that we, Lord, are truly thine.

Dearest Savior, help us see the times in our lives when you are working with us, showing us a new way. Help us accept your gifts of righteousness; help us understand your direction and let us follow you. Amen.

Tuesday, July 14 — Psalm 85:1–7
Deuteronomy 24:14–25:19; Luke 9:12–27

There shall once more be heard the voice of mirth and the voice of gladness, the voice of the bridegroom and the voice of the bride, the voices of those who sing, "Give thanks to the Lord of hosts, for the Lord is good, for his steadfast love endures forever!" Jeremiah 33:10-11

By pain and sorrow undeterred, 393*
I shall proceed in gladness:
we who rely on God's own word
see past this mortal sadness.
When cloudy and difficult winter is past,
God will work our great restoration.
Take heart in the coming of springtime at last!
Take heart in glad anticipation!

Jesus said to them, "The wedding guests cannot fast while the bridegroom is with them, can they?" Mark 2:19

Long ago apostles heard it 600
by the Galilean lake,
turned from home and work and fam'ly,
leaving all for his dear sake.

Holy Redeemer, thank you for being with us and inviting us to be part of your creation—and your family. You created us from dust making us your children, and we celebrate our lives in you. Amen.

Wednesday, July 15 — Psalm 85:8–13
Deuteronomy 26:1–27:13; Luke 9:28–36

The human mind may devise many plans, but it is the purpose of the Lord that will be established. Proverbs 19:21

Take my motives and my will, 647
all your purpose to fulfill.
Take my heart—it is your own;
it shall be your royal throne.

Therefore be serious and discipline yourselves for the sake of your prayers. Above all, maintain constant love for one another. 1 Peter 4:7-8

In loving service may our lives be spent, 587
in other's gladness finding sweet content,
striving to show God's fellowship to all.
To show God's loving work—the servants' call.
In loving service may our lives be spent.

Wise Father, you make everything work together for our good and for your will to be established on earth as it is in heaven. Help us always remember that your perfect plans give us hope and love for one another. Amen.

Thursday, July 16 — Psalm 86:1–10
Deuteronomy 27:14–28:24; Luke 9:37–50

Ho, everyone who thirsts, come to the waters. Isaiah 55:1

Water has held us, 408*
moved by creation.
Out of dark chaos,
broke forth the light.
Up from the deluge,
showing God's promise,
has come a rainbow,
gladdening sight.

Jesus said, "Those who drink of the water that I will give them will never be thirsty." John 4:14

The springs of salvation from Christ, 616
the rock, bursting
and flowing throughout all the world's wilderness
bring life and salvation to those who are thirsting
to drink from this spring of salvation by grace;
as streams through the desert refresh the ground
and make land once barren with green abound,
the pow'r of his Spirit our cold hearts o'er flowing,
renews us for service with lives bright and glowing.

Source of all love, may we drink from your fountain, the living water that restores our bodies and our souls. May we fill ourselves with your salvation, and your love, and share it with everyone who thirsts. Amen.

Friday, July 17 — Psalm 86:11–17
Deuteronomy 28:25–57; Luke 9:51–62

For the Lord your God is God of gods and Lord of lords, the great God, mighty and awesome, who is not partial and takes no bribe. Deuteronomy 10:17

This is my Father's world: 456
he shines in all that's fair;
in rustling grass I hear him pass—
he speaks to me ev'rywhere.
This is my Father's world:
why should my heart be sad?
The Lord is King, let heaven ring!
God reigns; let earth be glad.

Blessed are the pure in heart, for they will see God. Matthew 5:8

Blessed are the pure in heart, 584
for they shall see their God.
The secret of the Lord is theirs;
their soul is Christ's abode.

Perfect Lord, sometimes it's hard to have a soft heart in a world full of anger and despair, of war and unfairness. Help us see the way you see, love the way you love, and help us to stay pure-hearted. In Jesus' name, we pray. Amen.

Saturday, July 18 — Psalm 87
Deuteronomy 28:58–29:21; Luke 10:1–16

Yes, and from ancient days I am he. No one can deliver out of my hand. When I act, who can reverse it? Isaiah 43:13 NIV

Hail, Alpha and Omega, hail, 703
O Author of our faith,
the Finisher of all our hopes,
the Truth, the Life, the Path.

All of us must appear before the judgment seat of Christ. 2 Corinthians 5:10

As sure as I prove 608
your mercy and love,
as life you did gain
for me, and my comfort does ever remain.

Merciful Judge, who are we to be loved so fiercely by you? You judge us with mercy and love, that no one can contradict. You pardon us with your own sacrifice and tell us we are loved by you. Help us realize the immensity of your love. Amen.

Seventh Sunday after Pentecost

Watchword for the Week — Thus says the Lord, the King of Israel, and his Redeemer, the Lord of hosts: I am the first and I am the last; besides me there is no god. Isaiah 44:6

Sunday, July 19 — Isaiah 44:6-8; Psalm 86:11-17
Romans 8:12-25; Matthew 13:24-30,36-43

What are human beings that you are mindful of them, mortals that you care for them? Psalm 8:4

> Lifegiving Creator of both great and small; 457
> of all life the maker, the true life of all;
> we blossom, then wither like leaves on the tree,
> but you live forever who was and will be.

We are what he has made us, created in Christ Jesus for good works, which God prepared beforehand to be our way of life. Ephesians 2:10

> Just as I am; thy love unknown 762
> has broken every barrier down;
> now to be thine, yea, thine alone,
> O Lamb of God, I come, I come!

Mastermind of creation, when we look at all the intricacies of our world we are so amazed! Every tiny detail has been arranged by you. Help us to trust that you have prepared our way even when we can't see. Amen.

Monday, July 20 — Psalm 88:1–5
Deuteronomy 29:22–31:8; Luke 10:17–24

Listen to me, you stubborn-hearted, you who are now far from my righteousness. I am bringing my righteousness near, it is not far away. Isaiah 46:12-13 NIV

New songs of celebration render 545*
to God who has great wonders done;
awed by his love his foes surrender
and fall before the Mighty One.
He has made known his great salvation
which all his friends with joy confess;
he has revealed to ev'ry nation
his everlasting righteousness.

The grace of God has appeared, bringing salvation to all, training us to renounce impiety. Titus 2:11-12

God is our strength and song, 531
and his salvation ours;
then be his love in Christ proclaimed
with all our ransomed pow'rs.

God of salvation, you bring us—your erring and stubborn children—great gifts even when we wander from your direction. Help us push away the materialistic world and instead enrich our lives with your strength and righteousness. In Jesus' name, we pray. Amen.

Tuesday, July 21 — Psalm 88:6–12
Deuteronomy 31:9–32:9; Luke 10:25–42

I will give thanks to the Lord with my whole heart; I will tell of all your wonderful deeds.
Psalm 9:1

Thus, all my toilsome way along, 537
I sing aloud your praises,
that all may hear the grateful song
my voice unwearied raises.
Be joyful in the Lord, my heart,
both soul and body bear your part.
To God all praise and glory!

Give thanks in all circumstances; for this is the will of God in Christ Jesus for you.
1 Thessalonians 5:18

Then let us adore and give him his right, 565
all glory and pow'r and wisdom and might,
all honor and blessing, with angels above,
and thanks never ceasing for infinite love.

Merciful Creator and giver of all, help us remember to thank you everyday for all the gifts you give us. Help us to have grateful hearts—hearts that swell with gratitude everytime we think of you. Thank you God! Amen.

Wednesday, July 22 — Psalm 88:13–18
Deuteronomy 32:10–43; Luke 11:1–13

God does great things beyond understanding, and marvelous things without number. Job 9:10

Each little flow'r that opens, 467
each little bird that sings—
God made their glowing colors,
God made their tiny wings.

This is what the kingdom of God is like. A man scatters seed on the ground. Night and day, whether he sleeps or gets up, the seed sprouts and grows, though he does not know how. All by itself the soil produces grain. Mark 4:26-28 NIV

We plow the fields, and scatter 453
the good seed on the land,
but it is fed and watered
by God's almighty hand;
he sends the snow in winter,
the warmth to swell the grain,
the breezes and the sunshine
and soft refreshing rain.

God of wonder, help us to accept that your mysterious ways may never be understood by us, but that your plans are always the best and wisest choices. We surrender to the brilliant adventure that is our life in you. Amen.

Thursday, July 23 — Psalm 89:1–8
Deuteronomy 32:44–33:17; Luke 11:14–28

You are my witnesses, says the Lord. Isaiah 43:10

Witness, ye men and angels, now, 341r
before the Lord we speak;
to Him we make our solemn vow,
a vow we dare not break.

Go into all the world and proclaim the good news to the whole creation. Mark 16:15

Sing hallelujah, praise the Lord! 543
Sing with a cheerful voice;
exalt our God with one accord,
and in his name rejoice.
Ne'er cease to sing, O ransomed host,
praise Father, Son, and Holy Ghost,
until in realms of endless light
your praises shall unite.

Mighty God, good news is ours to tell! Give us the courage and the ability to love our neighbors, to produce fruit for you, and to let everyone know what a kind and loving Savior we have in you! Amen.

Friday, July 24 — Psalm 89:9–18
Deuteronomy 33:18–34:12; Luke 11:29–36

O that you would tear open the heavens and come down! Isaiah 64:1

Gracious God, I come before thee; 12r
come thou also down to me;
where we find thee and adore thee,
there a heaven on earth must be.
To my heart, O enter thou;
let it be your temple now.

Rescue us from the evil one. Matthew 6:13

Hear us, O Lord, as we now pray, 536*
dedicate us to your way;
lead us to work that bears your fruit,
giving knowledge of your truth.
Open our door and enter in,
rescue from darkness and from sin.
Strengthen according to your might,
share with us the promised life.

Patient God, please be with us in our times of despair. Heal our hearts and keep us vigilant. We know our shepherd's voice; let us never be led astray by worldly affairs. Keep our eyes on you, we pray. Amen.

Saturday, July 25 — Psalm 89:19–29
Joshua 1,2; Luke 11:37–54

Whoever is steadfast in righteousness will live, but whoever pursues evil will die. Proverbs 11:19

Through the valley and shadow of death 180r
though I stray,
since thou are my Guardian, no evil I fear.
Thy rod shall defend me,
thy staff be my stay,
no harm can befall with my Comforter near.

Blessed are those who hunger and thirst for righteousness, for they will be filled. Matthew 5:6

Blessed are the strong but gentle, 595
trained to served a higher will,
wise to know th'eternal purpose
which their Father shall fulfill.
Blessed are they who with true passion
strive to make the right prevail,
for the earth is God's possession
and his purpose will not fail.

Precious Lord, protect us from evil. Give us the desire to seek you and your righteousness over everything else this world offers. Keep us hungry for more of your wisdom and truth, and keep us always in your hands. Amen.

Eighth Sunday after Pentecost

Watchword for the Week — God, turn to me and be gracious to me, as is your custom toward those who love your name. Psalm 119:132

Sunday, July 26 —1 Kings 3:5-12; Psalm 119:129-136
Romans 8:26-39; Matthew 13:31-33,44-52

Whoever is kind to the needy honors God. Proverbs 14:31 NIV

Take my life that it may be 610
all you purpose, Lord, for me.
Take my moments and my days;
let them sing your ceaseless praise,
let them sing your ceaseless praise.

Jesus said, "Just as you did it to one of the least of these who are members of my family, you did it to me." Matthew 25:40

Let your heart be broken 582*
for a world in need—
feed the mouths that hunger,
soothe the wounds that bleed;
give the cup of water
and the loaf of bread—
be the hands of Jesus,
serving in his stead.

Benevolent God, help us share our possessions with those in need, blessing them by sharing our blessings. Help us see ourselves in the eyes of the needy, so that we may truly be generous with our lives and our wealth. Amen.

Monday, July 27 — Psalm 89:30–37
Joshua 3,4; Luke 12:1–12

The Lord gives wisdom; from his mouth come knowledge and understanding. Proverbs 2:6

God of wisdom, truth, and beauty, p132*
God of spirit, fire, and soul,
God of order, love, and duty,
God of purpose, plan, and goal:
grant us visions ever growing,
breath of life, eternal strength,
mystic spirit moving, flowing,
filling height and depth and length.

If any of you is lacking in wisdom, ask God, who gives to all generously and ungrudgingly, and it will be given you. James 1:5

God of grace and God of glory, 751**
on your people pour your power;
crown your ancient Church's story;
bring its bud to glorious flower.
Grant us wisdom, grant us courage
for the facing of this hour,
for the facing of this hour.

Giver of wisdom, we cry out for your wisdom and knowledge, for your understanding and grace. We ask that you bless us with the quiet peace that comes when our hearts and minds both feel your presence in our lives. Amen.

Tuesday, July 28 — Psalm 89:38–45
Joshua 5,6; Luke 12:13–21

Thus far the Lord has helped us. 1 Samuel 7:12

Bless, O Lord, we pray, your congregation; 445
bless each home and family;
bless the youth, the rising generation;
blessed may your dear children be;
bless your servants, grant them help and favor;
you to glorify be their endeavor.
Lord, on you we humbly call;
let your blessing rest on all.

We are afflicted in every way, but not crushed; perplexed, but not driven to despair. 2 Corinthians 4:8

Faith finds in Christ our ev'ry need 700
to save or strengthen us indeed;
we now receive the grace sent down,
which makes us share his cross and crown.

Sometimes we feel lost and confused, God, and we need your help to figure out what it is we need to do. Give us confidence that you are working in our lives and that you know what is best for us. Amen.

Wednesday, July 29 — Psalm 89:46–52
Joshua 7; Luke 12:22–34

Naked I came from my mother's womb, and naked I will depart. Job 1:21 NIV

Blessed are the poor in spirit, 595
claiming nothing as their own,
but as giv'n them by their Father
that his goodness may be shown.
Blessed are they who share the sorrow
of their God's unchanging love;
they shall know his presence with them
and his promised comfort prove.

We brought nothing into the world, so that we can take nothing out of it; but if we have food and clothing, we will be content with these. 1 Timothy 6:7-8

No offering of my own I have, 539r
nor works my faith to prove;
I can but give the gifts he gave
and plead his love for love.

Sustainer, help us to realize that you provide for our needs and that there is no need for us to pile up treasures here on earth—for your kingdom is our treasure and your love is our greatest reward. Amen.

Thursday, July 30 — Psalm 90
Joshua 8:1–29; Luke 12:35–48

Be silent before the Lord God! For the day of the Lord is at hand. Zephaniah 1:7

Amazing grace! How sweet the sound 783
that saved a wretch like me!
I once was lost, but now am found,
was blind, but now I see.

Let anyone with ears to hear listen! Mark 4:9

Jesus, great High Priest of our profession, 202r
we in confidence draw near;
condescend, in mercy, the confession
of our grateful hearts to hear;
thee we gladly own in every nation,
head and master of thy congregation,
conscious that in every place
thou dispensest life and grace.

There are times when we get so wrapped up in our busy lives, gracious Lord, we forget that pausing to be quiet and listening for your voice is all we need to find solace. Help us remember to seek your peace. In Jesus' name, we pray. Amen.

Friday, July 31 — Psalm 91:1–8
Joshua 8:30–9:27; Luke 12:49–59

You shall not spread a false report. Exodus 23:1

Keep me from saying words 615
that later need recalling;
guard me, lest idle speech
may from my lips be falling;
but when, within my place,
I must and ought to speak,
then to my words give grace,
lest I offend the weak.

Do your best to present yourself to God as one approved by him, a worker who has no need to be ashamed, rightly explaining the word of truth. 2 Timothy 2:15

Thanks we give and adoration 559
for your gospel's joyful sound.
May the fruits of your salvation
in our hearts and lives abound.
Ever faithful, ever faithful
to your truth may we be found.

Ruler of the universe, help us recognize our place as ambassadors to your kingdom. Let us be honest, respectful, and worthy in everything we do as we represent you to the world. Let them know we are Christians by our love. Amen.

Saturday, August 1 — Psalm 91:9–16
Joshua 10:1–28; Luke 13:1–17

I am coming to gather all nations and tongues; and they shall come and shall see my glory. Isaiah 66:18

We'll crowd your gates with thankful songs, 455
high as the heav'n our voices raise;
and earth, with her ten thousand tongues,
shall fill your courts with sounding praise.

There is no distinction between Jew and Greek; the same Lord is Lord of all and is generous to all who call on him. Romans 10:12

Proclaim to ev'ry people, tongue, and nation 618
that God, in whom they live and move, is love;
tell how he stooped to save his lost creation,
and died on earth that we might live in love.

We come to you this day from all over your world, O God, to lift up a prayer for all your people. May we all come to know you as one who willingly accompanies us along this day's journey. Amen.

Ninth Sunday after Pentecost

Watchword for the Week — The Lord is good to all, and his compassion is over all that he has made. Psalm 145:9

Sunday, August 2 — Isaiah 55:1-5; Psalm 145:8-9,14-21
Romans 9:1-5; Matthew 14:13-21

Remember the days of old, consider the years long past; ask your father, and he will inform you; your elders, and they will tell you. Deuteronomy 32:7

May those who teach, and those who learn, p91r
walk in the narrow road;
in every sphere of thought discern
an everpresent God.

Hold to the standard of sound teaching that you have heard from me, in the faith and love that are in Christ Jesus. 2 Timothy 1:13

Then let us praise the Father 391
and worship God the Son
and sing to God the Spirit,
eternal Three in One,
till all the ransomed number
who stand before the throne
ascribe all pow'r and glory
and praise to God alone.

O Holy Word, from you comes the truth that shall make us free. Bless all the teachers of the world who continue to share such a redeeming truth. Amen.

Monday, August 3 — Psalm 92:1–8
Joshua 10:29–11:23; Luke 13:18–30

The Lord gives grace to the humble.
Proverbs 3:34 NKJV

Make use of me, my God; 512r
let me not be forgot,
a broken vessel, cast aside,
one whom thou needest not.

Do nothing from selfish ambition or conceit, but in humility regard others as better than yourselves. Philippians 2:3

Let us each for others care, 672
each another's burden bear,
to your church a pattern give,
showing how believers live.

Gracious God, let our broken hearts live in concert with the broken hearts of others. Together, we are stronger. Together, we can make beautiful harmony for the world to hear. Amen.

Tuesday, August 4 — Psalm 92:9–15
Joshua 12:1–13:7; Luke 13:31–14:6

In the great congregation I will bless the Lord. Psalm 26:12

Bless your maker, all you creatures, 458
ever under God's control;
all throughout his vast dominion
bless the Lord of all, my soul!

What then shall we say, brothers and sisters? When you come together, each of you has a hymn, or a word of instruction, a revelation, a tongue, or an interpretation. Everything must be done so that the church may be built up. 1 Corinthians 14:26 NIV

The wise may bring their learning, 658
the rich may bring their wealth,
and some may bring their greatness,
and some their strength and health:
we too would bring our treasures
to offer to the King,
we have no wealth or learning—
what shall we children bring?

Thank you, O great Giver, for the gifts you impart to the whole congregation. May we all find ways to bless your name and build up your church no matter the amount of resources we may have. Amen.

Wednesday, August 5 — Psalm 93
Joshua 13:8–14:5; Luke 14:7–24

May the Lord, who is good, pardon everyone who sets their heart on seeking God. 2 Chronicles 30:18-19 NIV

O, to grace how great a debtor 782
daily I'm constrained to be!
Let that grace, Lord, like a fetter,
bind my wand'ring heart to thee.
Prone to wander, Lord, I feel it,
prone to leave the God I love,
here's my heart, O take and seal it;
seal it for thy courts above.

A man was there by the name of Zacchaeus; he was a chief tax collector and was wealthy. He wanted to see who Jesus was. Luke 19:2-3 NIV

Take my wealth, all I possess, 647
make me rich in faithfulness.
Take my mind that I may use
ev'ry pow'r as you should choose.

Oftentimes, Lord, we see you from a distance. Instead of doing everything we can to readjust our angle in life, we blindly go about our day. Forgive us, good Lord, and please make yourself at home in our hearts. Amen.

Thursday, August 6 — Psalm 94:1–11
Joshua 14:6–15:19; Luke 14:25–32

He does not deal with us according to our sins, nor repay us according to our iniquities. Psalm 103:10

Praise him for his grace and favor 529
to his people in distress.
Praise him, still the same forever,
slow to chide, and swift to bless.
Alleluia! Alleluia!
Glorious in his faithfulness!

We believe that we will be saved through the grace of the Lord Jesus. Acts 15:11

All our days, O Jesus, 770
hallow unto you;
may our lives be given
in your service true;
let us all experience,
to the end of days,
your abiding presence
and your loving grace.

Gracious God, our sins are too many to count and yet you refuse to number them when considering our worthiness to stand before you. May your grace continue to uphold us all our days. Amen.

Friday, August 7 — Psalm 94:12–23
Joshua 15:20–63; Luke 15:1–10

The Lord will again comfort Zion. Zechariah 1:17

"Comfort, comfort now my people; 264
tell of peace!" So says our God.
Comfort those who sit in darkness
bowed beneath oppression's load.
To God's people now proclaim
that God's pardon waits for them!
Tell them that their war is over;
God will reign in peace forever!

He who rescued us from so deadly a peril will continue to rescue us; on him we have set our hope. 2 Corinthians 1:10

Those who are by Christ directed, 717
trusting the Good Shepherd's care,
from all harm will be protected,
and no danger need to fear.

Restore us and revive us, O great First Responder. Be there by our side when there is destruction. May your healing touch give life to our bodies and souls. Amen.

Saturday, August 8 — Psalm 95
Joshua 16,17; Luke 15:11–32

My eyes are ever towards the Lord, for he will pluck my feet out of the net. Psalm 25:15

To the hills I lift my eyes, 729
the everlasting hills.
Streaming forth in fresh supplies,
my soul the Spirit feels;
will he not his help afford?
Help, while yet I ask, is giv'n;
God comes down, the God and Lord
who made both earth and heav'n.

Pray for us, so that the word of the Lord may spread rapidly and be glorified everywhere, just as it is among you, and that we may be rescued from wicked and evil people; for not all have faith. But the Lord is faithful; he will strengthen you and guard you from the evil one. 2 Thessalonians 3:1-3

We've a song to be sung to the nations, 621
that shall lift their hearts to the Lord,
a song that shall conquer evil
and shatter the spear and sword,
and shatter the spear and sword.

O God, when the affairs of this world entangle us and the naysayers encamp their criticisms around us, may we be ready to boldly share your gracious love even so. Amen.

Tenth Sunday after Pentecost

Watchword for the Week — Jesus spoke to the disciples and said, "Take heart, it is I; do not be afraid." Matthew 14:27

Sunday, August 9 — 1 Kings 19:9-18; Psalm 85:8-13
Romans 10:5-15; Matthew 14:22-33

The Lord gave them food from heaven in abundance. He opened the rock, and water gushed out; it flowed through the desert like a river. For he remembered his holy promise. Psalm 105:40-42

Sing, pray, and keep his ways unswerving, 712
offer your service faithfully,
and trust his word; though undeserving,
you'll find his promise true to be.
God never will forsake in need
the soul that trusts in him indeed.

Blessed be the God and Father of our Lord Jesus Christ, who has blessed us in Christ with every spiritual blessing in the heavenly places. Ephesians 1:3

Here is a pasture, rich and never failing, 593
here living waters in abundance flow;
none can conceive the grace with them prevailing,
who Jesus' shepherd-voice obey and know.
He banishes all fear and strife,
and leads them gently on to everlasting life.

Our cup runneth over with your blessings, O God, of every gift! May the river of nourishment flow through our souls to give us life in your name. Amen.

Monday, August 10 — Psalm 96:1–9
Joshua 18:1–19:9; Luke 16:1–15

Gideon said, "I will not rule over you; the Lord will rule over you." Judges 8:23

Come, holy Comforter, 555
your sacred witness bear
in this glad hour.
Your grace to us impart,
now rule in ev'ry heart,
never from us depart,
Spirit of pow'r!

It is not those who commend themselves that are approved, but those whom the Lord commends. 2 Corinthians 10:18

Mighty God, we humbly pray, 586
let your pow'r now lead the way
that in all things we may show
that we in your likeness grow.

Sovereign God, may we find favor in your sight this day. May your smiles outnumber your frowns as you look upon us. Thank you for your love, nonetheless. In your name, we pray. Amen.

Tuesday, August 11 — Psalm 96:10–13
Joshua 19:10–39; Luke 16:16–31

Let the righteous be joyful; let them exult before God; let them be jubilant with joy. Psalm 68:3

Joyful, joyful, we adore you, 544
God of glory, Lord of love;
hearts unfold like flow'rs before you,
op'ning to the sun above.
Melt the clouds of sin and sadness;
drive the dark of doubt away;
giver of immortal gladness,
fill us with the light of day!

Rejoice in the Lord always; again I will say, rejoice. Philippians 4:4

Rejoice, the Lord is King! 372
Your Lord and King adore.
Rejoice, give thanks and sing
and triumph evermore.
Lift up your heart, lift up your voice,
rejoice, again I say, rejoice!

Source of eternal joy, may our earthly happiness be transformed into true joy as we live alongside you. This joy carries us through all circumstances. So, regardless of what today brings, we rejoice! Amen!

Wednesday, August 12 — Psalm 97:1–6
Joshua 19:40–21:8; Luke 17:1–10

Let your eyes be open to the plea of your servant, and to the plea of your people Israel, listening to them whenever they call to you. 1 Kings 8:52

Lord, you have been our dwelling place p147
in every generation.
Your people still have known your grace
and your blest consolation.
Through ev'ry age you heard our cry,
through ev'ry age we found you nigh,
our strength and our salvation.

If in my name you ask me for anything, I will do it. John 14:14

Lord, teach us how to pray aright, 750
with rev'rence and with fear;
though dust and ashes in your sight,
we may, we must draw near.

May we courageously approach your throne of grace, O God. May we speak with confidence that you are near and hear us with open ears and a compassionate heart. What an example for us to follow! Amen.

August Thirteenth Festival† — Joshua 24:16-24; Psalm 133
1 John 4:1-13; John 17:1-2,6-19

Thursday, August 13 — Psalm 97:7–12
Joshua 21:9–45; Luke 17:11–19

By his bruises we are healed. Isaiah 53:5

What wondrous love is this, 328
O my soul, O my soul!
What wondrous love is this, O my soul!
What wondrous love is this
that caused the Lord of bliss
to bear the dreadful curse for my soul, for my soul,
to bear the dreadful curse for my soul?

Jesus was about to die for the nation, and not for the nation only, but to gather into one the dispersed children of God. John 11:51-52

May we all your loved ones be, 352
all one holy family,
loving, since your love we see:
hear us, holy Jesus.

Christ, we are united by your grace. You call us from all walks of life to gather at your cross. May the painful waters flow from your side into our wandering hearts to bring us together. Amen.

† On this date in 1727 in Berthelsdorf, Saxony (now Germany), a group of quarreling Christians experienced their unity in Christ through the power of the Holy Spirit. This new Pentecost marked the revival of the Unity of the Brethren, begun in 1457, and the beginning of the Renewed Moravian Church.

Friday, August 14 — Psalm 98
Joshua 22; Luke 17:20–25

Whom have I in heaven but you? And there is nothing on earth that I desire other than you. Psalm 73:25

God reveals his presence; 554
let us now adore him
and with awe appear before him.
God is in his temple;
all in us keep silence
and before him bow with reverence.
Him alone God we own;
he's our Lord and Savior.
Praise his name forever.

So Jesus asked the twelve, "Do you also wish to go away?" Simon Peter answered him, "Lord, to whom can we go? You have the words of eternal life. We have come to believe and know that you are the Holy One of God." John 6:67-69

To you, most holy Lord, 633
we sing with hearts and voices;
in you, with one accord,
your church on earth rejoices!
We bend before your throne
and humbly chant your praise;
we worship you alone,
whose love has crowned our days.

Our one and only Lord, may our loyalty to you never waver. The idols of the world are no match for you. Our greatest satisfaction is knowing that we are yours and you are ours. Amen.

Saturday, August 15 — Psalm 99
Joshua 23:1–24:13; Luke 17:26–37

Do not oppress the widow, the orphan, the alien, or the poor. Zechariah 7:10

From tender childhood's helplessness, 532r
from woman's grief, man's burdened toil,
from famished souls, from sorrow's stress
thy heart has never known recoil.

God chose what is low and despised in the world. 1 Corinthians 1:28

O Master, from the mountain side 532r
make haste to heal these hearts of pain;
among these restless throngs abide;
O tread the city's streets again.

Lord, help us to see you outside of the cathedrals and mansions of the world. May we find you among the vulnerable and be willing to work there alongside you. May every ear be afforded the sound of good news! Amen.

Eleventh Sunday after Pentecost

Watchword for the Week — Let the peoples praise you, O God; let all the peoples praise you. Psalm 67:5

Sunday, August 16 — Isaiah 56:1,6-8; Psalm 67
Romans 11:1-2a,29-32; Matthew 15:(10-20),21-28

He remembered us in our low estate, for his steadfast love endures forever. Psalm 136:23

O perfect Love, all human thought transcending, 427
lowly we kneel in prayer before your throne,
that theirs may be the love which knows no ending,
whom you forevermore unite in one.

Remember those who are in prison, as though you were in prison with them; those who are being tortured, as though you yourselves were being tortured. Hebrews 13:3

Fill us with your compassion, Lord, 338*
our fear and pride remove,
till all our lives enflesh your word
and bear your wounds of love.

Thank you, God, for looking past our stains and imperfections. Although we tend to allow them to hold us captive, your love breaks the chains of bondage. May we share that love with others who feel imprisoned. Amen.

Monday, August 17 — Psalm 100
Joshua 24:14–Judges 1:16; Luke 18:1–17

Let us go with you, for we have heard that God is with you. Zechariah 8:23

O yes, having found in the Lord our delight, 675
he is our chief object by day and by night;
this knits us together; no longer we roam;
we all have one Father, and heav'n is our home.

Every day they continued to meet together in the temple courts. They broke bread in their homes and ate together with glad and sincere hearts, praising God and enjoying the favor of all the people. Acts 2:46-47 NIV

When Christians shared agape meals, 395*
O Lord, your Spirit came
to bless and love the infant church
which gathered in your name
and set each heart aflame.

What a blessing to sit at the table with you, Lord! Jesus, come and take your place among us. Nourish us with your spirit. Let us leave the table feeling refreshed and energized for that which you have called us. Amen.

Tuesday, August 18 — Psalm 101
Judges 1:17–2:23; Luke 18:18–30

For the Lord is good; his steadfast love endures forever, and his faithfulness to all generations. Psalm 100:5

Now thank we all our God 533
with heart and hands and voices,
who wondrous things has done,
in whom his world rejoices;
who, from our mother's arms,
has blessed us on our way
with countless gifts of love,
and still is ours today.

When the goodness and loving kindness of God our Savior appeared, he saved us, not because of any works of righteousness that we had done, but according to his mercy. Titus 3:4-5

Through many dangers, toils, and snares, 783
I have already come;
'tis grace has brought me safe thus far,
and grace will lead me home.

We cannot fathom your infinite love for us, O loving God. How can we ever love you so much in return? We give you our hearts and trust that you will feel the love we have for you. Amen.

Wednesday, August 19 — Psalm 102:1–11
Judges 3; Luke 18:31–43

Moses said to the Lord, "Consider too that this nation is your people." Exodus 33:13

This is our Father's world: 456
O let us not forget
that though the wrong is often strong,
God is the ruler yet.
He trusts us with his world,
to keep it clean and fair—
all earth and trees, all skies and seas,
all creatures ev'rywhere.

God called you through our proclamation of the good news, so that you may obtain the glory of our Lord Jesus Christ. 2 Thessalonians 2:14

May the love of Jesus fill me 585
as the waters fill the sea;
him exalting, self abasing—
this is victory.

Almighty God, the world you created for us is suffering and we are to blame. Let us love and value your creation as if it were our very own. In the name of Jesus. Amen.

Thursday, August 20 — Psalm 102:12–22
Judges 4; Luke 19:1–10

Hatred stirs up strife, but love covers all offenses. Proverbs 10:12

Spirit of Love, transform our ways, 491*
fill with new feeling all of our days;
replace our hatred, our anger, our fear
with new compassion, new struggle to care.

By this everyone will know that you are my disciples, if you have love for one another. John 13:35

O that Jesus' love and merit 589
filled our hearts both night and day!
May the leading of his Spirit
all our thoughts and actions sway!
Then should we be ever ready
cheerfully to testify
how our spirit, soul and body
do in God our Savior joy.

God, teach us to love those with whom we struggle. May your heart, filled with compassion and love, be an example for us as we follow your lead. Amen.

Friday, August 21† — Psalm 102:23–28
Judges 5; Luke 19:11–27

You are wearied with your many consultations. Isaiah 47:13

My Shepherd will supply my need; 730
the Lord God is his name.
In pastures fresh he makes me feed,
beside the living stream.
He brings my wand'ring spirit back
when I forsake his ways,
and leads me for his mercy's sake
in paths of truth and grace.

The disciples came to Jesus and asked, "Who is the greatest in the kingdom of heaven?" He called a child, whom he put among them, and said, "Truly I tell you, unless you change and become like children, you will never enter the kingdom of heaven." Matthew 18:1-3

I am Jesus' little lamb; 723
ever glad at heart I am;
for my Shepherd gently guides me,
knows my need and well provides me,
loves me ev'ry day the same,
even calls me by my name.

May our child-like curiosity never lead us astray, great Teacher. May we be attentive to your words and always ready to welcome your children into our fellowship. Amen.

† On this day in 1732, the first missionaries departed from Herrnhut bound for St. Thomas.

Saturday, August 22 — Psalm 103:1–5
Judges 6; Luke 19:28–44

The king said to Daniel, 'Truly, your God is God of gods and Lord of kings.' Daniel 2:47

All praise to you, my God, this night 569
for all the blessings of the light.
Keep me, O keep me, King of kings,
beneath the shelter of your wings.

At the name of Jesus every knee should bend, in heaven and on earth and under the earth. Philippians 2:10

Jesus' name, Jesus' name, 324
source of life and happiness!
In this name true consolation
mourning sinners may possess;
here is found complete salvation.
Blessed Jesus, we your name will praise
all our days, all our days.

You alone, Lord, have the power to change us. May our hearts surrender to your transforming ways. In your holy name, we pray. Amen.

Twelfth Sunday after Pentecost

Watchword for the Week — Do not be conformed to this world, but be transformed by the renewing of your minds, so that you may discern what is the will of God—what is good and acceptable and perfect. Romans 12:2

Sunday, August 23 — Isaiah 51:1-6; Psalm 138
Romans 12:1-8; Matthew 16:13-20

Trust in him at all times, O people; pour out your heart before him; God is a refuge for us. Psalm 62:8

If you but trust in God to guide you 712
and place your confidence in him,
you'll find him always there beside you
to give you hope and strength within;
for those who trust God's changeless love
build on the rock that will not move.

And this is the boldness we have in him, that if we ask anything according to his will, he hears us. 1 John 5:14

Ask and it shall be given unto you, 605*
seek and you shall find,
knock and the door shall be opened unto you—
Allelu, alleluia!

God, in our weakness, we fail to come to you when we need you the most. When we do strike up the courage to approach you, may your inviting arms reassure us that we're always welcome. Amen.

Monday, August 24 — Psalm 103:6–18
Judges 7; Luke 19:45–20:8

You prepare a table before me in the presence of my enemies; you anoint my head with oil; my cup overflows. Psalm 23:5

Come, you thankful people, come, 450
raise the song of harvest-home;
all is safely gathered in,
ere the winter storms begin;
God, our Maker, does provide
for our needs to be supplied:
come with all his people, come,
raise the song of harvest-home.

While he was at Bethany in the house of Simon the leper, as he sat at the table, a woman came with an alabaster jar of very costly ointment of nard, and she broke open the jar and poured the ointment on his head. But some were there who said to one another in anger, "Why was the ointment wasted in this way?" But Jesus said, "Let her alone; why do you trouble her? She has performed a good service for me." Mark 14:3-4,6

Take my love; my Lord, I pour 647
at your feet its treasure store;
take myself, and I will be
yours for all eternity.

Open our eyes, Lord, to the various ways in which people worship you. May our variety of traditions and customs be a blessing to you, your church, and your children. Amen.

Tuesday, August 25 — Psalm 103:19–22
Judges 8; Luke 20:9–19

Lord, I rejoice in your salvation.
1 Samuel 2:1 NJKV

O enter then his gates with joy; 539
within his courts his praise proclaim.
Let thankful songs your tongues employ;
O bless and magnify his name.

Mary said, "My soul magnifies the Lord, and my spirit rejoices in God my Savior, for he has looked with favor on the lowliness of his servant." Luke 1:46-48

Praise to the Lord! 530
O, let all that is in me adore him!
All that has life and breath,
come now with praises before him!
Let the amen
sound from his people again.
Gladly forever adore him!

Gracious God, no other gift deserves as much praise as the one you gave the world two thousand years ago! What a blessing to inherit such a gift. May your name be forever praised! Amen!

Wednesday, August 26 — Psalm 104:1–9
Judges 9:1–33; Luke 20:20–26

You have burdened me with your sins; you have wearied me with your iniquities. I, I am he who blots out your transgressions for my own sake, and I will not remember your sins. Isaiah 43:24-25

For thinking you too far from us, 738*
for fearing you too close to us,
forgive us now, good Lord.
You dwell in high and holy place,
and yet touch all things with your grace.
Through all our lives be now adored.

Once you were alienated from God and were enemies in your minds because of your evil behavior. But now he has reconciled you by Christ's physical body through death to present you holy in his sight. Colossians 1:21-22 NIV

O God of unrelenting grace, 738*
whose judgment yet we daily face,
forgive us now, good Lord.
You are so distant and so near;
for you we long, yet you we fear,
O known, and yet beyond record.

Before you, great Judge, our sentence was merciless. Because of your great and radical decision, we were rescued from our initial destiny. This new life in you fills our hearts with hope. In your gracious name, we pray. Amen.

Thursday, August 27 — Psalm 104:10–18
Judges 9:34–10:18; Luke 20:27–40

The Lord our God protected us along all the way that we went. Joshua 24:17

He leadeth me: O blessed thought! 787
O words with heav'nly comfort fraught!
Whate'er I do, where'er I be,
still 'tis God's hand that leadeth me.

And remember, I am with you always, to the end of the age. Matthew 28:20

Lord God, Son, the Savior of the world, p35
be gracious unto us.
Lord God, Holy Spirit,
abide with us forever.

Companion, when the road is treacherous, guide our steps so we may not fall. When the road is smooth, guide our steps so we may not fall away. We are grateful for the adventurous path that awaits us. Amen.

Friday, August 28 — Psalm 104:19–23
Judges 11:1–27; Luke 20:41–21:4

O God, you are my God, I seek you, my soul thirsts for you. Psalm 63:1

Drop thy still dews of quietness, 739
till all our strivings cease.
Take from our souls the strain and stress;
and let our ordered lives confess
the beauty of thy peace.

Let anyone who is thirsty come to me. John 7:37

I need thee ev'ry hour; 740
teach me thy will,
and thy rich promises
in me fulfill.

Lord God, often we sit by the water's edge wondering when you will quench our thirst. Help us to find the courage to just dive into your vast ocean of blessings and nourishment. In Jesus' name, we pray. Amen.

Saturday, August 29 — Psalm 104:24–30
Judges 11:28–12:15; Luke 21:5–28

Hezekiah became sick and was at the point of death. He prayed to the Lord, and he answered him and gave him a sign. But Hezekiah did not respond according to the benefit done to him for his heart was proud. 2 Chronicles 32:24-25

Restrain me lest I harbor pride, 733
lest I in my own strength confide;
though I am weak, show me anew
I have my pow'r, my strength from you.

One of them, when he saw that he was healed, turned back, praising God with a loud voice. He prostrated himself at Jesus' feet and thanked him. Luke 17:15-16

Praise to God, immortal praise, p119
for the love that crowns our days!
Bounteous source of every joy,
let your praise our tongues employ;
all to you, our God, we owe,
source from which all blessings flow.

Creator God, everything comes from you. Let us always be mindful of your bounteous hand that provides all we need. Thank you for your great model of generosity. Amen.

Thirteenth Sunday after Pentecost

Watchword for the Week — Jesus said, "If any want to become my followers, let them deny themselves and take up their cross and follow me." Matthew 16:24

Sunday, August 30 — Jeremiah 15:15-21; Psalm 26:1-8
Romans 12:9-21; Matthew 16:21-28

The effect of righteousness will be peace, and the result of righteousness, quietness and trust forever. Isaiah 32:17

I've got peace like a river, 592
I've got peace like a river,
I've got peace like a river in my soul,
I've got peace like a river,
I've got peace like a river,
I've got peace like a river in my soul.

The kingdom of God is not food and drink but righteousness and peace and joy in the Holy Spirit. Romans 14:17

I've got joy like a fountain, 592
I've got joy like a fountain,
I've got joy like a fountain in my soul,
I've got joy like a fountain,
I've got joy like a fountain,
I've got joy like a fountain in my soul.

May we reflect on the day when our souls will be at rest in you, Lord. Is there solace for our current situation knowing that one day, all will be well? Lord, answer us in a comforting, yet powerful way. Amen.

Monday, August 31— Psalm 104:31–35
Judges 13; Luke 21:29–38

Know that the Lord is God. Psalm 100:3

Because the Lord our God is good, 539
his mercy is forever sure.
His truth at all times firmly stood,
and shall from age to age endure.

Indeed he is not far from each one of us. For 'In him we live and move and have our being'. Acts 17:27-28

Love divine, all loves excelling, 474
joy of heav'n, to earth come down!
Fix in us your humble dwelling,
all your faithful mercies crown.
Jesus, you are all compassion,
pure, unbounded love impart!
Visit us with your salvation,
enter ev'ry trembling heart.

Living God, we cannot do this thing called life by ourselves. It's too hard. Thank you for your life-giving spirit that breathes in us the will to keep going. Amen.

Tuesday, September 1 — Psalm 105:1–7
Judges 14,15; Luke 22:1–13

On that day the root of Jesse shall stand as a signal to the peoples. Isaiah 11:10

The word of God a promise told: 299
a king shall come, let all behold.
The world awaits his presence new,
a Child, a Son, a Savior true.

And just as Jesus was coming up out of the water, he saw the heavens torn apart and the Spirit descending like a dove on him. And a voice came from heaven, "You are my Son, the Beloved; with you I am well pleased." Mark 1:10-11

Teach me to love you as your angels love, 490
one holy passion filling all my frame:
the baptism of the heav'n-descended dove;
my heart an altar, and your love the flame.

Heavenly Father, that each of your sons and daughters is your beloved is the greatest blessing! May we lead lives reflective of that tremendous gift—offering love, tenderness, and forgiveness to others. Amen.

Wednesday, September 2 — Psalm 105:8–15
Judges 16,17; Luke 22:14–23

Praise him, sun and moon; praise him, all you shining stars! For he commanded, and they were created. Psalm 148:3,5

Praise the Lord! You heav'ns, adore him, 454
praise him, angels in the height;
sun and moon, rejoice before him;
praise him, all you stars and light.
Praise the Lord! For he has spoken;
worlds his mighty voice obeyed;
laws which never shall be broken
for their guidance he has made.

You are worthy, our Lord and God, to receive glory and honor and power, for you created all things, and by your will they existed and were created. Revelation 4:11

To him, enthroned by filial right, 469
all pow'r in heav'n and earth proclaim,
honor, and majesty, and might;
"Worthy the Lamb, for he was slain!"

Master Designer, with a majestic and gracious hand, you created all things bright and beautiful. We bow before you in worship because you alone are worthy of our thanks and praise. Amen.

Thursday, September 3 — Psalm 105:16–22
Judges 18; Luke 22:24–38

Anxiety weighs down the human heart, but a good word cheers it up. Proverbs 12:25

O bless his holy name, 452
and joyful thanks proclaim
through all the earth;
be grateful and receive
God's blessing; and believe;
his love does not deceive.
Now share your mirth!

Be kind to one another, tenderhearted, forgiving one another, as God in Christ has forgiven you. Ephesians 4:32

We now forgive each other's faults 785*
as we our own confess,
that we may love each other well
in Christian gentleness.

Lord, as your children we come to you sinful and selfish, yet you receive us with your never-failing love and with complete forgiveness. Enable us to extend the same grace to others. Amen.

Friday, September 4 — Psalm 105:23–36
Judges 19; Luke 22:39–51

The Lord bless you and keep you. Numbers 6:24

The Lord bless and keep you in his favor 446
as his chosen, cherished heir;
the Lord make his face shine on you ever
and enfold you in his care.
The Lord lift his countenance upon you,
may where'er you go his Spirit lead you,
and his peace on you bestow;
Amen, Amen, be it so.

From his fullness we have all received, grace upon grace. John 1:16

'Twas grace that taught my heart to fear 783
and grace my fears relieved;
how precious did that grace appear
the hour I first believed.

Thank you, God, for showering us with your grace. Like a lavish gift that is undeserved, we readily receive your grace daily and we delight in its splendor. Amen.

Saturday, September 5 — Psalm 105:37–45
Judges 20:1–31; Luke 22:52–62

You have been a refuge for the needy in his distress, a shelter from the storm and a shade from the heat. For the breath of the ruthless is like a storm. Isaiah 25:4 NIV

O God, our help in ages past, 461
our hope for years to come,
our shelter from the stormy blast,
and our eternal home!

These are the words of the first and the last, who was dead and came to life, "I know your affliction and your poverty." Revelation 2:8-9

O Lord of all the living, 763*
both banished and restored,
compassionate, forgiving
and ever caring Lord,
grant now that my transgressing,
my faithlessness may cease.
Stretch out your hand in blessing,
in pardon and in peace.

Compassionate Lord, you know each of us and the burden that each individual bears. Through the peace of Jesus, lighten our load. Amen.

Fourteenth Sunday after Pentecost

Watchword for the Week — Give me understanding, O God, that I may keep your law and observe it with my whole heart. Psalm 119:34

Sunday, September 6 — Ezekiel 33:7-11; Psalm 119:33-40 Romans 13:8-14; Matthew 18:15-20

The Lord will keep you from all evil; he will keep your life. Psalm 121:7

Faithful soul, pray, always pray, 729
and still in God confide;
he your stumbling steps shall stay,
and shall not let you slide;
safe from known or secret foes,
free from sin and Satan's hold,
when the flesh, earth, hell oppose,
he'll keep you in his fold.

May the God of peace himself sanctify you entirely; and may your spirit and soul and body be kept sound and blameless at the coming of our Lord Jesus Christ. 1 Thessalonians 5:23

Jesus, Master, I am yours; 614
keep me faithful, keep me near;
as your radiance through me pours
all my homeward way to cheer.
Jesus, at your feet I fall.
O be now my all in all!

Lord, on this Sabbath Day, we offer you praise. We ask for your protective and gracious eye to watch over us each day during the week ahead. Give us your peace. Amen.

Monday, September 7 — Psalm 106:1–5
Judges 20:32–21:25; Luke 22:63–71

Your eyes are open to all the ways of mortals. Jeremiah 32:19

God is my strong salvation, 769
no enemy I fear;
he hears my supplication,
dispelling all my care;
if he, my head and master,
defend me from above,
what pain or what disaster
can part me from his love?

We have our hope set on the living God, who is the Savior of all people, especially of those who believe. 1 Timothy 4:10

The ground of my profession 769
is Jesus and his blood;
he gives me the possession
of everlasting good.
To me his Holy Spirit
speaks many a precious word
of rest to one who's seeking
a refuge in the Lord.

Loving Lord, you keep watch over all your children. We find our hope in you, the living God. Thank you for your forgiveness through our Savior. Amen.

Tuesday, September 8 — Psalm 106:6–12
Ruth 1; Luke 23:1–12

You shall know that I am the Lord, when I deal with you for my name's sake, not according to your evil ways or corrupt deeds. Ezekiel 20:44

For God, in grace and tenderness, 519
regarded us in our distress;
yea, to our aid himself he came;
let all adore God's holy name.

He is kind to the ungrateful and the wicked. Luke 6:35

Most holy Lord and God, p203
holy, almighty God,
holy and most merciful Savior,
our eternal God!
Grant that we may never
lose the comforts from your death.
Have mercy, O Lord.

Merciful and ever-loving Lord, through your compassion our wrongs are made right. Our brokenness is restored. Our weakness becomes strength. And over and over again, we thank you for your mercy. Amen.

Wednesday, September 9 — Psalm 106:13–23
Ruth 2,3; Luke 23:13–31

Let those stand up and save you, who gaze at the stars and at each new moon predict what shall befall you. See, they are like stubble, the fire consumes them. Isaiah 47:13-14

"When through fiery trials your pathway shall lie, 709
my grace, all-sufficient, shall be your supply.
The flame shall not hurt you; I only design
your dross to consume and your gold to refine."

Do not be carried away by all kinds of strange teachings; for it is well for the heart to be strengthened by grace. Hebrews 13:9

By your holy word instruct them; 660
fill their minds with heav'nly light;
by your pow'rful grace constrain them
always to approve what's right;
let them know your yoke is easy,
let them prove your burden's light.

Thank you, gracious God, for your firm foundation, guiding hand, and never-failing love. You are the way, the truth, and the life. Forever. Amen.

Thursday, September 10 — Psalm 106:24–31
Ruth 4; Luke 23:32–43

God said, "I have set my bow in the clouds, and it shall be a sign of the covenant between me and the earth." Genesis 9:13

Water has held us, 408*
moved by creation.
Out of dark chaos,
broke forth the light.
Up from the deluge,
showing God's promise,
has come a rainbow,
gladdening sight.

So we who have found safety with him are greatly encouraged to hold firmly to the hope placed before us. Hebrews 6:18 GNT

I need your presence every passing hour. 807
What but your grace can foil the tempter's pow'r?
Who like yourself my guide and strength can be?
Through cloud and sunshine, O abide with me.

How blessed we are to embrace your promises, Lord! Thank you for never leaving us and always loving us. Amen.

* Used by permission of Marjean Postlethwaite.

Friday, September 11 — Psalm 106:32–39
1 Samuel 1:1–2:11; Luke 23:44–56

Hear my prayer, O Lord, and give ear to my cry; do not be silent at my tears. Psalm 39:12 NASB

O Lord, hear my prayer, 745
O Lord, hear my prayer:
when I call answer me.
O Lord, hear my prayer,
O Lord, hear my prayer.
Come and listen to me.

The Canaanite woman came and knelt before Jesus, saying, "Lord, help me." Matthew 15:25

Come, you thirsty, come and welcome, 765
God's free bounty glorify;
true belief and true repentance,
ev'ry grace that brings you nigh.

Lord, each of us is in need of your divine help. May we always trust in your provision and in your power, never hesitating to turn to you. In Jesus' name, we pray. Amen.

Saturday, September 12 — Psalm 106:40–48
1 Samuel 2:12–36; Luke 24:1–12

The earth is the Lord's and all that is in it, the world, and those who live in it. Psalm 24:1

Worship, honor, glory, blessing, p1
Lord, we offer unto you;
young and old, your praise expressing,
sing your mercies ever new.
All the saints in heav'n adore you;
we would bow before your throne.
As your angels serve before you,
so on earth your will be done.

Be careful then how you live, not as unwise people but as wise. Ephesians 5:15

Jesus, still lead on 799
till our rest be won;
heav'nly leader, still direct us,
still support, console, protect us,
till we safely stand
in the promised land.

Divine Teacher, for all the good you brought into being, we thank you. May we honor you with our lives as we seek your help to make wise choices that will bring glory to you. Amen.

Fifteenth Sunday after Pentecost

Watchword for the Week — Bless the Lord, O my soul, and do not forget all his benefits. Psalm 103:2

Sunday, September 13 — Genesis 50:15-21; Psalm 103:(1-7),8-13 Romans 14:1-12; Matthew 18:21-35

Ah Lord God! It is you who made the heavens and the earth by your great power and by your outstretched arm! Nothing is too hard for you. Jeremiah 32:17

What God's almighty pow'r has made, 537
in mercy he is keeping;
by morning glow or evening shade
his eye is never sleeping.
And where he rules in kingly might,
there all is just and all is right:
to God all praise and glory!

Jesus said, "All authority in heaven and on earth has been given to me. Go therefore and make disciples of all nations, baptizing them in the name of the Father and of the Son and of the Holy Spirit, and teaching them to obey everything that I have commanded you." Matthew 28:18-20

Lord, you call us to your service: 617*
"In my name baptize and teach."
That the world may trust your promise—
life abundant meant for each—
give us all new fervor, draw us
closer in community;
with the Spirit's gifts empow'r us
for the work of ministry.

Heavenly Redeemer, we have the tremendous privilege of serving you in your kingdom. We pray that we will always strive to bring honor to you. Amen.

Monday, September 14 — Psalm 107:1–9
1 Samuel 3,4; Luke 24:13–27

You shall rejoice in the Lord; in the Holy One of Israel you shall glory. Isaiah 41:16

Redeeming God, your arms embrace 385*
all now despised for creed or race;
let peace, descending like a dove,
make known on earth your healing love.

We even boast in God through our Lord Jesus Christ, through whom we have now received reconciliation. Romans 5:11

Lord, I'll praise thee now and ever, 108r
who for me wast crucified;
for thy agony, dear Savior,
for thy wounds and pierced side,
for thy love, so tried, unending,
for thy death, all deaths transcending.
For thy death and love divine,
Lord, I'll be forever thine.

Lord, there are no words that adequately express our deep gratitude for your gifts of forgiveness and reconciliation. Let us openly share that message with others. Amen.

Tuesday, September 15 — Psalm 107:10–16
1 Samuel 5:1–7:1; Luke 24:28–35

So Abram went, as the Lord had told him.
Genesis 12:4

Grant by guidance from above 586
that obedience, faith, and love
show our hearts to you are giv'n,
that our treasure is in heav'n.

Those who have faith are children of Abraham.
Galatians 3:7 NIV

We may not touch his hands and side, 713
nor follow where he trod;
yet in his promise we rejoice,
and cry, "My Lord and God!"

Gracious God, may we follow you more closely and love you more deeply, each and every day. Amen.

Ministers' Covenant Day†

Wednesday, September 16 — Psalm 107:17–22
1 Samuel 7:2–8:22; Luke 24:36–53

Honor the Lord with your wealth. Proverbs 3:9 NIV

We are called to faithful service 82s*
for the blessings from your hand,
to return the gifts you've granted,
stewards in your perfect plan.
Free us from our earthly treasure;
us unite in heav'nly pleasure.
May we sense from heav'n above
how to live out boundless love.

Lend, expecting nothing in return. Your reward will be great, and you will be children of the Most High. Luke 6:35

Is this our high calling, harmonious to dwell, 675
and thus in sweet concert Christ's praises to tell,
in peace and blessed union our moments to spend
and live in communion with Jesus our Friend?

Lord, out of the abundance you give, you only desire our hearts in return. Help us to set aside our selfishness and honor you with all we have. Amen.

† During a synodal conference in London, Jesus Christ was recognized as chief elder of the Brethren's Church. The day is observed as a covenanting day for servants of the church.

Thursday, September 17 — Psalm 107:23–32
1 Samuel 9; John 1:1–13

I, the Lord your God, hold your right hand; it is I who say to you, 'Do not fear, I will help you.' Isaiah 41:13

Lord, I would clasp thy hand in mine, 787
nor ever murmur nor repine,
content, whatever lot I see,
since 'tis my God that leadeth me.

But when Peter noticed the strong wind, he became frightened, and beginning to sink, he cried out, "Lord, save me!" Jesus immediately reached out his hand and caught him. Matthew 14:30-31

Eternal Father, strong to save, 725
whose arm has bound the restless wave,
who bade the mighty ocean deep
its own appointed limits keep:
O hear us when we cry to thee
for those in peril on the sea.

Like Peter, Master, we fear and falter. Yet also like Peter, you reach out to each of us. Precious Lord, may we take your hand. Amen.

Friday, September 18 — Psalm 107:33–43
1 Samuel 10; John 1:14–28

I the Lord love justice, I hate robbery and wrongdoing. Isaiah 61:8

Father, now your sinful child 779
through your love is reconciled.
By your pard'ning grace I live;
daily still I cry, forgive.

No one should wrong or take advantage of a brother or sister. The Lord will punish all those who commit such sins. 1 Thessalonians 4:6 NIV

Tis a pleasant thing to see 670
brothers in the Lord agree,
sisters of a God of love
live as they shall live above,
acting each a Christian part,
one in word and one in heart.

Loving Jesus, daily we fall short of your calling in our lives. Cleanse us from sin and fortify us with a desire to walk more closely with you. In you, we pray. Amen.

Saturday, September 19 — Psalm 108:1–5
1 Samuel 11,12; John 1:29–42

**God is wise in heart, and mighty in strength—
who has resisted him, and succeeded? Job 9:4**

O may this gracious God 533
through all our life be near us,
with ever joyful hearts
and blessed peace to cheer us,
and keep us in his grace,
and guide us when perplexed,
and free us from all ills
in this world and the next.

**Do not be haughty, but associate with the
lowly; do not claim to be wiser than you are.
Romans 12:16**

May we all so love each other 401*
and all selfish claims deny,
so that each one for the other
will not hesitate to die.
Even so our Lord has loved us;
for our lives he gave his life.
Still he grieves and still he suffers,
for our selfishness and strife.

Holy God, impart your wisdom so that we love and serve you first, others second, and ourselves last. Amen.

Sixteenth Sunday after Pentecost

Watchword for the Week — For to me, living is Christ and dying is gain. Philippians 1:21

Sunday, September 20 — Jonah 3:10-4:11; Psalm 145:1-8
Philippians 1:21-30; Matthew 20:1-16

Honor your father and your mother. Exodus 20:12

To you our vows with sweet accord, 677
head of your church, we pay;
we and our house will serve you, Lord;
your word we will obey.
Grant us and all our children grace
in word and deed your name to praise,
and in each family, your will
and purpose to fulfill.

Welcome one another, therefore, just as Christ has welcomed you, for the glory of God. Romans 15:7

O that such may be our union 673
as thine with the Father is,
and not one of our communion
e'er forsake the path of bliss;
may our light break forth with brightness,
from thy light reflected shine;
thus the world will bear us witness
that we, Lord, are truly thine.

Savior, we long to live in a right relationship with you and with our brothers and sisters. Help us share your love every day and in every place we go. Amen.

Monday, September 21 — Psalm 108:6–13
1 Samuel 13; John 1:43–51

I am shut in so that I cannot escape; my eye grows dim through sorrow. Every day I call on you, O Lord. Psalm 88:8-9

Make me a captive, Lord, 604
and then I shall be free;
force me to render up my sword,
and I shall conquer'r be.
I sink in life's alarms
when by myself I stand;
imprison me within your arms,
and strong shall be my hand.

Jesus prayed, "I am not asking you to take them out of the world, but I ask you to protect them from the evil one." John 17:15

I heard the voice of Jesus say, 606
"Come unto me and rest;
lay down, O weary one, lay down
your head upon my breast."
I came to Jesus as I was,
so weary, worn and sad,
I found in him a resting-place,
and he has made me glad.

There are times, Jesus, when we feel challenged, overwhelmed, defeated. Cover us with your blanket of protection, reminding us that you are greater than all of life's joys and sorrows. Amen.

Tuesday, September 22 — Psalm 109:1–7
1 Samuel 14:1–40; John 2:1–11

How long, O Lord? Will you forget me forever? How long will you hide your face from me? Psalm 13:1

Here, O my Lord, I see you face to face! 421
Here would I touch and handle things unseen,
here grasp with firmer hand eternal grace,
and all my weariness upon you lean.

In the world you face persecution. But take courage; I have conquered the world! John 16:33

Our Lamb has conquered: let us follow him, 587
with eagerness of heart and strength of limb,
brave in endeavor, with your vision clear,
and high thanksgiving for God's purpose here—
our Lamb has conquered: let us follow him.

Jesus, you defeated death and redeemed us so that we will spend eternity in your glorious kingdom! May our lives reflect that hope and joy. Amen.

Wednesday, September 23 — Psalm 109:8–20
1 Samuel 14:41–15:23; John 2:12–25

He will swallow up death forever. Isaiah 25:8

What rush of hallelujahs 394
fills all the earth and sky!
What ringing of a thousand harps
bespeaks the triumph nigh!
O day, for which creation
and all its tribes were made!
O joy, for all its former woes
a thousandfold repaid!

While we are in this tent, we groan and are burdened, because we do not wish to be unclothed but to be clothed instead with our heavenly dwelling, so that what is mortal may be swallowed up by life. 2 Corinthians 5:4 NIV

Savior, you came to give 380
those who in darkness live
healing and sight,
health to the sick in mind,
sight to the inward blind:
now to all humankind
let there be light!

Sovereign Lord, may the love and life of your son, Jesus, consume our lives so that we may share his light and the hope of eternity with others. Amen.

Thursday, September 24 — Psalm 109:21–31
1 Samuel 15:24–16:13; John 3:1–15

From the least to the greatest of them, everyone is greedy for unjust gain; and from prophet to priest, everyone deals falsely. They have treated the wound of my people carelessly, saying, "Peace, peace," when there is no peace. Jeremiah 6:13-14

Breathe on me, breath of God, 494
my will to yours incline,
until this selfish part of me
glows with your fire divine.

Each tree is known by its own fruit. Figs are not gathered from thorns, nor are grapes picked from a bramble bush. The good person out of the good treasure of the heart produces good. Luke 6:44-45

All the world is God's own field, 450
fruit unto his praise to yield,
wheat and weeds together sown,
unto joy or sorrow grown;
first the blade, and then the ear,
then the full corn shall appear;
Lord of harvest, grant that we
wholesome grain and pure may be.

Gracious God, forgive us and transform us. Help us to know you, to live for you, and to produce fruit through your spirit living in us. Amen.

Friday, September 25 — Psalm 110
1 Samuel 16:14–17:31; John 3:16–26

Great peace have those who love your law; nothing can make them stumble. Psalm 119:165

Apostles, prophets, martyrs, 391
and all the noble throng
who wear the spotless raiment
and raise the ceaseless song:
for them and those whose witness
is only known to you,
by walking in their footsteps,
we give you praise anew.

Let the word of Christ dwell in you richly; teach and admonish one another in all wisdom. Colossians 3:16

O teach me, Lord, that I may teach 646
the precious truths which you impart.
And wing my words that they may reach
the hidden depths of many a heart.

Beautiful Savior, as your children, we know your joy, your peace, and your truths. Make our steps sure as we witness to others. Amen.

Saturday, September 26 — Psalm 111
1 Samuel 17:32–58; John 3:27–36

I am with you, says the Lord, to save you. Jeremiah 30:11

Still he comes within us, 273
still his voice would win us
from the sins that hurt us;
would to truth convert us
from our foolish error,
ere he comes in terror.

At my first defense no one came to my support, but all deserted me. May it not be counted against them! But the Lord stood by me and gave me strength. 2 Timothy 4:16-17

Other refuge have I none; 724
hangs my helpless soul on thee;
leave, ah, leave me not alone,
still support and comfort me.
All my trust on thee is stayed,
all my help from thee I bring;
cover my defenseless head
with the shadow of thy wing.

God, our refuge, you are the anchor that holds firm. When troubles of this world disturb our calm, remind us of your abiding strength in our turbulent lives. Amen.

Seventeenth Sunday after Pentecost

Watchword for the Week — Let the same mind be in you that was in Christ Jesus. Philippians 2:5

Sunday, September 27 — Ezekiel 18:1-4,25-32; Psalm 25:1-9 Philippians 2:1-13; Matthew 21:23-32

The Lord has made his salvation known and revealed his righteousness to the nations. Psalm 98:2 NIV

Know that the Lord is God indeed; 539
he formed us all without our aid.
We are the flock he comes to feed,
the sheep who by his hand were made.

When Paul and Barnabas arrived, they called the church together and related all that God had done with them, and how he had opened a door of faith for the Gentiles. Acts 14:27

Highly favored congregation, 515
loved by Jesus and esteemed,
ne'er forget your destination,
why from this vain world redeemed.

Gracious God, as we your traveling pilgrims cross the threshold into this new week, may we go forth in faith. Strengthen and motivate us with your word and with your spirit. Amen.

Monday, September 28 — Psalm 112
1 Samuel 18:1–19:7; John 4:1–26

Remember your creator in the days of your youth, before the days of trouble come, and the years draw near when you will say, "I have no pleasure in them." Ecclesiastes 12:1

I search for you, Lord, 90s*
in the washing and churning of ocean's tide.
I look for your presence
in all of the brightness of morning's sky.
I wander in fields of clover and flowers
that smell so sweet.
I feel the brown earth and soft grass under my feet.
Lord, I know you're not far away.
God, I reach for you each day.
You are my life. You are my way.

Philip found Nathanael and said to him, "We have found him about whom Moses in the law and also the prophets wrote, Jesus son of Joseph from Nazareth." Nathanael said to him, "Can anything good come out of Nazareth?" Philip said to him, "Come and see." John 1:45-46

As with joyous steps they sped 94r
to that lowly manger bed,
there to bend the knee before
him whom heaven and earth adore;
so may we with willing feet
ever seek the mercy seat.

Sometimes life is hard, dear Lord, but you summon us to come, to taste, and to see that you are good. O let us seek and let us find. May we daily set aside the time we need to spend in your glorious presence. Amen.

* By Rick Sides and Jim Newsom, Jr. (1974). © 2013 IBOC and MMF.

Tuesday, September 29 — Psalm 113
1 Samuel 19:8–20:17; John 4:27–38

Love truth and peace! Zechariah 8:19

His is no earthly kingdom; 344*
it comes from heav'n above.
His rule is peace and freedom
and justice, truth, and love.
So let your praise be sounding
for kindness so abounding.

You will know the truth, and the truth will make you free. John 8:32

High King of heaven, my victory won, 719
may I reach heaven's joys, O bright heav'n's Sun!
Heart of my own heart, whatever befall,
still be my vision, O ruler of all.

You are a just and loving Lord. May we reflect your truth, peace, and love as we walk through this day. Amen.

Wednesday, September 30 — Psalm 114
1 Samuel 20:18–21:9; John 4:39–42

I kept my faith, even when I said, 'I am greatly afflicted'. Psalm 116:10

Through all the tumult and the strife, 701
I hear that music ringing.
It sounds and echoes in my soul;
how can I keep from singing?

Blessed is anyone who endures temptation. Such a one has stood the test and will receive the crown of life that the Lord has promised to those who love him. James 1:12

Take up your cross, and follow Christ, 758
nor think till death to lay it down;
for only those who bear the cross
may hope to wear the glorious crown.

Kind Jesus, none of us are worthy of your salvation. Yet we reach out to you, desperately in need of your mercy and grace. Forgive us, ever-loving Lord. Amen.

Thursday, October 1 — Psalm 115:1–8
1 Samuel 21:10–22:23; John 4:43–54

"Because your heart was penitent and you have humbled yourself before me, I also have heard you," said the Lord. 2 Chronicles 34:27

Give deep humility; the sense 750
of godly sorrow give,
a strong desiring confidence
to hear your voice and live.

I am the least of the apostles, unfit to be called an apostle, because I persecuted the church of God. But by the grace of God I am what I am. 1 Corinthians 15:9-10

Amazing grace! How sweet the sound 783
that saved a wretch like me!
I once was lost, but now am found,
was blind, but now I see.

God of grace, we come to you for forgiveness. Thank you for listening as we confess our sins and for giving us the hope of life eternal through your grace. Amen.

Friday, October 2 — Psalm 115:9–18
1 Samuel 23; John 5:1–15

I have seen their ways, but I will heal them; I will lead them and repay them with comfort. Isaiah 57:18

Come as a shepherd; guard and keep 432
your fold from all that fosters sin,
and nourish lambs, and feed the sheep,
the wounded heal, the lost bring in.

Jesus said, "Those who are well have no need of a physician, but those who are sick; I have come to call not the righteous but sinners." Mark 2:17

Christ bids each afflicted soul 416*
"Come that I may soothe your grief.
No one who is strong and whole
needs a doctor for relief;
therefore have no fear, draw nigh,
that your want I may supply."

Oh Lord, our shepherd. When we have lost our way and are hurting, you are always there to pick us up, comfort us, heal us, and bring us back to the fold. Thank you for caring so much. Amen.

Saturday, October 3 — Psalm 116:1–7
1 Samuel 24:1–25:17; John 5:16–30

The people who walked in darkness have seen a great light; those who lived in a land of deep darkness—on them light has shined. Isaiah 9:2

We've a story to tell to the nations, 621
that shall turn their hearts to the right,
a story of truth and mercy,
a story of peace and light,
a story of peace and light.

You may proclaim the mighty acts of him who called you out of darkness into his marvelous light. 1 Peter 2:9

We are called to be God's prophets, 635*
speaking for the truth and right,
standing firm for godly justice,
bringing evil things to light.
Let us seek the courage needed,
our high calling to fulfill,
that the world may know the blessing
of the doing of God's will.

God of light, before we knew you, we walked in darkness. We now know you and walk in your light. Show us the way to share our stories with those around us. Amen.

Eighteenth Sunday after Pentecost

Watchword for the Week — The stone that the builders rejected has become the chief cornerstone. This is the Lord's doing; it is marvelous in our eyes. Psalm 118:22,23

Sunday, October 4 — Isaiah 5:1-7; Psalm 80:7-15
Philippians 3:4b-14; Matthew 21:33-46

Trust in the Lord with all your heart, and do not rely on your own insight. In all your ways acknowledge him, and he will make straight your paths. Proverbs 3:5-6

Sing, pray, and keep his ways unswerving, 712
offer your service faithfully,
and trust his word; though undeserving,
you'll find his promise true to be.
God never will forsake in need
the soul that trusts in him indeed.

Therefore prepare your minds for action; discipline yourselves; set all your hope on the grace that Jesus Christ will bring you when he is revealed. 1 Peter 1:13

In mercy, Lord, this grace bestow, 643
that in your service we may do
with gladness and a willing mind
whatever is for us assigned.

Lord, we trust in you with all our heart and mind. Lead us in the right way to live and give us the strength to keep on your path to eternal life. Amen.

Monday, October 5 — Psalm 116:8–14
1 Samuel 25:18–44; John 5:31–47

Mortal, all my words that I shall speak to you receive in your heart and hear with your ears. Ezekiel 3:10

O give me Samuel's ear! 609
The open ear, O Lord,
alive and quick to hear
each whisper of thy word;
like him to answer at thy call,
and to obey thee first of all.

Therefore we must pay greater attention to what we have heard, so that we do not drift away from it. Hebrews 2:1

O let me hear you speaking 603
in accents clear and still,
above the storms of passion,
the murmurs of self-will.
O speak to reassure me,
to hasten or control;
and speak to make me listen,
O guardian of my soul.

In this world of noise and busyness, Lord, open our ears so we may hear you talking to us. Let us hear your words and store them in our hearts so we may follow you more closely. Amen.

Tuesday, October 6 — Psalm 116:15–19
1 Samuel 26,27; John 6:1–15

I will never again hide my face from them, when I pour out my spirit upon the house of Israel, says the Lord God. Ezekiel 39:29

The church is God's abiding place, 439
his altar is within,
and here by faith we see God's face,
are cleansed from stain of sin.
A sanctuary for the soul,
where love can cast out fear,
where broken spirits are made whole,
for God himself is here.

Now there are varieties of gifts, but the same Spirit; and there are varieties of services, but the same Lord; and there are varieties of activities, but it is the same God who activates all of them in everyone. To each is given the manifestation of the Spirit for the common good. 1 Corinthians 12:4-7

Gracious Spirit, in your wisdom 496*
grant your gifts to us anew;
hallow and transform our living;
breathe through all we say or do.

God, your people waited a long time for you to send the holy spirit. The spirit came, blessing us with gifts to help us serve you. Thank you for the gifts you have given each of us; may we use them wisely. Amen.

Wednesday, October 7 — Psalm 117
1 Samuel 28,29; John 6:16–24

Have I any pleasure in the death of the wicked, says the Lord God, and not rather that they should turn from their ways and live? Ezekiel 18:23

O Christians, haste, your mission high fulfilling, 618
to tell to all the world that God is light,
that he who made all nations is not willing
one life should perish, lost in shades of night.

I have come as light into the world, so that everyone who believes in me should not remain in the darkness. John 12:46

Christ is the world's light, Christ and none other; 562*
born in our darkness, he became our brother.
If we have seen him, we have seen the Father:
glory to God on high!

Before we knew you, Jesus, we lived in a world of darkness. You brought light to our lives and brought us out of the darkness. Praise to you! Amen.

Thursday, October 8 — Psalm 118:1–9
1 Samuel 30,31; John 6:25–42

Joshua said to the people, "You are witnesses against yourselves that you have chosen the Lord, to serve him." And they said, "We are witnesses." Joshua 24:22

And now, O God, our Father, 433
we pledge ourselves anew
by work and prayer and worship
to serve your kingdom too.
With grateful hearts we praise you
and pray, O Lord, that we
who are your church at present,
may serve you faithfully.

Do not let anyone disqualify you. Colossians 2:18

Help me walk in the paths of righteousness; 728*
be my aid when Satan and sin oppress.
I am trusting you whate'er may be.
Lead me, O Lord, lead me.

Lord God, help us turn away from the sin and the idols that keep us from loving and serving you. We dedicate ourselves to you—lead and guide us in the way you want us to go. Amen.

Friday, October 9 — Psalm 118:10–14
2 Samuel 1; John 6:43–51

"I have labored in vain, I have spent my strength for nothing and vanity; yet surely my cause is with the Lord, and my reward with my God." Isaiah 49:4

Sometimes I feel discouraged, 500
and think my work's in vain,
but then the Holy Spirit
revives my soul again.

Be steadfast, immovable, always excelling in the work of the Lord, because you know that in the Lord your labor is not in vain. 1 Corinthians 15:58

Lord Jesus Christ, we humbly pray: p228
O, keep us steadfast till that day
when each will be your welcomed guest
in heaven's high and holy feast.

There are days, Lord, when we question what we do. Keep us from being discouraged; you know what is in our hearts as we labor for you. Amen.

Saturday, October 10 — Psalm 118:15–21
2 Samuel 2; John 6:52–59

The Lord spoke and it came to be; he commanded, and it stood firm. Psalm 33:9

For the beauty of the earth, 538
for the glory of the skies,
for the love which from our birth
over and around us lies,
Lord of all, to you we raise
this our hymn of grateful praise.

Jesus woke up and rebuked the wind, and said to the sea, "Peace! Be still!" Then the wind ceased, and there was a dead calm. Mark 4:39

As you once calmed a storm on the sea, 88s*
and you spoke words of "Peace! Let it be!"
In my raging and doubt, fears within and without,
as you once calmed that storm, calm me.

All powerful and mighty God, when you speak, it is done. Open our ears and hearts to hear your words and obey them. Praise God! Amen.

* By David M. Henkelmann (1981). © 2013 by IBOC and MMF.

Nineteenth Sunday after Pentecost

Watchword for the Week — O Lord, you are my God; I will exalt you, I will praise your name; for you have done wonderful things. Isaiah 25:1

Sunday, October 11 — Isaiah 25:1-9; Psalm 23
Philippians 4:1-9; Matthew 22:1-14

The hearing ear and the seeing eye—the Lord has made them both. Proverbs 20:12

Eyes to see and ears to hear— 649
God's good gifts to me and you;
eyes and ears he gave to us
to help each other the whole day through.

Blessed are your eyes, for they see, and your ears, for they hear. Matthew 13:16

God gave us eyes to see them, 467
and lips that we might tell
how great is God Almighty,
who has made all things well.

Great God of creation, you gave us eyes to see your mighty works and ears to hear you calling us. Thank you for these great gifts; help us use them wisely. Amen.

Monday, October 12 — Psalm 118:22–29
2 Samuel 3:1–34; John 6:60–71

You are my Lord; I have no good apart from you. Psalm 16:2

We come to you, O Lord, with songs of gratitude, 65s*
for all that you have given us, our life, our food.
Our prayers ascend for this our native land
that it will choose your will.

And this is eternal life, that they may know you, the only true God, and Jesus Christ whom you have sent. John 17:3

We lift our voices singing 55s**
in grateful thanks and praise
to Christ whose love surrounds us
throughout our life-long days.

Lord, you are our God. Thank you for sending your son, Jesus. Because we know and believe in you, we have been given eternal life. Amen.

* By Willard R. Harstine (2004). © 2013 by IBOC and MMF.

** © 2004 by Thom Stapleton.

Tuesday, October 13 — Psalm 119:1–8
2 Samuel 3:35–5:16; John 7:1–13

David said to Solomon, "The Lord God will not fail you or forsake you, until all the work for the service of the house of the Lord is finished." 1 Chronicles 28:20

Like Solomon who was so wise, 46s*
  I journey with my Lord.
Built God a home, a heav'nly prize.
  I journey with my Lord.
My heart's the temple of God's will
  where I will worship God until
The holy promise is fulfilled.
  I journey with my Lord.

Think of us in this way, as servants of Christ and stewards of God's mysteries. 1 Corinthians 4:1

We are called to be God's people, 635**
showing by our lives his grace,
one in heart and one in spirit,
sign of hope for all the race.
Let us show how he has changed us,
and remade us as his own,
let us share our life together
as we shall around his throne.

We are your servants, Lord. Stand by us, as you did with Solomon, as we do your work. We know that with your guidance and protection, we can accomplish more of your work. Amen.

Wednesday, October 14 — Psalm 119:9–16
2 Samuel 5:17–6:23; John 7:14–24

Fear God, and keep his commandments; for that is the whole duty of everyone. Ecclesiastes 12:13

Unto such as keep God's cov'nant 458
and are steadfast in his way,
unto those who still remember
the commandments and obey.

Peter said, "I truly understand that God shows no partiality, but in every nation anyone who fears him and does what is right is acceptable to him." Acts 10:34-35

For God in Christ has made us one 781
from ev'ry land and race;
has reconciled us through the Son,
and met us all with grace.

Thank you, Lord, for giving the gift of salvation to all—no matter what race or color we are. All we need to do is accept your grace and follow your commandments. Amen.

Thursday, October 15 — Psalm 119:17–24
2 Samuel 7; John 7:25–44

Turn now, everyone of you, from your evil way and wicked doings. Jeremiah 25:5

Seek the Lord, whose willing presence 780*
moves your heart to make appeal.
Turn from wickedness and evil;
God will pardon, cleanse, and heal.

I delight in the law of God in my inmost self, but I see in my members another law at war with the law of my mind, making me captive to the law of sin that dwells in my members. Romans 7:22-23

O, to grace how great a debtor 782
daily I'm constrained to be!
Let that grace, Lord, like a fetter,
bind my wand'ring heart to thee.
Prone to wander, Lord, I feel it,
prone to leave the God I love,
here's my heart, O take and seal it;
seal it for thy courts above.

God of grace—keep us from doing evil and wicked things. We feel bad when we do wrong. Teach us the way to be obedient to you. Amen.

Friday, October 16 — Psalm 119:25–32
2 Samuel 8,9; John 7:45–52

He who keeps Israel will neither slumber nor sleep. Psalm 121:4

The Lord is never far away, 537
but through all grief distressing,
an everpresent help and stay,
our peace, and joy, and blessing.
As with a mother's tender hand,
he leads his own, his chosen band.
To God all praise and glory!

Jesus Christ will also strengthen you to the end. 1 Corinthians 1:8

O yes, having found in the Lord our delight, 675
he is our chief object by day and by night;
this knits us together; no longer we roam;
we all have one Father, and heav'n is our home.

Lord, you are always with us as we travel through life. Even when things don't go the way we want, you are there to comfort and strengthen us. Amen.

Saturday, October 17 — Psalm 119:33–40
2 Samuel 10,11; John 8:1–11

So now, O Israel, what does the Lord your God require of you? Only to fear the Lord your God, to walk in all his ways, to love him, to serve the Lord your God with all your heart and with all your soul. Deuteronomy 10:12

To serve the present age, 645
my calling to fulfill,
O may it all my pow'rs engage
to do my Master's will.

Be doers of the word, and not merely hearers. James 1:22

Christian workers, give your talents 75s*
to the holy plan.
Feed the hungry, house the homeless,
lend a helping hand.
Heal the sick, console the weak;
act through love, God's message speak.
Christian workers, be committed
to God's ministry.

Lord, you told us to not only listen to your word, but also to carry out your word. Help us go out and serve our neighbors. Amen.

Twentieth Sunday after Pentecost

Watchword for the Week — Sing to the Lord, bless his name; tell of his salvation from day to day. Psalm 96:2

Sunday, October 18 — Isaiah 45:1-7; Psalm 96:1-9,(10-13)
1 Thessalonians 1:1-10; Matthew 22:15-22

Surely, to obey is better than sacrifice. 1 Samuel 15:22

But we never can prove *
the delights of his love
until all on the altar we lay;
for the favor he shows,
for the joy he bestows,
are for them who will trust and obey.

Your obedience is known to all, so that I rejoice over you. Romans 16:19

When we walk with the Lord *
in the light of his word,
what a glory he sheds on our way!
While we do his good will,
he abides with us still,
and with all who will trust and obey.

Lord, you taught us that obedience to your word is what you want. Help us to be more obedient to your will. You know our hearts. Amen.

* *Trust and Obey* by John H. Sammis. Public Domain.

Monday, October 19 — Psalm 119:41–48
2 Samuel 12; John 8:12–30

The Lord sets the prisoners free. Psalm 146:7

The people who in darkness walked 320
have seen a glorious light;
on them broke forth the heav'nly dawn
who dwelt in death and night.

So if the son makes you free, you will be free indeed. John 8:36

Take full possession of my heart; 721
to me your lowly mind impart;
break nature's bonds, and let me see,
he whom you free indeed is free.

Lord, we are prisoners to sin and worldly treasurers. Help us see that you are the only one we need and trust. Then we will be fully free to live our lives to honor you. Amen.

Tuesday, October 20 — Psalm 119:49–56
2 Samuel 13:1–33; John 8:31–41

When times are good, be happy; but when times are bad, consider this: God has made the one as well as the other. Therefore, no one can discover anything about their future. Ecclesiastes 7:14 NIV

Teach me to feel that you are always nigh; 490
teach me the struggles of the soul to bear,
to check the rising doubt, the rebel sigh;
teach me the patience of unceasing prayer.

We know that all things work together for good for those who love God, who are called according to his purpose. Romans 8:28

Praise to the Lord, 530
who o'er all things is wondrously reigning,
shelt'ring you under his wings,
O, so gently sustaining.
Have you not seen
all you have needed has been
met by his gracious ordaining.

Lord, we know that you did not promise us a life of happiness when we decided to follow you. Help us understand, when we face hard times in our lives, you are there protecting us. Amen.

Wednesday, October 21 — Psalm 119:57–64
2 Samuel 13:34–14:33; John 8:42–59

Suddenly an angel touched Elijah and said to him, "Get up and eat." He got up, and ate and drank; then he went in the strength of that food forty days and forty nights to the mount of God. 1 Kings 19:5,8

O Father, who sustained them, 634*
O Spirit, who inspired,
Savior, whose love constrained them
to toil with zeal untired,
from cowardice defend us,
from lethargy awake!
Forth on your errands send us
to labor for your sake.

We have this treasure in clay jars, so that it may be made clear that this extraordinary power belongs to God and does not come from us. 2 Corinthians 4:7

We are God's house of living stones, 512
built for his own habitation;
he fills our hearts, his humble thrones,
granting us life and salvation.
Yet to this place, an earthly frame,
we come with thanks to praise his name;
God grants his people true blessing.

Lord, our bodies are frail. Some days we get so tired that we do not think we can work for you. Remind us that you are always with us—strengthening and feeding our souls. Then we can finish the tasks you have given us. Amen.

Thursday, October 22 — Psalm 119:65–72
2 Samuel 15:1–29; John 9:1–12

You have made my days a mere handbreadth; the span of my years is as nothing before you. Everyone is but a breath, even those who seem secure. Psalm 39:5 NIV

All that kills abundant living, 685*
let it from the earth be banned;
pride of status, race or schooling,
dogmas that obscure your plan.
In our common quest for justice
may we hallow life's brief span.

Our Savior Christ Jesus abolished death and brought life and immortality to light through the gospel. 2 Timothy 1:10

The strife is o'er, the battle done, 361
the victory of life is won;
the song of triumph has begun.
Alleluia! Alleluia! Alleluia!

God, the time we spend on earth is very short. Keep us from worrying about collecting riches on earth and help us remember that our reward comes from Jesus, who conquered death and gave us eternal life. Amen.

Friday, October 23 — Psalm 119:73–80
2 Samuel 15:30–16:23; John 9:13–34

I will make with you an everlasting covenant. Isaiah 55:3

Remembering what our fathers told 399
you did in their young day,
this solemn jubilee we hold.
May we, as then did they,
ourselves in covenant now bind
with soul and strength, with heart and mind,
through life, in death, on land, o'er sea
to you disciples be.

Now may the God of peace, who brought back from the dead our Lord Jesus, the great shepherd of the sheep, by the blood of the eternal covenant, make you complete in everything good so that you may do his will, working among us that which is pleasing in his sight. Hebrews 13:20-21

Thanks we give and adoration 559
for your gospel's joyful sound.
May the fruits of your salvation
in our hearts and lives abound.
Ever faithful, ever faithful
to your truth may we be found.

God, thank you for your gift of Jesus Christ, who came to save us all. You gave us the promise of eternal life if we believe and follow your word. Amen.

Saturday, October 24 — Psalm 119:81–88
2 Samuel 17; John 9:35–41

The Lord stirred up the spirit of all the people; and they came and worked on the house of the Lord of hosts, their God. Haggai 1:14

We built a sanctuary sure; 439
it stands on sacred sod.
A church erected to endure,
the temple of our God.
We come to worship in this place
with aspiration high;
it is the consecrated place,
where God himself draws nigh.

Do not neglect the gift that is in you. 1 Timothy 4:14

Teacher, Creator, God, 801*
enfold us in your arms;
be with us as we try our wings,
and keep us safe from harm.
All good and perfect gifts
come to us from your hand.
O help us use them carefully
and live by love's command.

Holy Creator, you know us and give each of us gifts to use for your honor. Sometimes the world gets in the way and we forget these gifts. When this happens, remind us what we are supposed to do. Amen.

Twenty-First Sunday after Pentecost

Watchword for the Week — You shall be holy, for I the Lord your God am holy. Leviticus 19:2

Sunday, October 25 — Leviticus 19:1-2,15-18; Psalm 1
1 Thessalonians 2:1-8; Matthew 22:34-46

Amos said, "I am a herdsman, and a dresser of sycamore trees, and the Lord took me from following the flock, and the Lord said to me, 'Go, prophesy to my people Israel.'" Amos 7:14-15

We have no mission but to serve 694*
in full obedience to our Lord,
to care for all, without reserve,
and spread his liberating word.

As Jesus passed along the Sea of Galilee, he saw Simon and his brother Andrew casting a net into the sea—for they were fishermen. And Jesus said to them, "Follow me and I will make you fish for people." Mark 1:16-17

Two fishermen, who lived along 611**
the Sea of Galilee,
stood by the shore to cast their nets
into an ageless sea.
Now Jesus watched them from afar,
then called them each by name;
it changed their lives, these simple men—
they'd never be the same.

Lord, you know the work that we do. Yet, like Amos, Simon, and Andrew, you call us to go beyond our daily tasks to spread your word to the world around us. Give us the courage to do your calling. Amen.

Monday, October 26 — Psalm 119:89–96
2 Samuel 18:1–30; John 10:1–10

I, I am he who comforts you; why then are you afraid of a mere mortal who must die? Isaiah 51:12

By pain and sorrow undeterred, 393*
I shall proceed in gladness:
we who rely on God's own word
see past this mortal sadness.
When cloudy and difficult winter is past,
God will work our great restoration.
Take heart in the coming of springtime at last!
Take heart in glad anticipation!

The one who is in you is greater than the one who is in the world. 1 John 4:4

With him as Lord to lead our way 308**
in want and in prosperity,
what need we fear in earth or space
in this new year of grace!

Holy Spirit, you are all powerful. There are times we fear circumstances that surround us in our lives, but we know that your power can help us through troubling times. Thank you. Amen.

Tuesday, October 27 — Psalm 119:97–104
2 Samuel 18:31–19:30; John 10:11–21

How can a man be in the right before God? If one wished to dispute with him, he could not answer him once in a thousand times. Job 9:2,3 NASB

God forgives all your transgressions, 458
all diseases gently heals,
God redeems you from destruction,
and with you so kindly deals.

The scribe said to Jesus, "You are right, Teacher; you have truly said that 'he is one, and besides him there is no other'; and 'to love him with all the heart, and with all the understanding, and with all the strength,' and 'to love one's neighbor as oneself,'—this is much more important than all whole burnt offerings and sacrifices." When Jesus saw that he answered wisely, he said to him, "You are not far from the kingdom of God." Mark 12:32-34

One our Master, one alone, 525
none but Christ as Lord we own;
"brethren of his law" are we—
"As I loved you, so love ye."
Branches we in Christ, the Vine,
living by his life divine;
as the Father with the Son,
so, in Christ, we all are one.

God of creation—all-knowing God—we face trials and days when things don't go the way we want. Help us to know that you are still by our side. You rule the world and know what the future holds for us. We lift our praise to you for being with us during the rough times when we can't see what our future holds. Amen.

Wednesday, October 28 — Psalm 119:105–112
2 Samuel 19:31–20:26; John 10:22–33

Who is a rock besides our God? Psalm 18:31

If you but trust in God to guide you 712
and place your confidence in him,
you'll find him always there beside you
to give you hope and strength within;
for those who trust God's changeless love
build on the rock that will not move.

No one can lay any foundation other than the one that has been laid; that foundation is Jesus Christ. 1 Corinthians 3:11

The church's one foundation 511
is Jesus Christ, her Lord;
she is his new creation
by water and the word;
from heav'n he came and sought her
to be his holy bride;
with his own blood he bought her,
and for her life he died.

Lord Jesus, you are our rock, a solid foundation for our lives. We face rough roads and mountains in our lives. Thank you for helping us meet these challenges and for supplying us a firm foundation. Amen.

Thursday, October 29 — Psalm 119:113–120
2 Samuel 21; John 10:34–42

You must neither add anything to what I command you nor take away anything from it, but keep the commandments of the Lord your God. Deuteronomy 4:2

In all things our Father, Lord and Savior, 397*
teaches us the law of love;
then let love determine our behavior,
for 'tis God's command to all;
may this motto live in all God's children
as we strive to follow love's direction;
may God bless us as we show
charity in all we do.

Beloved, I am writing you no new commandment, but an old commandment that you have had from the beginning; the old commandment is the word that you have heard. 1 John 2:7

We covenant with hand and heart p183
to follow Christ, our Lord;
with world, and sin, and self to part,
and to obey his word;
to love each other heartily,
in truth and with sincerity,
and under cross, reproach, and shame,
to glorify his name.

God, you gave us your greatest commandment that we should love you with all our hearts, souls, and minds. The second commandment is to love our neighbors as ourselves. Help us to keep these commandments without changing them to suit our needs. Amen.

Friday, October 30 — Psalm 119:121–128
2 Samuel 22:1–25; John 11:1–16

Six days you shall work, but on the seventh day you shall rest. Exodus 34:21

Holy Spirit, gracious God, 497*
source of Sabbath rest and joy,
gentle our hurts and still our cries;
comfort, heal, bless, make us wise.

Pay close attention to yourself and to your teaching; continue in these things. 1 Timothy 4:16

I would be true, for there are those who trust me; **
I would be pure, for there are those who care;
I would be strong, for there is much to suffer;
I would be brave, for there is much to dare,
I would be brave, for there is much to dare.

Lord, we work diligently for you, but it is in the moments of rest that we can be still and know that you are God. Help us to heal and recharge so we can go out refreshed in your name. Amen.

Saturday, October 31 — Psalm 119:129–136
2 Samuel 22:26–23:17; John 11:17–30

I will sing aloud of your steadfast love in the morning. For you have been a fortress for me and a refuge on the day of my distress. Psalm 59:16

I fully am persuaded 769
and joyfully declare
I'm never left unaided,
my Father hears my prayer;
his comforts never fail me,
he stands at my right hand;
when tempests fierce assail me,
they're calm at his command.

In the morning, while it was still very dark, Jesus got up and went out to a deserted place, and there he prayed. Mark 1:35

O Sabbath rest by Galilee! 739
O calm of hills above,
where Jesus knelt to share with thee
the silence of eternity,
interpreted by love!

Lord, we sing your praises because you are with us in times of good and in times of trials. May we make time to be still and listen to your guidance, knowing that you hear our prayer and are with us always. Amen.

All Saints Day
Twenty-Second Sunday after Pentecost

Watchword for All Saints Day — Salvation belongs to our God who is seated on the throne, and to the Lamb! Revelation 7:10

All Saints Day — Revelation 7:9-17; Psalm 34:1-10,22
1 John 3:1-3; Matthew 5:1-12

Watchword for the Week — O send out your light and your truth; let them lead me. Psalm 43:3

Sunday, November 1 — Micah 3:5-12; Psalm 43
1 Thessalonians 2:9-13; Matthew 23:1-12

The Lord, my God, lights up my darkness. Psalm 18:28

Open now the crystal fountain 790
where the healing waters flow;
let the fire and cloudy pillar
lead me all my journey through.
Strong deliv'rer, strong deliv'rer,
ever be my strength and shield;
ever be my strength and shield.

Jesus said to the blind man, "What do you want me to do for you?" The blind man said to him, "My teacher, let me see again." Jesus said to him, "Go; your faith has made you well." Immediately he regained his sight and followed him on the way. Mark 10:51-52

And then your touch brought life and health, 736*
gave speech, and strength, and sight;
and youth renewed and health restored,
claimed you, the Lord of light:
and so, O Lord, be near to bless,
almighty now as then,
in ev'ry street, in ev'ry home,
in ev'ry troubled friend.

O God, how can we thank you for caring for our every need, in sickness and in health? Let us follow the lamb and care for others. With the saints in glory, we praise your name. Amen.

Monday, November 2 — Psalm 119:137–144
2 Samuel 23:18–24:25; John 11:31–44

They have all gone astray, they are all alike perverse; there is no one who does good, no, not one. Psalm 14:3

We have sinned against your law. 760*
We have failed to do your will,
disobeyed your holy word.
Lord, have mercy on us still.

There is no distinction, since all have sinned and fall short of the glory of God; they are now justified by his grace as a gift, through the redemption that is in Christ Jesus. Romans 3:22-24

In the cross of Christ I glory, 332**
there for all was grace made free.
None deserving, yet receiving
life through death at Calvary.

Merciful God, yes, we are sinners; yes, we have all gone astray; yes, we have fallen short of your glory. How can you forgive even us? We are convinced that nothing will separate us from your unconditional love through Christ Jesus. We humbly offer thanks. Amen.

Tuesday, November 3 — Psalm 119:145–152
1 Kings 1:1–27; John 11:45–57

Rejoice with Jerusalem, and be glad for her, all you who love her; rejoice with her in joy, all you who mourn over her. Isaiah 66:10

Jerusalem the golden, 814
descending from above,
the city of God's presence,
the vision of God's love—
I know not, O I know not
what joys await us there,
what radiancy of glory,
what bliss beyond compare!

Anna began to praise God and to speak about the child to all who were looking for the redemption of Jerusalem. Luke 2:38

Christ, the model of the meek, 336*
though with the Godhead one,
God the Father's most beloved
and sole begotten Son,
set aside his majesty
to take the sinner's place.
Who would go so far as this
to show one's love and grace?

Teacher, stories of Jerusalem are complicated and sad. Help us to understand how the place of death and destruction becomes the image of light and joy. It can only happen through the transformation of the risen Christ. Thanks be to God. Amen.

Wednesday, November 4 — Psalm 119:153–160
1 Kings 1:28–53; John 12:1–11

Sing aloud, O daughter Zion; shout, O Israel! Rejoice and exult with all your heart, O daughter Jerusalem! The Lord has taken away the judgments against you. Zephaniah 3:14-15

Glorious things of you are spoken, 522
Zion, city of our God;
he whose word cannot be broken
formed you for his own abode;
on the rock of ages founded,
what can shake your sure repose?
With salvation's walls surrounded
you may smile at all your foes.

Jesus Christ is the atoning sacrifice for our sins, and not for ours only but also for the sins of the whole world. 1 John 2:2

Lord, for all that bought our pardon, 334
for the sorrows deep and sore,
for the anguish in the garden,
we will thank you evermore,
thank you for the groaning, sighing,
for the vict'ry of your dying,
for that last triumphant cry,
praise you evermore on high.

Gracious Lord, with joy and a grateful heart we recall the sacrifice made for us. Let us forgive and love our neighbors. In the name of Jesus, we pray. Amen.

Thursday, November 5 — Psalm 119:161–168
1 Kings 2:1–38; John 12:12–19

Not one of all the good promises that the Lord had made to the house of Israel had failed; all came to pass. Joshua 21:45

We come to you, our Father, 433
with thoughts of thanks and praise,
for your abundant mercy,
and all your love and grace;
we praise you for your goodness
and for your loving care,
for daily show'rs of blessing,
for answers to our prayers.

Now you, brothers and sisters, like Isaac, are children of promise. Galatians 4:28 NIV

By this promise that you love us, p190
by your gift of peace restored,
by your call to heav'n above us,
hallow all our lives, O Lord.

Giver of promises, you have been faithful in keeping your word to your people. Help us to be faithful stewards of your words of faith, love, and hope. Amen.

Friday, November 6 — Psalm 119:169–176
1 Kings 2:39–3:28; John 12:20–36

I am the Lord, and there is no other. I form light and create darkness, I make weal and create woe; I the Lord do all these things. Isaiah 45:6-7

The silence was broken when God sang the song, 382*
and light pierced the darkness and rhythm began,
and with its first birth-cries creation was born,
and creaturely voices sang praise to the morn.

May the Lord direct your hearts to the love of God and to the steadfastness of Christ. 2 Thessalonians 3:5

For God so loved us, he sent the Savior: 775
for God so loved us, and loves me too.

God, you are the creator and lover of all creation. Forgive us those times when we turn our backs on what your hands have made. Refocus our minds. We praise you, your creation, and your son, our savior. Amen.

Saturday, November 7 — Psalm 120
1 Kings 4:1–28; John 12:37–50

As my life was ebbing away, I remembered the Lord; and my prayer came to you. Jonah 2:7

God has given, he has taken, 667*
but his children ne'er forsaken;
his the loving purpose solely
to preserve them pure and holy.

Become imitators of those who through faith and patience inherit the promises. Hebrews 6:12

Lead us, Jesus, 418**
gently day by day.
Lead us, Jesus,
show us each the way
to walk your diff'rent walk,
from fears and hungers freed,
O, lead us, Jesus, lead us.

Lord, you are the one who cares for souls—souls that are ebbing away or souls who need a gentle nudge. Thank you for being there when no one else is. Where would we be without your tender care? Amen.

Twenty-Third Sunday after Pentecost

Watchword for the Week — Keep awake therefore, for you know neither the day nor the hour. Matthew 25:13

Sunday, November 8 — Amos 5:18-24; Psalm 70
1 Thessalonians 4:13-18; Matthew 25:1-13

Joseph said to his master's wife, who tried to seduce him, "How then could I do this great wickedness, and sin against God?" Genesis 39:9

Save us from weak resignation 751*
to the evils we deplore;
let the gift of your salvation
be our glory evermore.
Grant us wisdom, grant us courage
serving you whom we adore,
serving you whom we adore.

Paul wrote to Timothy: You then, my child, be strong in the grace that is in Christ Jesus. 2 Timothy 2:1

Stand up, stand up for Jesus, 752
stand in his strength alone;
the arm of flesh will fail you,
you dare not trust your own.
Put on the gospel armor,
each piece put on with prayer;
where duty calls, or danger,
be ever faithful there.

Lord, you give us grace when we need it most. We know what grace is when it comes. Help us to discern giving grace to others when they need it most. We humbly pray. Amen.

* Used by permission of Elinor Fosdick Downs.

Monday, November 9 — Psalm 121
1 Kings 4:29–5:18; John 13:1–17

I was ready to be sought out by those who did not ask, to be found by those who did not seek me. Isaiah 65:1

O lead me, Lord, that I may lead 646
the wand'ring and the wav'ring feet.
O feed me, Lord, that I may feed
your hungry ones with manna sweet.

For we hold that a person is justified by faith apart from works prescribed by the law. Romans 3:28

We walk by faith and not by sight; 713
no gracious words we hear
from Christ, who spoke as none e'er spoke;
but we believe him near.

God, there is so much we do not know, even if we think we do. Help us to accept the mysteries of our faith. We pray this in deep humility. Amen.

Tuesday, November 10 — Psalm 122
1 Kings 6; John 13:18–30

Turn to me and be gracious to me; give your strength to your servant. Psalm 86:16

Give me your courage, Lord, p150*
to speak whenever strong oppress the weak.
Should I myself as victim live,
rememb'ring you, may I forgive.

And my God will fully satisfy every need of yours according to his riches in glory in Christ Jesus. Philippians 4:19

You give yourself to us, O Lord; 417**
then selfless let us be
to serve each other in your name
in truth and charity.

God of strength, help us to be strong. Help us to give ourselves freely in love. Help us to serve others in your name. It is in giving that we receive. Fill us up, O gracious Lord. Amen.

Wednesday, November 11 — Psalm 123
1 Kings 7:1–33; John 13:31–38

Better is a little with the fear of the Lord than great treasure and trouble with it. Proverbs 15:16

The earth is the Lord's and its fulness, 656*
its mystery, splendor and wealth,
its bounty, fertility, kindness,
its beauty, its reason, its health;
then who is this wise-hearted steward
who faithfully carries this trust?
The generous, gentle, obedient,
the patient, the honest, the just.

What good is it for someone to gain the whole world, yet forfeit their soul? Mark 8:36 NIV

The earth is the Lord's own possession, 656*
not the tithe, nor the half, but the whole:
he made it, sustains it, and leads it
in love to its heavenly goal;
but the harmony of the creation
is broken by selfhood and vice
when the anxious, incompetent steward
in fear keeps back part of the price.

God, we try to balance the scale of having too much. However, the scale is only one measure. Our values seem out of alignment as well. Help us step back to gain a more comprehensive view and make adjustments to follow you. In Jesus' name, we pray. Amen.

Thursday, November 12 — Psalm 124
1 Kings 7:34–8:16; John 14:1–14

We your people, the flock of your pasture, will give thanks to you forever; from generation to generation we will recount your praise. Psalm 79:13

All people that on earth do dwell, 539
sing to the Lord with cheerful voice;
serve him with joy, his praises tell,
come now before him and rejoice.

Through Jesus, then, let us continually offer a sacrifice of praise to God, that is, the fruit of lips that confess his name. Hebrews 13:15

Join we all with one accord; 525
praise we all our common Lord;
for we all have heard his voice,
all have made his will our choice.
Join we with the saints of old,
no more strangers in the fold,
one the Shepherd who us sought,
one the flock his blood has bought.

Jesus, shepherd of our souls, we wander amid the flock. You know each name; you prepare a table for us; you keep us safe from danger. Thank you for counting us among your flock. Amen.

Chief Elder Festival

Chief Elder Festival† — Ezekiel 34:11-16,23-24; Psalm 8
Hebrews 4:14-16; John 10:1-10

Friday, November 13 — Psalm 125
1 Kings 8:17–53; John 14:15–24

I will pour water on the thirsty land, and streams on the dry ground; I will pour my spirit upon your descendants, and my blessing on your offspring. Isaiah 44:3

Bless, O Lord, we pray, your congregation; 445
bless each home and family;
bless the youth, the rising generation;
blessed may your dear children be;
bless your servants, grant them help and favor;
you to glorify be their endeavor.
Lord, on you we humbly call;
let your blessing rest on all.

Peter said, "The promise is for you, for your children, and for all who are far away, everyone whom the Lord our God calls to him." Acts 2:39

Our children, Lord, in faith and prayer, 409
we baptize in your name.
Let them your cov'nant mercies share
as we our faith proclaim.

Jesus, as our Chief Elder, you provide counsel, assurance, love, spiritual direction, and intercession with the Father for the growing Moravian Church. Keep our ears and eyes open to your voice. Amen.

† On this day in 1741, it was announced in all Moravian congregations that Jesus Christ had ben chosen Chief Elder of the Moravian Church. The Moravian Church has had no single human chief executive since then, and now observes this as a festival day.

Saturday, November 14 — Psalm 126
1 Kings 8:54–9:19; John 14:25–15:8

How great are your works, O Lord! Your thoughts are very deep! Psalm 92:5

When we've been there ten thousand years, 783
bright shining as the sun,
we've no less days to sing God's praise
than when we'd first begun.

The King of kings and Lord of lords. It is he alone who has immortality and dwells in unapproachable light, whom no one has ever seen or can see; to him be honor and eternal dominion. Amen. 1 Timothy 6:15-16

Look, O look, the sight is glorious, 406
see the man of sorrows now;
from the fight returned victorious,
ev'ry knee to him shall bow.
Crown him! Crown him!
Crown him! Crown him!
Crowns become the victor's brow.

We sing your highest praise, King of kings and Lord of lords. We stand in awe of your creation and powerful works. We have deep gratitude for your Son, Christ Jesus. Amen.

Twenty-Fourth Sunday after Pentecost

Watchword for the Week — So teach us, O God, to count our days that we may gain a wise heart. Psalm 90:12

Sunday, November 15 — Zephaniah 1:7,12-18; Psalm 90:1-8,(9-11),12 1 Thessalonians 5:1-11; Matthew 25:14-30

He has told you, O mortal, what is good; and what does the Lord require of you but to do justice, and to love kindness, and to walk humbly with your God? Micah 6:8

What does the Lord require 695*
for praise and offering?
What sacrifice, desire, or tribute bid you bring?
Do justly, love mercy, walk humbly with your God.

Pursue righteousness, faith, love, and peace, along with those who call on the Lord from a pure heart. 2 Timothy 2:22

Of all the Spirit's gifts to me, 598**
I pray that I may never cease
to take and treasure most these three:
love, joy and peace.

Lord, you require of us justice, mercy, humility, righteousness, faith, love, and peace. Over our lifetime we learn these challenges. We are imperfect; help our ineptitude. Give us opportunities every day to practice in real life—with the help of Jesus. Amen.

Monday, November 16 — Psalm 127
1 Kings 9:20–10:29; John 15:9–17

You shall love your neighbor as yourself: I am the Lord. Leviticus 19:18

Since, O Lord, you have demanded 401*
that our lives your love should show
so we wait to be commanded
forth into your world to go.
Kindle in us love's compassion
so that ev'ryone may see
in our faith and hope the promise
of a new humanity.

Let mutual love continue. Do not neglect to show hospitality to strangers, for by doing that some have entertained angels without knowing it. Hebrews 13:1-2

Blessed be the tie that binds 680
our hearts in Christian love;
the fellowship of kindred minds
is like to that above.

Visiting Stranger, we welcome you among us. Could you be the homeless man or woman? Could you be the immigrant child with parents? Could you be the gay man next door? Could you be the gang member downtown? Could you be the elder in the grocery store? We want to be ready. In Jesus' name, we pray. Amen.

Tuesday, November 17 — Psalm 128
1 Kings 11:1–25; John 15:18–16:4

For my name's sake I defer my anger, for the sake of my praise I restrain it for you, so that I may not cut you off. Isaiah 48:9

For God, in grace and tenderness, 519
regarded us in our distress;
yea, to our aid himself he came;
let all adore God's holy name.

God saved us and called us with a holy calling, not according to our works but according to his own purpose and grace. This grace was given to us in Christ Jesus. 2 Timothy 1:9

Jesus calls us; by your mercies, 600
Savior, may we hear your call,
give our hearts to your obedience,
serve and love you best of all.

God, you withhold your anger and show us mercy. You call us to service—not according to what we would like to do, but according to your design. You show us the path with purpose and grace through Jesus Christ. Thank you. Amen.

Wednesday, November 18 — Psalm 129
1 Kings 11:26–12:24; John 16:5–16

O Lord our God, other lords besides you have ruled over us, but we acknowledge your name alone. Isaiah 26:13

Before the Lord's eternal throne, 455
you nations, bow with sacred joy;
know that the Lord is God alone;
he can create, and he destroy.

We must obey God rather than any human authority. Acts 5:29

God's word forever shall abide, 788*
no thanks to foes who fear it;
for God himself fights by our side
with weapons of the Spirit.
Were they to take our house,
goods, honor, child, or spouse,
though life be wrenched away,
they cannot win the day.
The Kingdom's ours forever.

Lord our God, it is you and you alone we look to for calm in the midst of the clamor of a busy day; for joy in the peace of a woodland vacation; for rest in the middle of a sleepless night; for comfort in sorrow of a lost one. Thanks be to God. Amen.

Thursday, November 19 — Psalm 130
1 Kings 12:25–13:22; John 16:17–33

O taste and see that the Lord is good; happy are those who take refuge in him. Psalm 34:8

God is love; and love enfolds us, 463
all the world in one embrace;
with unfailing grasp God holds us,
ev'ry child of ev'ry race.
And when human hearts are breaking
under sorrow's iron rod,
then we find that self-same aching
deep within the heart of God.

Come; for everything is ready now. Luke 14:17

Open then our hearts and senses 684
to your Spirit's varied ways.
Overcome our self-defenses
so we hear the prayer and praise
which the folk of countless cultures
in new words and rhythms raise.

Delicious One, with our fruit of the spirit, we are prepared to share the joy and comfort we find in you. Melt us, mold us, fill us, use us. Spirit of the living God, fall afresh on us. Amen.

Friday, November 20 — Psalm 131
1 Kings 13:23–14:20; John 17:1–19

He changes times and seasons, deposes kings and sets up kings. Daniel 2:21

Unresting, unhasting, and silent as light, 457
nor wanting, nor wasting, you rule day and night;
your justice like mountains high soaring above
your clouds which are fountains of goodness and love.

Great and amazing are your deeds, Lord God the Almighty! Just and true are your ways, King of the nations! Lord, who will not fear and glorify your name? Revelation 15:3-4

Holy, holy, holy Lord God Almighty! 381
All thy works shall praise thy name
in earth and sky and sea.
Holy, holy, holy, merciful and mighty!
God in three persons, blessed Trinity!

Lord God, the almighty, you are in charge. We grow where you have planted us. We sing a new song in a sometimes strange land. We learn to love our work. We thank you for the gifts you have given. Amen.

Saturday, November 21 — Psalm 132
1 Kings 14:21–15:8; John 17:20–26

God, your steadfast love is better than life. Psalm 63:3

All time is yours, O Lord, to give; 804*
may we, in all the years we live,
find that each day of life is new,
a celebration, Lord, with you.

So we have known and believe the love that God has for us. God is love, and those who abide in love abide in God, and God abides in them. 1 John 4:16

O love, how deep, how broad, how high, 485
beyond all thought and fantasy,
that God, the Son of God, should take
our mortal form for mortals' sake.

God of love, it is reassuring to know that those who abide in love—abide in God and God abides in them. Our world desperately needs this kind of love. Help us to spread it far and wide. Amen.

Reign of Christ (Christ the King Sunday)

Watchword for the Week — God says, "I will seek the lost, and I will bring back the strayed, and I will bind up the injured, and I will strengthen the weak." Ezekiel 34:16

Sunday, November 22 — Ezekiel 34:11-16,20-24; Psalm 95:1-7a Ephesians 1:15-23; Matthew 25:31-46

I, I am the Lord, and besides me there is no savior. Isaiah 43:11

Let God be God wherever life may be; 459*
let ev'ry tongue bear witness to the call;
all humankind is one by God's decree;
let God be God, let God be God for all.

One Lord, one faith, one baptism, one God and Father of all, who is above all and through all and in all. Ephesians 4:5-6

One member may not know another here, 516
and yet their fellowship is true and near;
one is their Savior, and their Father one;
one Spirit rules them, and among them none
lives to one's self.

Omnipresent One, today we celebrate the reign of Christ. Let us raise the image of Christians throughout the world who sing your praise—in Africa, Central America, West Indies, Europe, North America, Nepal, South America, Middle East, and throughout the world. Amen.

Monday, November 23 — Psalm 133
1 Kings 15:9–16:14; John 18:1–11

I dwell in the high and holy place, and also with those who are contrite and humble in spirit, to revive the spirit of the humble, and to revive the heart of the contrite. Isaiah 57:15

For thinking you too far from us, 738*
for fearing you too close to us,
forgive us now, good Lord.
You dwell in high and holy place,
and yet touch all things with your grace.
Through all our lives be now adored.

Jesus saw a great crowd; and he had compassion for them, because they were like sheep without a shepherd. Mark 6:34

Thou, Lord, wilt not forsake me, 795
though I am oft to blame;
as thy reward, O take me
anew, just as I am;
grant me henceforth, dear Savior,
through all my pilgrim years
to look to thee and never
give way to anxious fears.

Jesus Christ, you have a knack for turning things upside down. You elevate the humble and lowly. You are the shepherd who dies for sheep who love to wander. You pay the debts your servants owe. You show us paradoxes of the Christian faith. Help us to know your ways, we pray. Amen.

Tuesday, November 24 — Psalm 134
1 Kings 16:15–17:24; John 18:12–24

All the ends of the earth have seen the salvation of our God. Psalm 98:3 NIV

Eternal thanks we sing, 488
great author of salvation,
who sinful hearts did bring
to heed your invitation.
We are your property.
O may we yours remain;
this is our only plea,
since you for us were slain.

Is a lamp brought in to be put under the bushel basket, or under the bed, and not on the lampstand? Mark 4:21

Do not let the bushel cover up your light, *
keep your lamp in order,
trimmed and burning bright;
try to be a blessing, brighten up the night:
let the Gospel light shine out.

Light of the world, we would put our light under a bushel, except for you. We would let the candles extinguish, except for you. We want your light to shine through us. Amen.

* *Let the Gospel Light Shine Out* by Johnson Oatman. Public Domain.

Wednesday, November 25 — Psalm 135:1–12
1 Kings 18; John 18:25–40

You drink wine by the bowlful and use the finest perfumes, but you do not mourn over the ruin of Israel. Amos 6:6 GNT

God of our weary years, 707
God of our silent tears,
thou who hast brought us thus far on the way,
thou who hast by thy might
led us into the light,
keep us forever in the path, we pray.
Lest our feet stray from the places,
our God, where we met thee,
lest our hearts, drunk with the wine
of the world, we forget thee,
shadowed beneath thy hand,
may we forever stand,
true to our God, true to our native land.

As for those who in the present age are rich, command them not to be haughty, or to set their hopes on the uncertainty of riches, but rather on God who richly provides us with everything for our enjoyment. They are to do good, to be rich in good works, generous, and ready to share, thus storing up for themselves the treasure of a good foundation for the future, so that they may take hold of the life that really is life. 1 Timothy 6:17-19

We give you but your own 657
in any gifts we bring;
all that we have is yours alone,
a trust from you, our King.

Lord, we have been blessed. Help us to share those blessings with others in humility. Help us to empty ourselves and fill with your spirit. In your name, we pray. Amen.

Thursday, November 26 — Psalm 135:13–21
1 Kings 19; John 19:1–11

And now, our God, we give thanks to you and praise your glorious name. 1 Chronicles 29:13

Praise him for his grace and favor 529
to his people in distress.
Praise him, still the same forever,
slow to chide, and swift to bless.
Alleluia! Alleluia!
Glorious in his faithfulness!

Give thanks to God the Father at all times and for everything in the name of our Lord Jesus Christ. Ephesians 5:20

Praise the Lord, praise the Lord, 550
let the earth hear his voice!
Praise the Lord, praise the Lord, let the people rejoice!
O come to the Father through Jesus the Son,
and give him the glory—great things he has done!

God our Father, we give you thanks for the bounty of the earth. We give you thanks for the presence of your son, Jesus Christ, who teaches us to give praise at all times. Amen.

Friday, November 27 — Psalm 136
1 Kings 20:1–21; John 19:12–24

O Lord, all my longing is known to you; my sighing is not hidden from you. Psalm 38:9

Make me your abode, 608
a temple of God,
a vessel of grace,
prepared for your service and formed to your praise.

You know that the testing of your faith produces endurance. James 1:3

Lead on, O King eternal! 753
The day of march has come;
henceforth in fields of conquest
your tents will be our home:
through days of preparation
your grace has made us strong,
and now, O King eternal,
we lift our battle song.

Lord, you know our inward thoughts and worries. We share these with you all day long. Sometimes we need help getting back on track, and we turn to you for guidance. We pray in Jesus' name. Amen.

Saturday, November 28 — Psalm 137
1 Kings 20:22–21:16; John 19:25–37

As a mother comforts her child, so I will comfort you. Isaiah 66:13

As a mother looks with favor 659
on the new life in her arms,
searching ev'ry small expression,
sav'ring moments filled with charm,
so God smiles on ev'ry person,
so God takes such keen delight
in the praises that we offer;
we are precious in God's sight.

Jesus said, "I will not leave you orphaned; I am coming to you. Because I live, you also will live." John 14:18,19

O then what raptured greetings 394
on Canaan's happy shore;
what knitting severed friendships up,
where partings are no more!
Then eyes with joy shall sparkle
that brimmed with tears of late,
no orphans left without a home,
nor mourners desolate.

God, you act as a mother would, providing comfort and assurance. Thinking of the assurance that hymns bring, we can hear you singing these two verses. A smile comes to our faces. Amen.

First Sunday of Advent

Watchword for the Week — Then they will see 'the Son of Man coming in clouds' with great power and glory. Mark 13:26

Sunday, November 29 — Isaiah 64:1-9; Psalm 80:1-7,17-19
1 Corinthians 1:3-9; Mark 13:24-37

May the Lord cause you to flourish, both you and your children. Psalm 115:14 NIV

God made from one blood 678*
all the families of earth,
the circles of nurture that raised us from birth,
companions who join us to walk through each stage
of childhood and youth and adulthood and age.

His mercy is for those who fear him from generation to generation. Luke 1:50

Lord, you have been our dwelling place p147
in every generation.
Your people still have known your grace
and your blessed consolation.
Through every age you heard our cry,
through every age we found you nigh,
our strength and our salvation.

Steadfast Lord, your mercies are shared throughout the world and over time. The richness of scripture reveals your mercies across generations, across time, and across miles. Praise be to God. Amen.

Monday, November 30 — Psalm 138:1–5
1 Kings 21:17–22:28; John 19:38–20:9

Thus said the Lord of hosts, "Truly, one who touches you touches the apple of my eye." Zechariah 2:8

I love your church, O God! 513
Her walls before you stand,
dear as the apple of your eye,
and graven on your hand.

Who will bring any charge against God's elect? It is God who justifies. Romans 8:33

Elect from ev'ry nation, 511
yet one o'er all the earth,
her charter of salvation:
one Lord, one faith, one birth;
one holy name she blesses,
partakes one holy food;
and to one hope she presses
with ev'ry grace endued.

God, your beloved church is a refuge in this world. Although forces work to destroy the church, through the faithful one, your church remains strong and focused on spreading your love throughout the world. Thank you for the witness of your church on earth. Amen.

Tuesday, December 1 — Psalm 138:6–8
Kings 22:29–53; John 20:10–23

The Lord said to Isaac, "Reside in this land as an alien, and I will be with you, and will bless you." Genesis 26:3

Lord, for thy coming us prepare; p8
may we, to meet thee without fear,
at all times ready be;
in faith and love preserve us sound;
O let us day and night be found
waiting with joy to welcome thee.

Live in reverent fear during the time of your exile. 1 Peter 1:17

Faith is a living power from heav'n 700
that grasps the promise God has giv'n,
a trust that can't be overthrown
fixed heartily on Christ alone.

Holy God, in our waiting we prepare for the promise that is Jesus Christ. Open our hearts and minds to loving and knowing you more deeply and expansively than the day before. Amen.

Wednesday, December 2 — Psalm 139:1–6
Kings 1:1–2:18; John 20:24–31

In the Lord I take refuge; how can you say to me, "Flee like a bird to the mountains." Psalm 11:1

Help me the slow of heart to move 735
by some clear, winning word of love;
teach me the wayward feet to stay,
and guide them in the homeward way.

Jesus said, "Peace I leave with you; my peace I give to you. I do not give to you as the world gives. Do not let your hearts be troubled, and do not let them be afraid." John 14:27

In hope that sends a shining ray 735
far down the future's broad'ning way,
in peace that only you can give;
with you, O Master, let me live.

Prince of peace, within the chaos and turmoil of our lives, guide us to your presence, filling us with shalom that only comes from you. Amen.

Thursday, December 3 — Psalm 139:7–12
2 Kings 2:19–3:27; John 21:1–14

All shall give as they are able, according to the blessing of the Lord your God that he has given you. Deuteronomy 16:17

We'll bring him hearts that love him, 658
we'll bring him thankful praise,
and souls forever striving
to follow in his ways:
and these shall be the treasures
we offer to the King,
and these are gifts that even
our grateful hearts may bring.

If the eagerness is there, the gift is acceptable according to what one has—not according to what one does not have. 2 Corinthians 8:12

God loves the person who loves to give, 39s*
giving cheerfully her smile, his time, their wealth.
You may ask what you have that is worth offering,
you can graciously give yourself.
A kind word praises God.
A kind word praises God.
A gentle hand can bless the soul.
A kind word praises God.

Creator God, we offer ourselves to be shaped and molded as you would have us be. Move us to release your generosity to the many who long to be loved and cared for with compassion. Amen.

Friday, December 4 — Psalm 139:13–16
2 Kings 4:1–37; John 21:15–25

It is vain for you to rise up early, to retire late, to eat the bread of painful labors; for he gives to his beloved even in his sleep. Psalm 127:2 NASB

No longer need we sorrow 268*
nor worry night and day
how we might draw him to us
within our heart's embrace.
He of his own will find us
and full of love and grace
take up each anxious burden
and bless each soul with peace.

Your Father knows what you need before you ask him. Matthew 6:8

The sure provisions of my God 730
attend me all my days;
O may your house be my abode
and all my work be praise.
There would I find a settled rest,
while others go and come—
no more a stranger or a guest,
but like a child at home.

Loving God, how blessed we are that you give us the best you have to offer. As we search our needs and acknowledge your gifts, may we be empowered to see and respond to the needs of those around us. Amen.

Saturday, December 5 — Psalm 139:17–24
2 Kings 4:38–5:14; Acts 1:1–14

A father of the fatherless and a judge for the widows, is God in His holy habitation. God makes a home for the lonely; he leads out the prisoners into prosperity. Psalm 68:5-6 NASB

God is our refuge, strength and home, 20s*
our help and peace today.
Though pow'rs may fail and sorrows come,
God's light will show the way.

That evening, at sunset, they brought to Jesus all who were sick or possessed with demons. And the whole city was gathered around the door. And he cured many. Mark 1:32-34

Be still and know our Lord is God, 20s*
whose love attends our prayers.
Each whispered word, each silent hope
finds comfort in God's care.

Great Helper of the helpless, we bow in humility before you, asking you to heal the broken areas of our lives. Restore us to be the people you desire us to be. Amen.

Second Sunday of Advent

Watchword for the Week — He will feed his flock like a shepherd; he will gather the lambs in his arms, and carry them in his bosom. Isaiah 40:11

Sunday, December 6 — Isaiah 40:1-11; Psalm 85:1-2,8-13
2 Peter 3:8-15a; Mark 1:1-8

It is my pleasure to tell you about the miraculous signs and wonders that the most high God has performed for me. Daniel 4:2 NIV

God gave us eyes to see them, 467
and lips that we might tell
how great is God Almighty,
who has made all things well.

This life was revealed, and we have seen it and testify to it, and declare to you the eternal life that was with the Father and was revealed to us. 1 John 1:2

Proclaim to ev'ry people, tongue, and nation 618
that God, in whom they live and move, is love;
tell how he stooped to save his lost creation,
and died on earth that we might live in love.

Gracious loving God, on this Lord's day we give you thanks for revealing yourself to us through the abundance of divine love and generous grace. Give us the courage to reveal your love and grace to others. Amen.

Monday, December 7 — Psalm 140:1–5
2 Kings 5:15–6:23; Acts 1:15–26

Those who are wise shall shine like the brightness of the sky, and those who lead many to righteousness, like the stars forever and ever. Daniel 12:3

Apostles, prophets, martyrs, 391
and all the noble throng
who wear the spotless raiment
and raise the ceaseless song:
for them and those whose witness
is only known to you,
by walking in their footsteps,
we give you praise anew.

So we are ambassadors for Christ, since God is making his appeal through us; we entreat you on behalf of Christ, be reconciled to God. 2 Corinthians 5:20

I will seek God's help in all my life; 51s*
to follow the way in calm or strife;
to flourish in faith with God as guide:
enfolded in love I will abide.

God of love, as we continue in our Advent preparations, may we hear your call to love and serve others more loudly and more strongly. Like Mary, may we ponder in our hearts what your coming to us means. Amen.

Tuesday, December 8 — Psalm 140:6–13
2 Kings 6:24–7:20; Acts 2:1–13

The day of the Lord is coming, it is near. Joel 2:1

Lead on, O King eternal, 753
till sin's fierce war shall cease,
and holiness shall whisper
the sweet amen of peace;
for not with sword's loud clashing,
nor roll of stirring drums,
but deeds of love and mercy,
the heav'nly kingdom comes.

In accordance with his promise, we wait for new heavens and a new earth, where righteousness is at home. 2 Peter 3:13

The Spirit and the church p84
"O come!" are now entreating;
let all who hear their voice
"O come!" be loud repeating:
amen! Lord Jesus, come;
we still wait faithfully.
Soon, we implore you, come,
your glory let us see.

Loving Savior, we wait for your coming with anticipation of creating newness in our lives. We need only to turn to you to lay aside the burdens that weigh us down so our relationship with you is reenergized and renewed. Amen.

Wednesday, December 9 — Psalm 141:1–4
2 Kings 8; Acts 2:14–28

The Lord your God is bringing you into a good land, a land with flowing streams, with springs and underground waters welling up in valleys and hills. Deuteronomy 8:7

He leadeth me: O blessed thought! 787
O words with heav'nly comfort fraught!
Whate'er I do, where'er I be,
still 'tis God's hand that leadeth me.

God who did not withhold his own Son, but gave him up for all of us, will he not with him also give us everything else? Romans 8:32

To God be the glory—great things he has done! 550
So loved the the world that he gave us his Son,
who yielded his life an atonement for sin,
and opened the lifegate that all may go in.

Holy God, how we marvel at the care you provide for us. When we are distracted, far away, or indisposed, still you care for us and love us despite ourselves. What more can we say other than "Thank You!"? Amen.

Thursday, December 10 — Psalm 141:5–10
2 Kings 9; Acts 2:29–47

The glory of the Lord shall be revealed, and all people shall see it together, for the mouth of the Lord has spoken. Isaiah 40:5

Straight shall be what long was crooked, 264
and the rougher places plain!
Let your hearts be true and humble,
as befits his holy reign!
For the glory of the Lord
now on earth is shed abroad,
and all flesh shall see the token
that God's word is never broken.

We have seen his glory, the glory as of a father's only son, full of grace and truth. John 1:14

Savior of the nations, come! 265
Virgin's Son, make here your home.
Marvel now, both heav'n and earth,
that the Lord chose such a birth.

Glorious heavenly Father, your unrelenting revelation calls to us, cries to us, sings with us, and speaks to us through all of life's experiences. In the chaos of earthly life, your glory is seen, recognized, and honored. Amen.

Friday, December 11 — Psalm 142
2 Kings 10; Acts 3:1–10

He is the living God, enduring forever. His kingdom shall never be destroyed. Daniel 6:26

E'en so I love you and will love, 602
and in your praise will sing,
solely because you are my God
and my eternal King.

Jesus Christ is the same yesterday and today and forever. Hebrews 13:8

Yesterday, today, fore'er the same, 756*
lo, the heritage of all who bear your name;
to ransom them from sin the Savior came:
Saranam, Saranam, Saranam.

Lord Jesus Christ, because of you, we see God; because of you, we hear God; because of you, we love God. In you, we are joined with God and receive peace within. May we dwell in that peace forever. Amen.

Saturday, December 12 — Psalm 143:1–6
2 Kings 11; Acts 3:11–26

O Lord, be gracious to me; heal me, for I have sinned against you. Psalm 41:4

Be still my soul: the Lord is on your side. 757
Bear patiently the cross of grief or pain;
leave to your God to order and provide;
in ev'ry change God faithful will remain.
Be still, my soul: your best, your heav'nly friend
through thorny ways leads to a joyful end.

The prayer of faith will save the sick, and the Lord will raise them up; and anyone who has committed sins will be forgiven. James 5:15

Here does the Lord of life proclaim p198
to all the world his saving name;
repenting souls, in him believe;
you wounded, look on him and live.

Lord of life, we cannot rise to our full potential unless we are released from the burden of sin we create in our lives. We name our sins and offer them to you for our souls' liberation. Amen.

Third Sunday of Advent

Watchword for the Week — May the God of peace sanctify you entirely; and may your spirit and soul and body be kept sound and blameless at the coming of our Lord Jesus Christ. 1 Thessalonians 5:23

Sunday, December 13 — Isaiah 61:1-4,8-11; Psalm 126
1 Thessalonians 5:16-24; John 1:6-8,19-28

There is none like you, O Lord; you are great, and your name is great in might. Jeremiah 10:6

Praise to the Lord, the almighty, 530
the King of creation!
O my soul, praise him,
for he is your health and salvation!
Let all who hear
now to his temple draw near,
joining in glad adoration.

We have seen and do testify that the Father has sent his Son as the Savior of the world. 1 John 4:14

Born your people to deliver, 262
born a child and yet a king,
born to reign in us forever,
now your gracious kingdom bring.
By your own eternal Spirit
rule in all our hearts alone;
by your all-sufficient merit
raise us to your glorious throne.

Creator God, we worship and adore you, for there is no end to your creative powers. You create life anew within us and inspire us to lives of service by sending your Son to redeem us and show us the way. Amen.

Monday, December 14 — Psalm 143:7–12
2 Kings 12,13; Acts 4:1–12

When your judgments come upon the earth, the people of the world learn righteousness. Isaiah 26:9 NIV

O come, Desire of Nations, bind 274
all peoples in one heart and mind;
bid envy, strife and quarrels cease;
fill the whole world with heaven's peace.

He who supplies seed to the sower and bread for food will supply and multiply your seed for sowing and increase the harvest of your righteousness. 2 Corinthians 9:10

As you, Lord, have lived for others, 648
so may we for others live;
freely have your gifts been granted;
freely may your servants give.
Yours the gold and yours the silver,
yours the wealth of land and sea;
we but stewards of your bounty
held in solemn trust will be.

Lord, freely have you given to us and freely may we bring your story of the good news to those who live in darkness and long to be free. Amen.

Tuesday, December 15 — Psalm 144:1–4
2 Kings 14; Acts 4:13–22

Solomon prayed, "You have kept the promise you made to my father David; today every word has been fulfilled." 1 Kings 8:24 GNT

In his temple now behold him, 314
see the long-expected Lord;
ancient prophets had foretold him,
God has now fulfilled his word.
Now to praise him, his redeemed
shall break forth with one accord.

Blessed be the Lord God of Israel, for he has looked favorably on his people and redeemed them. He has raised up a mighty savior for us in the house of his servant David. Luke 1:68-69

Welcome, O my Savior, now! 261
Joyful, Lord, to you I bow.
Come into my heart, I pray;
O, prepare yourself a way!

God of the covenants, thank you for your steadfastness and for honoring your promise to come to us as one of us. May our loyalty be directed solely to you and "soul-y" to you. Amen.

Wednesday, December 16 — Psalm 144:5–8
2 Kings 15; Acts 4:23–37

**You are the God who works wonders;
you have displayed your might among the peoples. Psalm 77:14**

Great Father of glory, pure Father of light, 457
your angels adore you, all veiling their sight;
all praise we would render, O lead us to see
the light of your splendor, your love's majesty.

To his saints God chose to make known how great among the Gentiles are the riches of the glory of this mystery, which is Christ in you, the hope of glory. Colossians 1:26-27

Name him, Christians, name him— 480
strong your love as death—
but with awe and wonder,
and with life-filled breath;
he is God the Savior,
he is Christ the Lord,
ever to be worshiped,
evermore adored.

Loving Savior, in this time of preparation, lead us boldly into the mystery that is you. Open our hearts and minds so that your dwelling within us reveals outer signs of service and mission. Amen.

Thursday, December 17 — Psalm 144:9–15
2 Kings 16:1–17:6; Acts 5:1–11

There is hope for your future, says the Lord. Jeremiah 31:17

Pardon for sin and a peace that endureth, 460*
thine own dear presence to cheer and to guide;
strength for today and bright hope for tomorrow,
blessings all mine, with ten thousand beside!

Listen! I am standing at the door, knocking; if you hear my voice and open the door, I will come in to you and eat with you, and you with me. Revelation 3:20

Be known to us in breaking bread, 411
but do not then depart;
Savior, abide with us, and spread
your table in our heart.

Bread of life, feed our souls, inspire our spirits, and strengthen us for your mission of building God's kingdom here; a kingdom where all are fed and loved beyond compare. Amen.

Friday, December 18 — Psalm 145:1–7
2 Kings 17:7–41; Acts 5:12–16

Hear the word of the Lord, because the Lord has a charge to bring against you who live in the land: "There is no faithfulness, no love, no acknowledgment of God in the land." Hosea 4:1 NIV

Now we bring ourselves to you; 741
cleanse us, Lord, we humbly pray;
undeserving though we be,
draw us closer ev'ry day.
Lord, our refuge, hope, and strength!
Keep, O keep us safe from harm,
shield us through our earthly life
by your everlasting arm.

Repent, for the kingdom of heaven has come near. Matthew 3:2

For the herald's voice is crying 264
in the desert far and near,
calling us to true repentance,
since the Kingdom now is here.
O, that warning cry obey!
Now prepare for God a way!
Let the valleys rise to meet him,
and the hills bow down to greet him!

Holy God, we confess we often turn away from you allowing ourselves to be led in troubling and dangerous directions. May our repentance be revealed in noticeable changes in thoughts, words, and deeds. Amen.

Saturday, December 19 — Psalm 145:8–16
2 Kings 18; Acts 5:17–40

Your eyes beheld my unformed substance. In your book were written all the days that were formed for me. Psalm 139:16

His sov'reign pow'r without our aid 455
formed us of clay and gave us breath;
and when like wand'ring sheep we strayed,
he saved us from the pow'r of death.

Rejoice that your names are written in heaven. Luke 10:20

We'll crowd your gates with thankful songs, 455
high as the heav'n our voices raise;
and earth, with her ten thousand tongues,
shall fill your courts with sounding praise.

Creator of all that is, you love and care for us more than we can imagine. In the midst of our Advent preparations, may we raise our songs of praise to you and wait with anticipation for the coming of your son. Amen.

Fourth Sunday of Advent

Watchword for the Week — The Mighty One has done great things for me, and holy is his name. Luke 1:49

Sunday, December 20 — 2 Samuel 7:1-11,16; Luke 1:47-55
Romans 16:25-27; Luke 1:26-38

May those who love your salvation say continually, "Great is the Lord!" Psalm 40:16

Sing praise to God who reigns above, 537
the God of all creation,
the God of pow'r, the God of love,
the God of our salvation.
My soul with comfort rich he fills,
and ev'ry grief he gently stills:
to God all praise and glory!

He destined us for adoption as his children through Jesus Christ, according to the good pleasure of his will. Ephesians 1:5

By love's closest bonds united, 515
as the Lord's own family,
be to serve his name excited,
be to him a fruitful tree.

God, how blessed we are to follow Christ into your family. We live this day and everyday as your beloved, and show in all that we do and say that we strive to live into our name, Christian. Amen.

Monday, December 21 — Psalm 145:17–21
2 Kings 19:1–28; Acts 5:41–6:7

These people draw near with their mouths and honor me with their lips, while their hearts are far from me. Isaiah 29:13

O God of unrelenting grace, 738
whose judgment yet we daily face,
forgive us now, good Lord.
You are so distant and so near;
for you we long, yet you we fear,
O known, and yet beyond record.

Little children, let us love, not in word or speech, but in truth and action. 1 John 3:18

Grant, Lord, that with thy direction, 673
"Love each other," we comply,
aiming with unfeigned affection
thy love to exemplify;
let our mutual love be glowing;
thus the world will plainly see
that we, as on one stem growing,
living branches are in thee.

Loving God, living savior, we confess that in this season we are distracted by schedules, to-do lists, and worldly obligations that decrease our sincere worship of you. We ask your forgiveness; redirect us to your truth. Amen.

Tuesday, December 22 — Psalm 146
2 Kings 19:29–20:21; Acts 6:8–7:3

God, you remain the same, and your years will never end. Psalm 102:27

Wide as the world is your command, 455
vast as eternity your love;
firm as a rock your truth must stand,
when rolling years shall cease to move.

"I am the Alpha and the Omega," said the Lord God, who is and who was and who is to come, the Almighty. Revelation 1:8

Of the Father's love begotten 483
ere the worlds began to be,
he is Alpha and Omega—
he the source, the ending he
of the things that are, that have been,
and that future years shall see
evermore and evermore.

Holy God, you break down the barriers of time and space as well as our inner obstacles of fear and doubt. Help us to understand and acknowledge your presence and its perpetuity. Amen.

Wednesday, December 23 — Psalm 147:1–6
2 Kings 21:1–22:10; Acts 7:4–16

I lie down and sleep; I wake again, for the Lord sustains me. Psalm 3:5

Through the long night watches, 567
may your angels spread
their bright wings above me,
watching round my bed.

Truly I tell you, anyone who will not receive the kingdom of God like a little child will never enter it. Mark 10:15 NIV

Gracious Savior, gentle Shepherd, 660
children all are dear to you;
may your loving arms enfold them
in your care their whole life through;
fondly tend and safely keep them
in your mercy strong and true.

Loving Savior, our preparation is drawing to a close and we are eager to receive you anew. Anticipation builds within us. Open our hearts, gracious Lord, so we may arrive at the manger with deep humility and a strong desire to serve you. Amen.

Thursday, December 24 — Psalm 147:7–14
2 Kings 22:11–23:20; Acts 7:17–29

My soul thirsts for God, for the living God. When shall I come and behold the face of God? Psalm 42:2

My God will lead me to a spot 794
where, all my cares and griefs forgot,
I shall enjoy sweet rest.
As pants for cooling streams the hart,
I languish for my heavenly part,
for God, for God, my refuge blessed.

Wise men from the East came to Jerusalem, asking, "Where is the child who has been born king of the Jews? For we observed his star at its rising, and have come to pay him homage." Matthew 2:1-2

As they offered gifts most rare p190
at that manger rude and bare;
so may we with holy joy,
pure and free from sin's alloy,
all our costliest treasures bring;
Christ, to you our heav'nly King.

God of all, you remain faithful to the prophet's messages and are about to reveal yourself to us in love and grace. The waiting is almost over; soon we will see your love revealed in a simple manger and amidst the candle glow. Amen.

Nativity of the Lord (Christmas Day)

Watchword for Christmas Day — Jesus is the reflection of God's glory and the exact imprint of God's very being, and he sustains all things by his powerful word. Hebrews 1:3

Nativity of the Lord — Isaiah 52:7-10; Psalm 98
Hebrews 1:1-4,(5-12); John 1:1-14

Friday, December 25 — Psalm 147:15–20
2 Kings 23:21–24:20; Acts 7:30–43

Happy are the people whose God is the Lord. Psalm 144:15

Yea, Lord, we greet thee, 283
born this happy morning;
Jesus, to thee be all glory giv'n;
word of the Father, now in flesh appearing!
O come, let us adore him,
O come, let us adore him,
O come, let us adore him, Christ, the Lord.

See—I am bringing you good news of great joy for all the people: to you is born this day in the city of David a Savior, who is the Messiah, the Lord. Luke 2:10-11

Christ is born! Christ is born! 29s*
Prophets' word of old foretold
the coming of a Savior
who would remain forever
God's gift of love,
a promise, the Prince of Peace, Messiah.
Long expected! Incarnation!
Wondrous Jesus! Our Salvation!
God the Son to earth is come.

O, bright morning Star, how brightly your love burns within us! As we welcome you to earth, you welcome us into God's kingdom with abundant, everlasting life. With all of creation, we sing your praises. Amen.

Saturday, December 26 — Psalm 148:1–6
2 Kings 25; Acts 7:44–60

I will bring health and healing to it; I will heal my people and will let them enjoy abundant peace and security. Jeremiah 33:6 NIV

Sing praise to God the Father, 43s*
sing praise to God above,
for all God has created,
for daily gifts of love.

The shepherds said to one another, "Let us go now to Bethlehem and see this thing that has taken place, which the Lord has made known to us." Luke 2:15

Shepherds come! Shepherds come 29s**
quickly to the manger bed
in rev'rent awe and wonder
to see the infant Jesus,
on bended knee, adoring,
for such a gift, rejoicing!
God is with us! Shout with glory!
God is with us! Spread the story!
God the Son to earth is come.

Glory to you, Child divine! We celebrate with shepherds and angels to sing and shout of God now with us. May our celebration of your presence have no end. Accept our praise given in both loud acclaims and quiet, mindful reflections. Amen.

First Sunday after Christmas Day

Watchword for the Week — But when the fullness of time had come, God sent his Son, born of a woman, born under the law, in order to redeem those who were under the law, so that we might receive adoption as children. Galatians 4:4,5

Sunday, December 27 — Isaiah 61:10-62:3; Psalm 148
Galatians 4:4-7; Luke 2:22-40

Happy are those who make the Lord their trust. Psalm 40:4

To the hills I lift my eyes, 729
the everlasting hills.
Streaming forth in fresh supplies,
my soul the Spirit feels;
will he not his help afford?
Help, while yet I ask, is giv'n;
God comes down, the God and Lord
who made both earth and heav'n.

So we have the prophetic message more fully confirmed. You will do well to be attentive to this as to a lamp shining in a dark place, until the day dawns and the morning star rises in your hearts. 2 Peter 1:19

Jesus, Lord of life and light, 26s*
ev'ry soul's salvation,
glowing hope in sin's dark night,
love's bright affirmation:
on the earth on Christmas night
you were born in meekness,
leaving all your heav'nly might
to embrace our weakness.

Bright morning Star, you left the heavenly realm and came to show us our Father's abundant love and mercy. Turn our faces and our hearts to your light so it may shine within us to gather others to you. Amen.

* By C. Daniel Crews (2001).

Monday, December 28 — Psalm 148:7–14
1 Chronicles 1:1–37; Acts 8:1–8

The Lord God has given me the tongue of disciples, that I may know how to sustain the weary one with a word. Isaiah 50:4 NASB

Lord, speak to me, that I may speak 646
in living echoes of your tone.
As you have sought, so let me seek
your erring children lost and lone.

We may be able to console those who are in any affliction with the consolation with which we ourselves are consoled by God. 2 Corinthians 1:4

Candle gleaming, 63s*
my face beaming,
let me rise and go
while he leads me,
where he needs me,
in this world below.

Holy Servant, you nourish us with the bread of life and refresh us with endless streams of water. At your manger, you call us to your light to guide us. Amen.

* By Allen W. Schattschneider (1939), alt. © 2013 by IBOC and MMF.

Tuesday, December 29 — Psalm 149:1-4
1 Chronicles 1:38–2:17; Acts 8:9–25

For you who revere my name the sun of righteousness shall rise, with healing in its wings. Malachi 4:2

Visit, then, this soul of mine, 475
pierce the gloom of sin and grief;
fill me, radiancy divine;
scatter all my unbelief;
more and more yourself display,
shining to the perfect day!

He came to what was his own, and his own people did not accept him. But to all who received him, who believed in his name, he gave power to become children of God. John 1:11-12

Then forth they went, with tongues of flame 396
in one blessed theme delighting;
the love of Jesus, and his name,
God's children all uniting.
That love our theme and watchword still;
the law of love may we fulfill—
give love as love we're given.

Christ divine, how blessed we are that, through you, we are adopted into God's family and are called "Beloved." Of this we are certain: God loves us today and always, thanks to you, O Savior. Amen.

Wednesday, December 30 — Psalm 149:5-9
1 Chronicles 2:18–55; Acts 8:26–40

See, I will create new heavens and a new earth. The former things will not be remembered. Isaiah 65:17 NIV

For lo, the days are hast'ning on, 286
by prophet bards foretold,
when with the ever-circling years
comes round the age of gold,
when the new heav'n and earth shall own
the Prince of Peace their King
and the whole world send back the song
which now the angels sing.

Your kingdom come. Your will be done, on earth as it is in heaven. Matthew 6:10

O may I never do my will, 733
but yours, and only yours, fulfill;
let all my time and all my ways
be spent and ended to your praise.

Creator God, when we imagine you building new heavens and a new earth, we never would have thought it would begin with an infant. How marvelous are your ways! Your surprises enlighten and we are inspired. Amen.

Thursday, December 31 — Psalm 150
1 Chronicles 3; Acts 9:1–9

The Lord has heard my supplication, the Lord accepts my prayer. Psalm 6:9

Each day unto my heart 737
new life and grace impart.
Do now my needs supply
lest I should droop and die.
Continually I've need
by faith on you to feed.

Ask and you will receive, so that your joy may be complete. John 16:24

Joy to the world, the Lord is come! 294
Let earth receive her king;
let ev'ry heart prepare him room,
and heav'n and nature sing,
and heav'n and nature sing,
and heav'n and heav'n and nature sing.

Savior who reigns within and about us, lead us into new directions for the sake of your kingdom. May we dedicate the coming year to proclaiming your glory while loving and serving your people. We are so blessed! Thank you, Jesus! Amen.

To order *Moravian Daily Texts*, contact:

The Interprovincial Board of Communication (IBOC)
Moravian Church in America
1021 Center St.
Bethlehem, PA 18018
1.800.732.0591, ext. 38

To order online and
view our complete catalog, visit:
store.moravian.org

The *Moravian Daily Texts* are available in
paperback, hardcover, large print and journal editions,
plus German and Spanish translations.

Also available for the
Amazon Kindle and Apple iBooks

The *Moravian Daily Texts* app is available
for iOS and Android devices on
the iTunes Store and Google Play.

To subscribe to the *Moravian Daily Texts* e-mail and to
learn more about the Moravian Church, visit
www.moravian.org

2020 Directory & Statistics

The Moravian Church in America

1021 Center St., Bethlehem, PA 18018
459 South Church St., Winston-Salem, NC 27101

Published by the Interprovincial Board of Communication
Moravian Church in America
www.moravian.org

Contents

ADDRESSES OF CHURCHES

The following code indicates the Province and/or District (of the Northern Province) that a church is associated with:

NP = Northern Province
SP = Southern Province
CD = Canadian District
ED = Eastern District
WD = Western District

ALBERTA, CANADA (NP, CD)

Calgary

Christ
Rev. Stephen A. Gohdes
600 Acadia Dr. SE
Calgary, AB T2J 0B8
O: 403.271.2700
F: 403.271.2810
moravian@nucleus.com
www.christmoravian.com

Good Shepherd Community
6311 Norfolk Dr. NW
Calgary, AB T2K 5J8
O: 403.274.4888
F: 403.451.1556
moravian@telus.net
www.goodshepherdmoravian.org

Edmonton

Edmonton
Rev. Rebecca Craver
9540 83 Ave. NW
Edmonton, AB T6C 1B9
O: 780.439.1063
F: 780.756.7898
edmontonmoravian@shaw.ca
https://edmontonmoravian.com

Heimtal
The Rev. Matthew J. Gillard
5315-127 St.
Edmonton, Alberta T6Y 0A5
O: 780.955.7305
heimtal@telus.net
www.heimtal.com

Millwoods
Rev. Aaron Linville
2304 38th St. NW
Edmonton, AB T6L 4K9
O: 780.463.7427
F: 780.461.3058
office@mcchurch.ca
www.mcchurch.ca

Rio Terrace
Rev. James LaVoy
15108 76 Ave. NW
Edmonton, AB T5R 2Z9
O/F: 780.487.0211
rioterracemoravian@gmail.com
www.rioterracechurch.org

Sherwood Park

Good News
Rev. Ian D. Edwards
2 Primrose Blvd.
Sherwood Park, AB T8H 1G2
O: 780.467.0337
goodnewschurch@yahoo.com
www.goodnewschurch.ca

Note: Pastors associated with each congregation currrent as of August 1, 2019. Subject to change.

CALIFORNIA (NP, WD)

Banning

Morongo
Rev. Gregg Schafer
47765 Foothill Rd.
PO Box 352
Banning, CA 92220-0352
O: 951.849.3067
morongomoravian@verizon.net

DISTRICT OF COLUMBIA (NP, ED)

Washington

Faith
Rev. Bevon White
405 Riggs Rd. NE
Washington, DC 20011-2515
O: 202.634.9012/9013
F: 202.635.9014
pastor@faithmoravianchurch.org
www.faithmoravianchurch.org

FLORIDA (SP)

Longwood

Rolling Hills
Rev. Wilma E. Israel
1525 State Road 434 W
Longwood, FL 32750-3877
O: 407.332.8380
rhmcoffice@centurylink.net
www.rhmoravian.org

Miami

King of Kings
Gregorio Moody, acolyte
1880 NW 183rd St.
Miami, FL 33056
kokmoravian@att.net

New Hope
Gregorio Moody, acolyte
6001 SW 127th Ave.
Miami, FL 33183-1427
O/F: 305.273.4047
nhmiami@yahoo.com

Prince of Peace
1880 NW 183rd St
Miami, FL 33056
O: 305.628.2061
F: 305.625.5365
popmc@bellsouth.net
www.floridamoravian.org

West Palm Beach

Palm Beach
Evette Campbell, acolyte
297 27th St
West Palm Beach, FL 33407
O: 561.832.1363
F: 561.832.1363 (call first)
pbmoravan@yahoo.com

GEORGIA (SP)

Stone Mountain

First of Georgia
Rev. Elroy Christopher, Interim
4950 Hugh Howell Rd.
Stone Mountain, GA 30087
O: 770.491.7250
F: 770.414.5678
firstmoravian@gmail.com
www.gamoravian.org

ILLINOIS (NP, WD):

West Salem

West Salem
Rev. Reid Lauderman
257 E. Church St.
PO Box 27
West Salem, IL 62476-0027
O: 618.456.8532
wsmor12@gmail.com
www.westsalemmoravianchurch.webs.com

INDIANA (NP, WD)

Hope

Hope
Rev. Andrew Kilps
202 Main St.
Hope, IN 47246
O: 812.546.4641
office@hopemoravianchurch.org
pastor@hopemoravianchurch.org
www.hopemoravianchurch.org

MARYLAND (NP, ED)

New Carrollton

Trinity
Rev. Tammie L. Rinker
7011 Good Luck Rd.
New Carrollton, MD 20784
O: 301.441.1814
trinitymoravianoffice@gmail.com
www.trinitymoravianchurch.org

Thurmont

Graceham
Rev. Sue Koenig
8231A Rocky Ridge Rd.
Thurmont, MD 21788
O: 301.271.2379
secretary@gracehammoravian.org
pastorsue@gracehammoravian.org
www.gracehammoravian.org

Upper Marlboro

St. Paul's
Rev. Dr. William T. Andrews
8505 Heathermore Blvd.
Upper Marlboro, MD 20772
O: 301.627.4200
F: 301.627.4204
spmoravian@gmail.com
www.spmoravian.org

MICHIGAN (NP, WD)

Daggett

Daggett
Rev. James T. Hicks
102 Old US Highway 41
Daggett, MI 49821
Mail: c/o James Hicks
1460 Woodmont Way
Green Bay, WI 54313
daggett@new.rr.com

Unionville

Unionville
Rev. Timothy Naisby
2711 Cass St.
Unionville, MI 48767
O: 989.674.8686
moravian@airadv.net
www.unionvillemoravian.org

Westland

Grace
31133 Hively Ave.
Westland, MI 48185
O/F: 734.721.9290
gracemoravian@gmail.com

MINNESOTA (NP, WD)

Altura

Our Savior's
Rev. Gregory Behrend
37 Chapel Dr. NW
PO Box 161
Altura, MN 55910-0161
O: 507.796.5612
oursaviorsmoravian@gmail.com
www.oursaviorsmoravian.org

Chaska

Chaska
115 E 4th St.
Chaska, MN 55318
O: 952.448.4000
office@chaskamoravian.org
www.chaskamoravian.org

MINNESOTA (Cont.)

Maple Grove

Christ's Community
Rev. Jonathan C. Lee
13250 93rd Ave.
Maple Grove, MN 55369
O: 763.420.7187
christscommunitymoravian@gmail.com
www.ccc-mg.org

Northfield

Northfield
713 Division St. South
Northfield, MN 55057
O: 507.645.7566
church.northfieldmoravian@gmail.com
www.mainstreetmoravianchurch.org

Saint Charles

Berea
Rev. Franklin Jones
12730 Berea Dr.
PO Box 402
St. Charles, MN 55972-0402
O: 507.932.3584
bereamor@bereamoravian.org

Victoria

Lake Auburn
7460 Victoria Dr.
PO Box 160
Victoria, MN 55386
O/F: 952.443.2051
lakeauburnchurch@centurylink.net
www.lakeauburnchurch.org

Waconia

Waconia
Rev. Dr. Amy Gohdes-Luhman
209 E 2nd St.
Waconia, MN 55387
O: 952.442.2920
wmoravian@gmail.com
www.waconiamoravian.org

NEW JERSEY (NP, ED)

Cinnaminson

Palmyra
Rev. Laura Gordon
1921 Cinnaminson Ave.
Cinnaminson, NJ 08077
O: 856.829.2886
palmyramoravian@gmail.com
www.palmyramoravian.org

Egg Harbor

Egg Harbor City
Rev. Bruce Weaknecht
245 Boston Ave.
Egg Harbor City, NJ 08215
O: 609.965.1920
wknt03@aol.com
www.eggharborcitymoravian.org

Riverside

First, Riverside
Rev. Rebecca Sisley
228 E. Washington St.
Riverside, NJ 08075-3629
O: 856.461.0132
F: 856.764.7032
riversidemoravianchurch@gmail.com
www.riversidemoravian.org

Union

Battle Hill
777 Liberty Ave.
Union, NJ 07083
O: 908.686.5262
F: 908.378.5866
bhcmchurch777@gmail.com
or ironpreacher@aol.com
www.battlehillmoravian.wordpress.com

NEW YORK (NP, ED)

Bronx

Tremont Terrace
1621 Pilgrim Ave.
Bronx, NY 10461
O: 718.829.2156
F: 718.829.0044
tremontterrace@verizon.net

Brooklyn

Fellowship
Rev. Wellesley Ferguson
(Meeting at Church of the Evangel UCC)
1950 Bedford Ave.
Brooklyn, NY 11225
O: 718.287.7200
fellowshipmoravian@gmail.com

John Hus
Rev. Dr. Michael E. Johnson
153 Ocean Ave.
Brooklyn, NY 11225
O: 718.856.2200
F: 718.856.2201
johnhusmoravian@optonline.net
www.johnhusmoravianchurch.com

New York City

First, New York
Rev. Charles C. Harewood
154 Lexington Ave.
New York, NY 10016
Mail: PO Box 1874
Murray Hill Station
New York, NY 10156-0609
O: 212.683.4219
F: 212.683.9734
firstmoravian@verizon.net

United
Rev. Desna Henry Goulbourne
200 E 127th St.
New York, NY 10035
O: 212.722.2109
F: 212.987.2818
unitedmoravian@gmail.com
www.unitedmoravian.org

Queens

Grace
Rev. Earl Goulbourne
178-38 137th Ave.
Springfield Gardens, NY 11434
O: 718.723.2681
F: 718.723.4288
gracemoravian@verizon.net
www.gracemoravianchurchny.org

Staten Island

Castleton Hill
Rev. Lance Fox
1657 Victory Blvd.
Staten Island, NY 10314
O: 718.442.5215 or 718.442.5309
F: 718.442.5211
office@castletonhill.org
www.castletonhill.org

Great Kills
Rev. Dr. Tracy A. Pryor
62 Hillside Terr.
Staten Island, NY 10308
O: 718.317.7788
F: 718.356.2826
office@greatkillsmoravian.org
www.greatkillsmoravian.org

New Dorp
Rev. Duane E. Ullrich
2205 Richmond Rd.
Staten Island, NY 10306-2557
O: 718.351.0090
F: 718.351.0290
ndmcthree.moravian@verizon.net
office@newdorpmoravian.org
www.newdorpmoravian.org

Vanderbilt Avenue
Rev. Wellesley Ferguson
285 Vanderbilt Ave.
Staten Island, NY 10304
O: 718.447.2966
office@vanderbiltmoravian.org
www.vanderbiltmoravian.org

NORTH CAROLINA (SP)

Advance

Macedonia
Rev. Zachary Dease
700 NC Highway 801 N
Advance, NC 27006
O: 336.998.4394
F: 336.940.5317
macedonia@yadtel.net
https://macedoniamoravian.org

Bethania

Bethania
5545 Main St.
PO Box 170
Bethania, NC 27010-0170
O: 336.922.1284
F: 336.922.1294
bethaniaoffice@triad.4wcbc.com
www.bethaniamoravianchurch.org

Charlotte

Little Church on the Lane
522 Moravian Lane
Charlotte, NC 28207
O: 704.334.1381
F: 704.333.2281 (call first)
www.littlechurchonthelane.com

Peace
Rev. Rusty Rushing
9303 Monroe Rd., Suite H-1
Charlotte, NC 28270
O: 980.339.7609
general@peacemoravian.com
www.peacechurchcharlotte.org

Clemmons

Clemmons
Rev. Chris Thore
3535 Spangenberg Ave.
Clemmons, NC 27012
Mail: PO Box 730
Clemmons, NC 27012-0730
O: 336.766.6273
F: 336.766.3794
office@clemmonsmoravian.org
www.clemmonsmoravian.org

Durham

Christ the King
c/o 459 South Church St.
Winston-Salem, NC 27101
O: 336.725.5811

Eden

Leaksville
Rev. John Rainey
712 McConnell Ave.
Eden, NC 27288
Mail: PO Box 35
Eden, NC 27289-0035
O: 336.623.9440
leaksvillemoravian@gmail.com
www.leaksvillemoravianchurch.org

Greensboro

First, Greensboro
Rev. Tony Hayworth
304 S. Elam Ave.
Greensboro, NC 27403
O: 336.272.2196
F: 336.275.7800
office@greensboromoravian.org
www.greensboromoravian.org

Huntersville

New Beginnings
Rev. Russ Williams
211 Seagle St.
Huntersville NC 28077
Mail: PO Box 2278
Huntersville, NC 28078
O: 704.992.2003
F: 704.992.2002
newbeginnings100@bellsouth.net
www.newbeginningsmoravian.org

Kernersville

Kernersville
504 S Main St.
Kernersville, NC 27284
O: 336.993.3620
F: 336.993.7052
www.kernersvillemoravian.org

King

King
Rev. Doug Rights
228 W. Dalton Rd.
King, NC 27021
O: 336.283.5322
office@kingmoravianchurch.org
www.kingmoravianchurch.org

Lewisville

Unity
Rev. Barry Foster
8300 Concord Church Rd.
Lewisville, NC 27023
O: 336.945.3801 or 336.945.3877
unitymc@unitymoravianchurch.org
www.unitymoravian.org

Lexington

Enterprise
Arkon Stewart, Interim
2733 Enterprise Rd.
Lexington, NC 27295-9233
O: 336.764.1281
emcpastor@bellsouth.net

Mayodan

Mayodan
Rev. Judith Justice, Interim
104 S. 3rd Ave.
PO Box 245
Mayodan, NC 27027-0245
O: 336.548.2645
F: 336.548.2645 (call first)
mayodanmoravian@triad.twcbc.com

Mt. Airy

Grace
Rev. Dr. Neil Routh
1401 N. Main St.
Mt. Airy, NC 27030
O: 336.786.5627
F: 336.786.2896
office@gracemoravianchurch.org
www.gracemoravianchurch.org

Newton

New Hope
Rev. Betty Helms
2897 Sandy Ford Rd.
Newton, NC 28658
O: 828.294.4802
F: 828.294.1237
newhopemoravian@gmail.com
www.newhopemoravian.org

Oak Ridge

Moravia
Rt. Rev. Carol Foltz
2920 Oak Ridge Rd.
Oak Ridge, NC 27310
O/F: 336.643.5166
moraviamoravianchurch@gmail.com
www.moraviamoravianchurch.org

Raleigh

Raleigh
Rev. Dr. Craig S. Troutman
1816 Ridge Rd.
Raleigh, NC 27607
O: 919.787.4034
F: 919.787.4250
office@raleighmoravian.org
www.raleighmoravian.org

NORTH CAROLINA (Cont.)

Rural Hall

Mizpah
Rev. Fran Saylor
3165 Mizpah Church Rd.
Rural Hall, NC 27045
O: 336.924.1661
mizpahmoravianchurch@windstream.net
www.mizpahmoravianchurch.org

Rural Hall
7939 Broad St.
PO Box 487
Rural Hall, NC 27045-0487
O: 336.969.9488
F: 336.450.1535
secretary@rhmc.org
www.rhmc.org

Walnut Cove

Fulp
Mr. Chuck Harmon, acolyte
1556 US 311 Highway S
Walnut Cove, NC 27052
O/F: 336.591.7940
office@fulpmoravian.org
www.fulpmoravian.org

Wilmington

Covenant
Rev. Jeff Jones
4126 S. College Rd.
Wilmington, NC 28412
O/F: 910.799.9256
office@covenantmoravian.org
www.covenantmoravianwilmington.org

Winston-Salem

Advent
Rev. Dr. Timothy G. Sapp
1514 W. Clemmonsville Rd.
Winston-Salem, NC 27127
O: 336.788.4951
F: 336.788.0739
amchurch@triad.rr.com
www.adventmoravian.org

Ardmore
2013 W. Academy St.
Winston-Salem, NC 27103
O: 336.723.3444
F: 336.723.5710
offfice@ardmoremoravian.org
www.ardmoremoravian.org

Bethabara
2100 Bethabara Rd.
Winston-Salem, NC 27106
O/F: 336.924.8789
bethabaraoffice@windstream.net
www.bethabara.org

Calvary
Rt. Rev. Lane A. Sapp
Rev. Chaz Snider
600 Holly Ave.
Winston-Salem, NC 27101
O: 336.722.3703
office@calvarymoravian.org
www.calvarymoravian.org

Christ
919 W. Academy St.
Winston-Salem, NC 27101-5103
O: 336.722.2007
F: 336.724.1704
office@christmoravianchurch.org
www.christmoravianchurch.org

Fairview
Rev. Jeff Coppage, Interim
6550 Silas Creek Pkwy.
Winston-Salem, NC 27106
O: 336.768.5629
F: 336.768.5637
fmc@fairviewmoravianchurch.org
www.fairviewmoravianchurch.org

Friedberg
Rev. James C. Newsome
Rev. Dan Nelson
2178 Friedberg Church Rd.
Winston-Salem, NC 27127-9073
O: 336.764.1830
F: 336.764.4524
info@friedbergmoravian.org
www.friedbergmoravian.org

Friedland
Rev. Wayne Byerly, Interim
Rev. Adam Goodrich
2750 Friedland Church Rd.
Winston-Salem, NC 27107
O: 336.788.2652
F: 336.784.1534
office@friedlandmoravian.org
www.friedlandmoravian.org

Fries Memorial
Rev. Worth Green, Interim
251 N. Hawthorne Rd. NW
Winston-Salem, NC 27104
O: 336.722.2847
F: 336.722.2132
frieschurch@gmail.com
www.frieschurch.org

Home
Rev. Virginia Tobiassen
Rev. Andrew Heil
529 S. Church St.
Winston-Salem, NC 27101
O: 336.722.6171
F: 336.723.5085
home1771@homemoravian.org
www.homemoravian.org

Hope
Rev. David Merritt, Interim
2759 Hope Church Rd.
Winston-Salem, NC 27127
O: 336.765.8017
hopemoraviannc@triad.rr.com
www.hopemoraviannc.org

Hopewell
Rev. Walter Bishop
701 Hopewell Church Rd.
Winston-Salem, NC 27127
O: 336.788.2289
hmc701@triad.twcbc.com
www.hopewellmoraviannc.org

Immanuel New Eden
Rev. Cheryl Cottingham
3680 Old Lexington Rd.
Winston-Salem, NC 27107
O: 336.788.1561

Konnoak Hills
Rev. John D. Rights
3401 Konnoak Dr.
Winston-Salem, NC 27127
O: 336.788.9321
F: 336.785.0211
khmc3401@bellsouth.net
www.khmoravian.org

Messiah
Rev. Gerald Harris
1401 Peace Haven Rd.
Winston-Salem, NC 27104-1397
O: 336.765.5961
F: 336.659.6642
messiah1401@gmail.com
www.messiahmoravian.org

New Philadelphia
Rev. Joe Moore
Rev. Larry Jones, Interim
4440 Country Club Rd.
Winston-Salem, NC 27104
O: 336.765.2331
F: 336.768.5961
worth@newphilly.org
www.newphilly.org

Oak Grove
David Berrier, acolyte
120 Hammock Farm Rd.
Winston-Salem, NC 27105
O: 336.595.8167
oakgrovemoravian@embarqmail.com

NORTH CAROLINA (Cont.)

Olivet
Rev. Matthew W. Allen
2205 Olivet Church Rd.
Winston-Salem, NC 27106
O: 336.924.8063
F: 336.922.9005
olivet@windstream.net
www.olivetmoravian.org

Pine Chapel
Rev. James Demby
324 Goldfloss St.
Winston-Salem, NC 27127
O: 336.723.7118
pinechapelmoravian@att.net

Providence
929 Old Hollow Rd
Winston-Salem, NC 27105
O/F: 336.767.8234

St. Philips
Rev. Dr. Bill McElveen, Interim
911 S. Church St.
Winston-Salem, NC 27101
office@stphilipsmoravian.org
www.stphilipsmoravian.org

Trinity
Rev. John P. Jackman
220 E. Sprague St.
Winston-Salem, NC 27127
O: 336.724.5541 or 336.724.5542
F: 336.724.1246
office@trinitymoravian.org
www.trinitymoravian.org

Union Cross
4295 High Point Rd.
Winston-Salem, NC 27107
O: 336.769.2411
ucmc@unioncrossmoravian.org
www.unioncrossmoravian.org

NORTH DAKOTA (NP, WD)

Davenport

Canaan
Rev. Martin Avery
4465 159th Ave. SE
Davenport, ND 58021
O: 701.347.4730
canaannews@aol.com
www.moraviannd.com

Durbin

Goshen
Rev. Joel Russell
4201 153rd Ave. SE
Durbin, ND 58059
Mail: PO Box 336
Leonard, ND 58052
O: 701.645.2466

Fargo

Shepherd of the Prairie
Rev. Eric D. Renner
6151 25th St. S
Fargo, ND 58104
O: 701.235.5711
pastor@shepherdfargo.org
www.shepherdfargo.org

Leonard

Bethel
Rev. Joel Russell
State Highway 18
PO Box 336
Leonard, ND 58052
O: 701.645.2466

OHIO (NP, ED)

Dover

First, Dover
Rev. John Wallace
319 N. Walnut St.
Dover, OH 44622
O: 330.364.8831
pastor@firstmoravianchurch.org
www.doverfirstmoravianchurch.org

Dublin

Church of the Redeemer
3883 Summitview Rd.
Dublin, OH 43016-8426
O: 614.766.5030 or 614.766.5032
info@redeemermoravian.org
www.redeemermoravian.org

Gnadenhutten

Gnadenhutten
Rev. David Geyer
133 S. Walnut St.
PO Box 126
Gnadenhutten, OH 44629-0126
O: 740.254.4374
gnadenmor2@yahoo.com

New Philadelphia

Fry's Valley
Rev. David Geyer
594 Fry's Valley Rd SW
New Philadelphia, OH 44663-7830
O: 740.254.9373
fvmc1857@gmail.com

Schoenbrunn Community
Rev. Benjamin Lippert
2200 E. High Ave.
New Philadelphia, OH 44663
O: 330.339.1940
pastor@scmchurch.org
www.scmchurch.org

Sharon
Rev. Lloyd Gooden
4776 Moravian Church Rd. SE
New Philadelphia, OH 44663
O: 740.922.5507
secretary@sharonmoravian.org
www.sharonmoravian.org

Uhrichsville

First, Uhrichsville
Rev. David Geyer
315 N Water St.
Uhrichsville, OH 44683
O: 740.922.0886
uhrichsvillemoravian@gmail.com

ONTARIO, CANADA (NP, ED)

Toronto

New Dawn
Rev. F. Rowan Simmons
7 Glenora Ave.
Toronto, ON M6C 3Y2
Canada
O: 416.560.0473
newdawnmoravian@bellnet.ca
newdawnmoravianchurch.com

PENNSYLVANIA (NP, ED)

Allentown

Calvary
Rev. Janel R. Rice
948 N. 21st St.
Allentown, PA 18104-3785
O: 610.435.6881
calvarym@ptd.net
www.calvarymoravian.net

PENNSYLVANIA (Cont.)

Bethlehem

Advent
Rev. Melissa Johnson
3730 Jacksonville Rd.
Bethlehem, PA 18017
O: 610.866.1402 or 610.868.0477
F: 610.868.0507
office@adventmoravianbethlehem.org
www.adventmoravianbethlehem.org

Central
Rt. Rev. C. Hopeton Clennon
Rev. Dr. M. Lynnette Delbridge
73 W. Church St.
Bethlehem, PA 18018-5821
O: 610.866.5661 or 610.866.0607
F: 610.866.7256
office@centralmoravianchurch.org
www.centralmoravianchurch.org

College Hill
72 W. Laurel St.
Bethlehem, PA 18018
O: 610.867.8291
F: 610.865.3067
church@collegehillmoravian.org
www.collegehillmoravian.org

East Hills
Rev. Derek A. French
1830 Butztown Rd.
Bethlehem, PA 18017
O: 610.868.6481
office@easthillsmc.org
www.easthillsmc.org

Edgeboro
Rev. Daniel M. Miller
645 Hamilton Ave.
Bethlehem, PA 18017
O: 610.866.8793
churchoffice@edgeboromoravian.org
www.edgeboromoravian.org

West Side
Rev. Christine Johnson
402 3rd Ave.
Bethlehem, PA 18018-5699
O: 610.865.0256
westsidemoravian@gmail.com
www.westsidemoravian.org

Coopersburg

MorningStar
Rev. Jay Petrella
234 S. Main St.
Coopersburg, PA 18036
O/F: 610.282.1908

Easton

First, Easton
Rev. Patricia D. Honszer
225 N. 10th St.
Easton, PA 18042
O: 610.258.6317
eastonmoravian@rcn.com
www.firstmoravianeaston.org

Palmer Township
Rev. Darrell Johnson
2901 John St.
Easton, PA 18045-2544
O: 610.253.2510
F: 610.253.7401
pmc@palmermoravian.org
www.palmermoravian.org

Emmaus

Emmaus
Rev. Brian Dixon
146 Main St.
Emmaus, PA 18049
O: 610.965.6067
F: 610.965.5420
emmauspastorbrian@gmail.com
www.emmausmoravian.org

Hellertown

Mountainview
Rev. Jodie Harney
331 Constitution Ave.
Hellertown, PA 18055
O: 610.838.9344
F: 610.838.2807
mountainviewmoravianchurch@gmail.com
www.mountainviewmoravian.org

Lancaster

Lancaster
Rev. Mandy Mastros
227 N. Queen St.
PO Box 1327
Lancaster, PA 17608
O: 717.397.9722
office@lancastermoravian.org
www.lancastermoravian.org

Lebanon

Lebanon
1115 Birch Rd.
Lebanon, PA 17042-9123
O: 717.273.5864
lebmoravian@comcast.net
www.lebanonmoravian.com

Lititz

Lititz
Rev. Dean Jurgen
Rev. Mark V. Breland
8 Church Square
Lititz, PA 17543
O: 717.626.8515
F: 717.626.8258
office@lititzmoravian.org
www.lititzmoravian.org

Nazareth

Nazareth
Rev. Jeffrey D. Gehris, Sr.
4 S Main St.
PO Box 315
Nazareth, PA 18064-0315
O: 610.759.3163
F: 610.759.3175
nazmoroffice@rcn.com
www.nazarethmoravian.org

Schoeneck
Rev. Garritt Fleming
Rev. Sanette Fleming
316 N. Broad St. Ext.
Nazareth, PA 18064
O: 610.759.0376
F: 610.759.9762
schoeneck@schoeneckmoravian.org
www.schoeneckmoravian.org

Newfoundland

Newfoundland
Rev. Mark Newman
Route 191
PO Box 221
Newfoundland, PA 18445-0221
O: 570.676.8201
newfoundlandmoravianchurch@gmail.com

Philadelphia

Redeemer
Rev. Nasel Ephraim
2950 S 70th St.
Philadelphia, PA 19142
O: 215.365.6448
2950redeemer@gmail.com
www.redeemermoravianphiladelphia.net

PENNSYLVANIA (Cont.)

York

Covenant
Rev. John Fritts
901 Cape Horn Rd.
York, PA 17402
O: 717.755.3269
covenantyork@gmail.com
www.covenantmoravianyork.org

First, York
Rev. Sayward E. Lippincott
39 N. Duke St.
York, PA 17401
O: 717.843.2239
firstmoravianchurch@verizon.net
www.yorkfirstmoravian.org

VIRGINIA (SP)

Ararat

Willow Hill
Kenny King, acolyte
577 Will Hill Rd.
Ararat, VA 24053
info@willowhillmoravian.org
www.willowhillmoravian.org

Cana

Crooked Oak
Gary Easter, acolyte
3574 Bear Trail Rd.
Cana, VA 24317
riddlonc@yahoo.com

Mt. Bethel
Rev. Charles Fishel
127 Mt. Bethel Church Rd.
Cana, VA 24317
O: 276.755.4690

WISCONSIN (NP, WD)

Appleton

Freedom
Rev. James Heroux
W3471 Center Valley Rd.
Appleton, WI 54913-8937
O: 920.734.1278
freedommoravian@gmail.com

Cambridge

London
Rev. Barbara Berg
N5610 Hwy. O
PO Box 45
Cambridge, WI 53523-0045

DeForest

Christian Faith
Rev. Jason Andersen
805 E. Holum St.
DeForest, WI 53532-1320
O: 608.846.5876
cfmcoffice@gmail.com
www.cfmoravianchurch.org

Ephraim

Ephraim
Rev. Dawn E. Volpe
9970 Moravia St.
PO Box 73
Ephraim, WI 54211-0073
O: 920.854.2804
worship@ephraimmoravian.org
www.ephraimmoravian.org

Green Bay

West Side
Rev. Marian Boyle Rohloff
1707 S. Oneida St.
Green Bay, WI 54304
O: 920.499.4433
F: 920.499.9966
office@wsmoraviangb.org
www.wsmoraviangb.org

Lake Mills

Lake Mills
Rev. David W. Sobek
301 College St.
Lake Mills, WI 53551-1494
O: 920.648.5412
F: 920.648.3669
office@lakemillsmoravianchurch.org
www.lakemillsmoravianchurch.org

Madison

Glenwood
Rev. Staci Marrese-Wheeler
725 Gilmore St.
Madison, WI 53711
O: 608.233.8709
F: 608.233.2595
glenwoodmoravian@gmail.com
www.glenwoodmoravian.org

Lakeview
Rev. Staci Marrese-Wheeler
3565 Tulane Ave.
Madison, WI 53714
O: 608.249.1973
lakeviewrev@sbcglobal.net
www.lakeviewmoravianchurch.org

Pittsville

Veedum
Rev. Wanda Veldman
County Road E
PO Box 244
Pittsville, WI 54466-0244
O: 715.884.6911

Sister Bay

Sister Bay
Rev. Kerry D. Krauss
10924 Old Stage Rd.
PO Box 1010
Sister Bay, WI 54234-1010
O: 920.854.4080
sisterbaymoravian@gmail.com
www.sisterbaymoravianchurch.org

Sturgeon Bay

Sturgeon Bay
Rev. Dr. Matthew R. Knapp
323 S. 5th Ave.
Sturgeon Bay, WI 54235
O: 920.743.6218
sbmc@sbmoravian.org
www.sbmoravian.org

Watertown

Ebenezer
Rev. Katie Van Der Linden
N8095 High Rd.
Watertown, WI 53094
Mail: N8071 High Rd
Watertown, WI 53094
O: 920.206.0222
emc1853@aol.com
www.ebenezermoravianchurch.org

Watertown
Rev. Kurt Liebenow
510 Cole St.
Watertown, WI 53094
O: 920.261.7494
F: 920.206.9030
watertownmoravianchurch@yahoo.com

Wisconsin Rapids

Wisconsin Rapids
Rev. Beth Rohn-Habhegger
310 First Ave. S
Wisconsin Rapids, WI 54495-4155
O: 715.423.0180
moravian@wctc.net
www.wrmoravian.org

NEW & EMERGING MINISTRIES

ALBERTA, CANADA

Sherwood Park

The Common Ground Alberta Community Café
150, 161 Festival Way
Sherwood Park, AB T8A 4X2
Canada
supervisor.commonground@gmail.com
www.commongroundcommunitycafe.org

NORTH CAROLINA

Winston-Salem

Come and Worship
Rev. Russ May
Winston-Salem, N.C.
www.comeandworship.net

Meeting location:
Liberty Arts Coffee House
526 N. Liberty St.
Winston-Salem, NC 27101
Sundays at 10:00 a.m.
bsj3bennett@earthlink.net

Anthony's Plot
Rev. Russ May
2323 Sunnyside Ave.
Winston-Salem, NC 27127

Meeting location:
Anthony's Plot Community
2323 Sunnyside Ave.
Winston-Salem, NC 27127
O: 336-306-3562
info@anthonysplot.org
russ@anthonysplot.org
volunteer@anthonysplot.org
www.anthonysplot.org

Estamos Unidos Ministry
Rev. Angelica Regalado
angelica.regalado.cieza@gmail.com

Meeting location:
319 Haled St.
Winston-Salem, NC 27125
336-575-3530

PENNSYLVANIA

Lehigh Valley

Iglesia Esperanza for Bethlehem
Rev. Tracy Robinson
Rev. Rhonda Robinson
Church Planters
(Home) 724 East 6th St.
Bethlehem, PA 18015
O: 610.504.9127

Meeting location:
1240 East 4th St.
Bethlehem, PA 18015
www.esperanzaforbethlehem.org
pastortracy@
esperanzaforbethlehem.org or
pastorrhonda@
esperanzaforbethlehem.org

WISCONSIN

Milwaukee

Tricklebee Cafe
Rev. Christie Melby-Gibbons
Church Planter
2339 N. Sherman Blvd.
Milwaukee, WI 53210

Meeting location:
4424 W. North Ave.
Milwaukee, WI 53208
tricklebeecafe@gmail.com
www.tricklebeecafe.org

FELLOWSHIPS

CALIFORNIA

Hope Fellowship

Gina Antonio
1311 Windmere Ave.
Menlo Park, CA 94025
H: 650-630-5779
hazelmh2@gmail.com

Meeting location:
1852 Bay Rd.
East Palo Alto, CA 94303

FLORIDA

Margate Fellowship

Jeffrey Mason, Coordinator
1880 NW 183rd St.
Miami, FL 33056
O: 305.628.2061, F: 305.625.5365

Meeting location:
957 SW 71 Ave.
North Lauderdale, FL 33068
margatemoravian@gmail.com

New Covenant Fellowship

1621 Quail Lake Dr., Bldg. B203
West Palm Beach, FL 33409
H: 561.313.3651

Meeting location:
Executive Centre
Palm Beach Lakes Blvd.
West Palm Beach, FL 33409

Nueva Esperanza Fellowship

Illovis Gonzalez, acolyte
15910 SW 105 Ave.
Miami, FL 33157

Suriname Moravian Fellowship

Alfred Yorks, coordinator
245 NE 191 St., Unit #3009
Miami, FL 33179
O: 305.401.5479

Meeting location:
Prince of Peace Moravian Church

Tampa Fellowship

Federico Velasquez, Coordinator
6602 North 24th St.
Tampa, FL 33610-1310
O: 813.476.7969
C: 813.431.1917

Meeting location:
St. Paul Lutheran Church
5103 North Central Ave.
Tampa, FL 33610

NORTH CAROLINA

Community Fellowship

Welcome-Arcadia Rd.
Welcome, NC 27374
O: 336.731.8265
Mail: PO Box 397
Welcome, NC 27374-0397

Mountain Laurel Fellowship

Rev. Ted Burcaw, Coordinator
303 Wake Dr.
Winston-Salem, NC 27106
H: 336.657.3032
rtburcaw@aol.com

Meeting location:
Transou UMC
Laurel Springs, NC 28644
Sundays at 11:00am

SOUTH CAROLINA

Palmetto Fellowship
Patricia L. Bald, Coordinator
223 North Church St.
Spartanburg, SC 29306
O: 864.597.0200
palmettomoravian@aol.com
www.palmettomoravianfellowship.org

Meeting location:
Cannon Memorial Chapel
Central United Methodist Church
233 North Church St.
Spartanburg, SC 29307

WASHINGTON

Northwest Fellowship
Joan Thomas
20904 3rd Ave. S
Des Moines, WA 98198
O: 206.824.6411
mimisgiftbooksjoan@gmail.com

WISCONSIN

Mamre Fellowship
Don Wegner, Coordinator
W5884 Church Rd.
Johnson Creek, WI 53038-9736
H: 920.699.3272

Meeting location:
N9015 County Highway Q
Watertown, WI 53094
wegnerd1771@gmail.com

CHURCH ANNIVERSARY DATES

Organization dates of congregations in the United States and Canada.

Advent, Bethlehem, Pennsylvania (formerly First, South Bethlehem)	December 25, 1862
Advent, Winston-Salem, North Carolina	June 21, 1924
Ardmore, Winston-Salem, North Carolina	June 29, 1924
Battle Hill, Union, New Jersey (formerly in Elizabeth, New Jersey, begun 1866)	June 12, 1955
Berea, St. Charles, Minnesota	December 4, 1874
Bethabara, Winston-Salem, North Carolina	November 17, 1753
Bethania, North Carolina	April 4, 1760
Bethel, Leonard, North Dakota	February 2, 1891
Calvary, Allentown, Pennsylvania	March 5, 1939
Calvary, Winston-Salem, North Carolina	November 13, 1898
Canaan, Davenport, North Dakota	October 23, 1881
Castleton Hill, Staten Island, New York	August 31, 1893
Central, Bethlehem, Pennsylvania	June 25, 1742
Chaska, Minnesota	January 1, 1858
Christ the King, Durham, North Carolina	November 24, 1991
Christ, Calgary, Alberta	April 27, 1969
Christ, Winston-Salem, North Carolina	October 25, 1896
Christian Faith, DeForest, Wisconsin (formerly Windsor)	April 13, 1885
Christ's Community, Maple Grove, Minnesota	May 22, 1983
Church of the Redeemer, Dublin, Ohio	October 20, 1985
Clemmons, North Carolina	August 30, 1900
College Hill, Bethlehem, Pennsylvania	December 11, 1887
Covenant, Wilmington, North Carolina	February 12, 1978
Covenant, York, Pennsylvania (merger of Bethany [formerly 2nd Moravian, 1902, named Bethany, 1915], and Olivet, 1906)	November 13, 1965
Crooked Oak, Cana, Virginia	July 17, 1927
Daggett, Michigan	September 10, 1911
East Hills, Bethlehem, Pennsylvania	June 9, 1957
Ebenezer, Watertown, Wisconsin	June 17, 1853
Edgeboro, Bethlehem, Pennsylvania	October 25, 1914
Edmonton, Alberta	June 12, 1905

CHURCH ANNIVERSAY DATES (cont.)

Egg Harbor City, New Jersey	April 13, 1859
Emmaus, Pennsylvania	July 30, 1747
Enterprise, Arcadia, North Carolina	April 11, 1898
Ephraim, Wisconsin	May 26, 1853
Fairview, Winston-Salem, North Carolina	May 5, 1895
Faith Church of the Nation's Capital, Washington, DC	May 25, 1986
Fellowship, Brooklyn, New York	June 26, 1988
First, Dover, Ohio	December 27, 1842
First, Easton, Pennsylvania	April 1, 1888
First, Greensboro, North Carolina	October 5, 1908
First, New York, New York	December 27, 1748
First, Riverside, New Jersey	December 31, 1865
First, Stone Mountain, Georgia	March 23, 1975
First, Uhrichsville, Ohio	October 24, 1874
First, York, Pennsylvania	March 25, 1752
Freedom, Appleton, Wisconsin	December 22, 1866
Friedberg, Winston-Salem, North Carolina	April 4, 1773
Friedland, Winston-Salem, North Carolina	September 3, 1780
Fries Memorial, Winston-Salem, North Carolina	June 25, 1876
Fry's Valley, New Philadelphia, Ohio	June 11, 1857
Fulp, Walnut Cove, North Carolina	November 11, 1893
Glenwood, Madison, Wisconsin	April 7, 1929
Gnadenhutten, Ohio (Heckewelder Memorial)	July 6, 1800
Good News, Sherwood Park, Alberta	April 10, 1988
Good Shepherd, Calgary, Alberta (formerly Calgary)	May 18, 1902
Good Shepherd, Kernersville, North Carolina	February 12, 1989
Goshen, Durbin, North Dakota	May 24, 1878
Grace, Mount Airy, North Carolina	March 15, 1925
Grace, Queens, New York	November 9, 1980
Grace, Westland, Michigan	June 21, 1958
Graceham, Thurmont, Maryland	October 8, 1758
Great Kills, Staten Island, New York	March 14, 1886
Heimtal, South Edmonton, Alberta	July 26, 1896
Home, Winston-Salem, North Carolina	November 13, 1771
Hope, Indiana	June 17, 1830

CHURCH ANNIVERSARY DATES (cont.)

Hope, Winston-Salem, North Carolina	August 26, 1780
Hopewell, Winston-Salem, North Carolina	June 18, 1932
Immanuel-New Eden, Winston-Salem, North Carolina (merger of Immanuel 1912 and New Eden 1923)	October 7, 2002
John Hus, Brooklyn, New York	March 27, 1966
Kernersville, North Carolina	November 10, 1867
King of Kings, Miami, Florida	March 21, 1993
King, North Carolina	October 5, 1924
Konnoak Hills, Winston-Salem, North Carolina	January 21, 1951
Lake Auburn, Victoria, Minnesota	October 31, 1858
Lake Mills, Wisconsin	December 21, 1856
Lakeview, Madison, Wisconsin	March 28, 1954
Lancaster, Pennsylvania	November 30, 1746
Leaksville, Eden, North Carolina	April 21, 1929
Lebanon, Pennsylvania	December 19, 1747
Lititz, Pennsylvania (formerly known as Warwick)	February 9, 1749
London, Cambridge, Wisconsin	October 6, 1889
Macedonia, Advance, North Carolina	May 24, 1856
Main Street, Northfield, Minnesota (formerly Northfield)	September 5, 1869
Mayodan, North Carolina	November 29, 1896
Messiah, Winston-Salem, North Carolina	November 18, 1951
Millwoods, Edmonton, Alberta (formerly Bruderfeld)	June 27, 1895
Mizpah, Rural Hall, North Carolina	September 13, 1896
Moravia, Oak Ridge, North Carolina	October 3, 1896
Morningstar, Coopersburg, Pennsylvania (merger of Coopersburg, 1883, and Grace, 1955)	January 1, 2010
Morongo, Banning, California (result of Native American mission work begun 1889)	February 3, 1957
Mount Bethel, Cana, Virgina	November 25, 1852
Mountainview, Hellertown, Pennsylvania	March 14, 1951
Nazareth, Pennsylvania	June 25, 1747
New Beginnings, Huntersville, North Carolina	May 19, 2002
New Dawn, Toronto, Ontario	September 16, 1984
New Dorp, Staten Island, New York	July 6, 1763
New Hope, Miami, Florida	January 5, 1992

CHURCH ANNIVERSAY DATES (cont.)

New Hope, Newton, North Carolina	February 13, 1983
New Philadelphia, Winston-Salem, North Carolina	July 26, 1846
Newfoundland, Pennsylvania	August 13, 1837
Oak Grove, Winston-Salem, North Carolina	September 25, 1887
Olivet, Winston-Salem, North Carolina	April 6, 1851
Our Savior's, Altura, Minnesota (merger of Bethany, 1867, and Hebron, 1868)	April 21, 1976
Palm Beach, West Palm Beach, Florida	January 28, 1996
Palmer Township, Easton, Pennsylvania	April 10, 1949
Palmyra, Cinnaminson, New Jersey	May 17, 1863
Peace, Charlotte, North Carolina (renamed from Park Road in 1999)	November 24, 1963
Pine Chapel, Winston-Salem, North Carolina	November 16, 1924
Prince of Peace, Miami, Florida	November 30, 1986
Providence, Winston-Salem, North Carolina	November 21, 1880
Raleigh, North Carolina	October 4, 1953
Redeemer, Philadelphia, Pennsylvania	May 22, 1966
Rio Terrace, Edmonton, Alberta	January 19, 1964
Rolling Hills, Longwood, Florida	October 8, 1967
Rural Hall, North Carolina	May 3, 1931
Schoenbrunn, New Philadelphia, Ohio	December 31, 1947
Schoeneck, Nazareth, Pennsylvania	October 3, 1762
Sharon, Tusacarawas, Ohio	January 1, 1815
Shepherd of the Prairie, Fargo, North Dakota (formerly Fargo)	June 12, 1943
Sister Bay, Wisconsin	April 3, 1896
St. Paul's, Upper Marlboro, Maryland	January 31, 1971
St. Philip's, Winston-Salem, North Carolina	May 5, 1822
Sturgeon Bay, Wisconsin	January 30, 1864
The Little Church on the Lane, Charlotte, North Carolina	November 7, 1920
Tremont Terrace, Bronx, New York (formerly New York II)	April 27, 1852
Trinity, New Carrollton, Maryland	February 2, 1964
Trinity, Winston-Salem, North Carolina	July 14, 1912
Union Cross, Winston-Salem, North Carolina	September 13, 1893
Unionville, Michigan	February 13, 1870

CHURCH ANNIVERSAY DATES (cont.)

United, New York (merger of New York III, 1901, and New York IV, 1908)	January 1, 1968
Unity, Lewisville, North Carolina	November 16, 1980
Vanderbilt Avenue, Staten Island, New York (formerly Stapleton)	October 18, 1889
Veedum, Pittsville, Wisconsin	April 9, 1917
Waconia, Minnesota	January 1, 1915
Watertown, Wisconsin	September 11, 1854
West Salem, Illinois	May 25, 1844
West Side, Bethlehem, Pennsylvania	May 6, 1860
West Side, Green Bay, Wisconsin (formerly Fort Howard)	November 17, 1850
Willow Hill, Ararat, Virginia	June 5, 1898
Wisconsin Rapids, Wisconsin	January 20, 1889

FESTIVAL AND MEMORIAL DAYS OF THE UNITAS FRATRUM

March 1	Founding of the Unitas Fratrum (1457)
April 30	Day of Prayer and Covenanting for Widows
May 4	Day of Prayer and Covenanting for Single Sisters
May 12	Adoption of the Brotherly Agreement and Statutes (Covenant for Christian Living) at Herrnhut (1727)
June 4	Day of Prayer and Covenanting for Older Girls
June 17	Beginning of Herrnhut by emigrants from Moravia (1722)
July 6	Martyrdom of Jan Hus (1415)
July 9	Day of Prayer and Covenanting for Older Boys (alternate October 21)
August 13	Spiritual renewal of the Unitas Fratrum at Herrnhut (1727)
August 17	Day of Prayer and Covenanting for the Children
August 21	Beginning of Moravian missions (1732)
August 29	Day of Prayer and Covenanting for Widowers
September 7	Day of Prayer and Covenanting for Married Brethren and Sisters
September 16	Day of Prayer and Covenanting for the ministers of the Unitas Fratrum, commemorating a powerful experience (1741) of the fact that Jesus Christ is the Chief Elder of his church [See November 13.]
November 13	Formal acknowledgment that Jesus Christ is the Chief Elder of his church (1741) [See September 16.]

PRAYER DAYS AND SPECIAL EMPHASES

The following prayer days or special emphases have been authorized by the Northern Provincial Synod or by the Provincial Elders' Conferences of the Northern and Southern Provinces of the Moravian Church in America:

Ecumenical Sunday: The last Sunday in January

For Retired Ministers (optional): The last Sunday in January

For Moravian Unity Work: The first Sunday in March

Moravian Music Sunday: Fifth Sunday of Easter (fourth Sunday after Easter)

For Moravian Retirement Community (Southern Province): The second Sunday in May

For Outdoor Ministries (Northern Province): The Sunday after Trinity

For Camps & Conferences (Southern Province): The Sunday after Trinity

For World Peace and Nuclear Disarmament (Northern Province): The first Sunday in August

For Public Education and Moravian Educational Institutions (Southern Province): The last Sunday in August

For Public Education (Northern Province): The last Sunday in August

Moravian Day of Service: The weekend nearest to September 16

For Christian Education: The second Sunday in September

For Church Development (Northern Province): The third Sunday in September

For the Church's Ministry to Older Adults (Northern Province): The fourth Sunday in September

For Older Adults (Southern Province): The fourth Sunday in September.

For Children: A Sunday in October

For World Mission: The second Sunday in October

For Peace with Justice and Freedom (Northern Province): The third Sunday in October.

Prayer Day for Prison Ministry (Southern Province): The third Sunday in October

Prayer Day for Violence Against Women (Northern Province): The fourth Sunday in October

Moravian Women's Sunday (Northern Province): The first Sunday in November (date optional)

For the Bible Society: The Sunday before Thanksgiving

For Moravian College and Theological Seminary (Northern Province): The Sunday on or immediately after November 20

World AIDS Day: December 1

MORAVIAN CHURCH IN AMERICA

PROVINCIAL AND DISTRICT OFFICES

The Provincial Elders' Conference, Northern Province

The Rev. Dr. Elizabeth D. Miller, President
Office: 1021 Center St., Bethlehem, PA 18018
O: 610.867.3137 or 800.732.0591, F: 610.866.9223
email: betsy@mcnp.org
www.mcnp.org • www.moravian.org/northern

Northern Province District Executive Boards

Canadian District

Greg Weir, President
230 Arbour Cliff Close NW, Calgary, AB T3K3W7
O: 403.860.6302
email: greg@mcnp.org
Office: 600 Acadia Dr. SE, Calgary, AB T2J 0B8
email: moravian@nucleus.com
www.moravian.org/canada

Eastern District

The Rev. David E. Bennett, President
1021 Center St., Bethlehem, PA 18018
O: 610.865.0302, 800.732.0591, F:610.866.9223
email: daveb@mcnp.org
www.moravian.org/eastern

Western District

The Rev. Bruce Nelson, President
221 E. Mills Drive, Lake Mills, WI 53551
O: 920.253.9030
email: bruce@mcnp.org
www.moravian.org/western

The Provincial Elders' Conference, Southern Province

The Rev. David Guthrie, President
459 S. Church St., Winston-Salem, NC 27101
O: 336.725.5811, 888.725.5811 F: 336.723.1029
email: dguthrie@mcsp.org
www.mcsp.org • www.moravian.org/southern

Northern Province Church Causes

Members and friends of the Moravian Church can show continuing interest in its work by making the Church a beneficiary in their will or by making an outright monetary gift. For the address of any corporation listed below, please see pages immediately preceding. The programs of the Northern Province are administered by the following incorporated boards:

Auburn Homes & Services
Board of World Mission of the Moravian Church
Canadian Moravian Foundation
The Executive Board of the Canadian District, Northern Province
The Executive Board of the Eastern District, Northern Province
The Executive Board of the Western District, Northern Province
Hope Conference and Renewal Center
Interprovincial Board of Communication
Linden Hall School for Girls
Marquardt Village
Moravian Academy
The Moravian Archives
Moravian Church, Northern Province
Moravian College
Moravian Hall Square Historic District, Inc.
Moravian Larger Life Foundation
Moravian Manors, Inc.
Moravian Music Foundation, Inc.
Moravian Open Door, Inc.
Moravian Theological Seminary
Morningstar Senior Living, Inc.
Mt. Morris Camp and Conference Center
The Provincial Women's Board
The Society for Promoting the Gospel
Van-Es Camp and Conference Centre

REMITTANCES

Contributions for provincial or general church causes should be sent to the Northern Province Treasurer:

Brenda Cahill, Controller
1021 Center St.
Bethlehem, PA 18018

PLANNED GIFTS AND BEQUESTS:

For information about estate plans or information about charitable trusts, annuities and other forms of planned gifts to support one or more of the above ministries or your church, contact:

Chris Spaugh, President
Moravian Ministries Foundation
119 Brookstown Ave., Suite 305
Winston-Salem, NC 27101
Phone: 1.888.722.7923

Southern Province Church Causes

Members and friends of the Moravian Church can show continuing interest in its work by making the Church a beneficiary in their will or by making an outright monetary gift. For the address of any corporation listed below, please see pages immediately preceding. The programs of the Southen Province are administered by the following incorporated boards:

The Board of Cooperative Ministries*
Board of World Mission of the Moravian Church
Interprovincial Board of Communication
Laurel Ridge, Moravian Camp, Conference, & Retreat Center*
Mission Society of the Moravian Church, South, Inc.
Moravian Music Foundation, Inc.
Moravian Theological Seminary)
The Provincial Elders' Conference
Provincial Support Services*
Provincial Women's Board*
Salem Academy and College
Salemtowne
Sunnyside Ministry*

**Not incorporated. Bequests to these boards and agencies should be made for their use to the Moravian Church in America, Southern Province.*

REMITTANCES
Contributions for provincial or general church causes should be sent to the provincial treasurer:

SOUTHERN PROVINCE:
Robyn Glance, Chief Financial Officer
459 South Church St.
Winston-Salem, NC 27101

PLANNED GIFTS AND BEQUESTS: *For information about estate plans or information about charitable trusts, annuities and other forms of planned gifts to support one or more of the above ministries or your church, contact*

Chris Spaugh, President
Moravian Ministries Foundation
119 Brookstown Ave., Suite 305,
Winston-Salem, NC 27101
Phone: 1.888.722.7923

THE UNITAS FRATRUM STATISTICS

International Moravian Church for Year Ending Dec. 31, 2018†

Province	C	O	M	T
Alaska	22	2	10	1,688
America, North	85	3	88	19,611
America, South	53	8	47	14,406
Angola	13			1,200
Belize***/*	7	---	---	165
Burundi**	37	133	36	26,741
D. R. Congo	80	---	40	22,506
Costa Rica	3	1	3	1,956
Cuba***/*	8	9	3	600
Czech Republic	29	2	50	3,800
Czech Mission Province**/*	9	7	8	650
Eastern West Indies	52	2	46	16,000
Eastern Congo ***	13	37	14	3,500
European Continental	24	29	52	13,700
Garifuna*	16	---	18	9,000
Great Britain	30	---	16	1,200
Guyana	8	---	5	904
Haiti***/*	9	---	---	4,500
Honduras	94	---	46	27,622
Honduras Mission Province**/*	74	---	27	16,868
Jamaica & Cayman Islands	65	---	33	8,093
Kenya***	10	---	6	500
Labrador**/*	4	---	1	1,900
Malawi**	12	---	10	4,981
Nicaragua	226	---	106	102,084
Peru***/*	4	3		50
Ruvuma & Njombe***	9	4	12	8,197
Rwanda***	46	---	11	8,804
Sierra Leone***	3	1	1	125
South Africa	87	178	68	98,000
South Asia***/*	5	---	---	385
Suriname	66	---	37	30,000
Tanzania, East	71	---	70	24,597
Tanzania, Iringa	25			3,217
Tanzania, Lake Tanganyika	35	---	43	32,150
Tanzania, Mbozi	98		112	90,000
Tanzania, Northern	24	8	31	3,556
Tanzania, Rukwa	351	---	106	71,353
Tanzania, Southern	192	---	210	250,000
Tanzania, South West	113	---	178	210,000
Tanzania, Western*	61	270	110	110,000
Uganda***	5	---	2	287
Zambia*	17	49	14	5,210
Zanzibar***	1	4	1	146
Total, Dec. 31, 2016†	**2,196**		**1,671**	**1,250,252**

C = Congregations O = Outstations M = Ordained Ministers COM = Communicants T = Total Membership
*no update or only partly updated since 2013 ** Mission Province *** Mission Area
† Most recent statistics available from the Unitas Fratrum; provided by the Unity Board

OFFICIAL HEADS OF FULL UNITY PROVINCES COMPRISING THE MORAVIAN UNITY

Phone numbers do not include international access code numbers. The international direct dial access code from U.S. phones is 011 except for calls to Labrador, Eastern West Indies, and Jamaica.

President of the Unity Board

The Rev. Dr. Cortroy Jarvis
President, Eastern West Indies
Cashew Hill
PO Box 504
St. John's Antigua,
West Indies
O: 268.560.0185
F: 268.462.0643
cjarvis.ewip@gmail.com
www.moravians.net

Unity Board Administrator

The Rev. Dr. Jørgen Bøytler, Ph.D.
Lindegade 26
DK–6070 Christiansfeld
Denmark
O: 45.7456.1420
C: 45.4036.1420
boytler@ebu.de

Alaska

The Rev. Clifford Jimmie
481b 3rd Ave.
PO Box 545
Bethel, AK 99559-0545
O: 907.543.2478
F: 907.543.3942
cjimmie@alaskamoravianchurch.org
www.alaskamoravianchurch.org

America (North)

The Rev. Dr. Elizabeth D. Miller
1021 Center St.
Bethlehem, PA 18018
O: 610.865.3137
F: 610.866.9223
betsy@mcnp.org
www.mcnp.org

America (South)

The Rev. David Guthrie
459 South Church St.
Winston-Salem, NC 27101
O: 336.725.5811
F: 336.723.1029
dguthrie@mcsp.org
www.mcsp.org

D.R. Congo

The Rt. Rev. Jean Claude Ntambwe
Eglise Morave au Congo
PO Box 126
Muene-Ditu, Congo
O: 24.381.999.5615
jeanclaudentambwe4@gmail.com

Costa Rica

Dr. Leopold Pixley, Ph.D.
Iglesia Morava en Costa Rica
Apartado Postal 1327-1011Y
Griega 10106
San José, Costa Rica
Central America
O/F: 506.227.1542
lpixley@costarricense.cr

Czech Republic

The Rev. Peter Krasny
Bozeny Nemcove 54/9
CZ 460 05 Liberec V
Czech Republic
O: 420.484.847916
krasny@jbcr.info
www.jbcr.info

MORAVIAN UNITY (Continued)

Eastern West Indies

The Rev. Dr. Cortroy Jarvis
Cashew Hill
PO Box 504
St. John's Antigua, West Indies
O: 268.560.0185
F: 268.462.0643
cjarvis.ewip@gmail.com
www.moravians.net

European Continental

The Rev. Raimund Hertzsch
Badwasen 6
D–73087 Bad Boll, Germany
O: 49.7164.942130
F: 49.7164.942199
raimund.hertzsch@bb.ebu.de
www.ebu.de

Guyana

Mr. Noel Adonis
The Moravian Church in Guyana
53 New Garden St.
Queenstown Georgetown
Guyana, South America
O: 592.226.2524
F: 592.227.4590
ensinoda@yahoo.com

Great Britain and Ireland

Sr. Roberta Hoey
Moravian Church House
5-7 Muswell Hill
London N10 3TJ, United Kingdom
O: 44.208.883.3409
F: 44.208.365.3371
Roberta.hoey@moravian.org.uk
www.moravian.org.uk

Honduras

The Rev. Raby Becam
Iglesia Morava, Puerto Lempira
Depto. Gracias a Dios
Honduras, Central America
O: 504.8886.9295
F: 504.441.0627
rabybecamboscat@gmail.com

Jamaica & Cayman Islands

The Rev. Phyllis Smith-Seymour
The Moravian Church Office
PO Box 8369
3 Hector St.
Kingston CSO
Jamaica, West Indies
O: 876.928.1861
F: 876.928.8336
rayphyl@yahoo.com
www.jamaicamoravian.org

Malawi

The Rev. Geoffrey Chiona
Moravian Church in Malawi
PO Box 119
Karonga, Malawi
moravian_cmm@yahoo.com

Nicaragua

The Rev. Joseph Rivera
Iglesia Morava en Nicaragua
Puerto Cabezas RAAN Nicaragua
Central America
O/F: 505.792.2222
M: 505.835547
josephrivera27@hotmail.es

South Africa

The Rev. Godfrey R. Cunningham
PO Box 24111
Lansdowne
7780 South Africa
O: 27.21.761.4030
F: 27.21.761.4046
mcsa@iafrica.com

Suriname

The Rev. Desire Peerwijk
Evangelische Broeder Gemeente
PO Box 1811 Maagdenstraat 50
Paramaribo, Suriname
South America
O: 597.473073
F: 597.475794
ebgs@sr.net
djpeerbar@yahoo.com
www.moravianchurch.sr

Tanzania, Eastern

The Rev. Saul Kajula
PO Box 16416
Dar Es Salaam, Tanzania
O: 255.71.539.1929
moravian07@gmail.com

Tanzania, Lake Tanganyika

The Rev. Charles Katale
PO Box 1267
Kigoma, Tanzania
revckatale@yahoo.com

Tanzania, Northern

The Rev. Peter Malema
PO Box 12320
Arusha, Tanzania
O/F: 255.27.250.7901
mcnt2007@yahoo.com

Tanzania, Rukwa

The Rev. Erord Simae
PO Box 378
Sumbawanga Rukwa
Tanzania, East Central Africa
O: 255.25.280.2714
F: 255.25.280.2079
es.moravian@gmail.com

Tanzania, Southern

The Rev. Y. Mwambeta
Moravian Church in Tanzania
PO Box 32
Rungwe Tukuyu
Tanzania, East Central Africa
O: 255.25.255.2030
F: 255.25.255.2298
ymwambeta@yahoo.com

Tanzania, Southwest

The Rev. Z. E. Sichone
PO Box 377
2643 Mbeya
Tanzania, East Central Africa
O: 255.25.250.2643
mctswp@hotmail.com

Tanzania, Western

The Rev. Ezekiel Yona
PO Box 29
Tabora, Tanzania
East Central Africa
O/F: 255.26.260.4822
ezekielyoha@yahoo.com

Zambia

The Rev. Peter Chipson Mayembe
Moravian Church in Zambia
PO Box 38508
Lusaka, Zambia
O: 260.262.1215 or 260.976.051433
mayembep@yahoo.com

MORAVIAN UNITY MISSION PROVINCES

Burundi Bujambura

The Rev. Pascal Benimana
pascalbenimana@yahoo.fr

Cuba

The Rev. Tania Sanchez
Iglesia Morava en Cuba
Calle 72 #2305, Entre 23 y 25
Municipio Playa
La Habana, Cuba
moravos@cic.co.cu

Czech Republic

The Rev. Ondrej Halama
NA Sbore 80, 511 01 Turnov
Czech Republic
(00 42) 481 320 058
(00 42) 737 967 030
ondrej.halama@tiscali.cz

Honduras

Rev. Jose A Smith-Mejia
Puerto Lempira,Depto.
Gracias A Dios
Ahuas, Honduras
josesmithpalkaka@gmail.com

Labrador

Sarah Jensen
PO Box 220 Station B
Happy Valley-Goose Bay
Labrador A0P 1E0 Canada
O: 709.923.2262
moravianhv@hotmail.com
www.labradormoravian.blogspot.com

MORAVIAN UNITY MISSION AREAS

(Parenthesis indicate the supervising province - correspondence should be directed to the supervising province)

Moravian Church in Albania
(European Continental)

Moravian Church in Angola
(Congo)

Moravian Church in Belize
(Honduras)

Moravian Church in Central South Tanzania
(Tanzania - Western)

Moravian Church in Sud Kivu and Katanga, Eastern Congo
(Tanzania - Lake Tanganyika)

Moravian Church in Fr. Guiana
(Suriname)

Moravian Church in Garifuna
(Honduras)

Moravian Church in Haiti
(Jamaica)

Moravian Church in Iringa
(Tanzania - Southwest)

Moravian Church in Kenya
(Tanzania - Western)

Moravian Church in Kiwele
(Tanzania - Western)

Moravian Church in Mbozi, Tanzania
(Tanzania – Southwest)

Moravian Church in Peru
(USA - Board of World Mission)

Moravian Church in Ruvuma -Njombe
(Tanzania - Southern)

Moravian Church in Rwanda
(Tanzania - Western)

Moravian Church in Sierra Leone
(USA - Southern Province)

Moravian Church in South Asia
(Great Britain)

Moravian Church in Uganda
(Tanzania - Western)

Moravian Church in Zanzibar
(Tanzania - Eastern)

UNITY UNDERTAKINGS & AGENCIES

(Parenthesis indicate the supervising province)

Star Mountain Rehabilitation Center

(European Continental Province)

Director:

Ghada Naser
PO Box 199
Ramallah, Palestine
O: 972.2.296.2705
F: 972.2.296.2715
starmountaincenter@gmail.com www.starmountain.org

Unity Women's Desk

459 S. Church St.
Winston-Salem, NC 27101
O: 336.725.6413
www.unitywomensdesk.org

Coordinator :

Julie Tomberlin, Ph.D.
unitywomen2011@gmail.com

Advisory Board:

Africa Region: Rachel Lwali
lrachaeljuliana@yahoo.com

American Region:
Rt. Rev. Blair Couch
mblairc@gmail.com

Latin America/Caribbean Region:
Muriel Held
muriheld@gmail.com

European Region:
Rev. Erdmute Frank
e.enkelmann@gmx.net

Unity Archive of the Moravian Church

Director:

Rudiger Kroger
PO Box 21
Zittauerstrasse 24 D-02745
Herrnhut Germany
O: 49.358.734.8731
F: 49.358.734.8766
unitaetsarchiv@ebu.de

Related to the American Provinces

Unity of the Brethren in Texas

President of Synodical Committee

Rev. Dr. Larry Koslovsky
4311 Fir Valley Dr.
Kingwood, TX 77345-1366
Office:
P.O. Box 599
Crosby, TX 77532
281/328-2442 (o)
713/594-4518 (c)
lwkoslo@aol.com

2020

JANUARY

S	M	T	W	T	F	S
…	…	…	1	2	3	4
5	6	7	8	9	10	11
12	13	14	15	16	17	18
19	20	21	22	23	24	25
26	27	28	29	30	31	…
…	…	…	…	…	…	…

FEBRUARY

S	M	T	W	T	F	S
…	…	…	…	…	…	1
2	3	4	5	6	7	8
9	10	11	12	13	14	15
16	17	18	19	20	21	22
23	24	25	26	27	28	29
…	…	…	…	…	…	…

MARCH

S	M	T	W	T	F	S
1	2	3	4	5	6	7
8	9	10	11	12	13	14
15	16	17	18	19	20	21
22	23	24	25	26	27	28
29	30	31	…	…	…	…
…	…	…	…	…	…	…

APRIL

S	M	T	W	T	F	S
…	…	…	1	2	3	4
5	6	7	8	9	10	11
12	13	14	15	16	17	18
19	20	21	22	23	24	25
26	27	28	29	30	…	…
…	…	…	…	…	…	…

MAY

S	M	T	W	T	F	S
…	…	…	…	…	1	2
3	4	5	6	7	8	9
10	11	12	13	14	15	16
17	18	19	20	21	22	23
24	25	26	27	28	29	30
31	…	…	…	…	…	…

JUNE

S	M	T	W	T	F	S
…	1	2	3	4	5	6
7	8	9	10	11	12	13
14	15	16	17	18	19	20
21	22	23	24	25	26	27
28	29	30	…	…	…	…
…	…	…	…	…	…	…

JULY

S	M	T	W	T	F	S
…	…	…	1	2	3	4
5	6	7	8	9	10	11
12	13	14	15	16	17	18
19	20	21	22	23	24	25
26	27	28	29	30	31	…
…	…	…	…	…	…	…

AUGUST

S	M	T	W	T	F	S
…	…	…	…	…	…	1
2	3	4	5	6	7	8
9	10	11	12	13	14	15
16	17	18	19	20	21	22
23	24	25	26	27	28	29
30	31	…	…	…	…	…

SEPTEMBER

S	M	T	W	T	F	S
…	…	1	2	3	4	5
6	7	8	9	10	11	12
13	14	15	16	17	18	19
20	21	22	23	24	25	26
27	28	29	30	…	…	…
…	…	…	…	…	…	…

OCTOBER

S	M	T	W	T	F	S
…	…	…	…	1	2	3
4	5	6	7	8	9	10
11	12	13	14	15	16	17
18	19	20	21	22	23	24
25	26	27	28	29	30	31
…	…	…	…	…	…	…

NOVEMBER

S	M	T	W	T	F	S
1	2	3	4	5	6	7
8	9	10	11	12	13	14
15	16	17	18	19	20	21
22	23	24	25	26	27	28
29	30	…	…	…	…	…
…	…	…	…	…	…	…

DECEMBER

S	M	T	W	T	F	S
…	…	1	2	3	4	5
6	7	8	9	10	11	12
13	14	15	16	17	18	19
20	21	22	23	24	25	26
27	28	29	30	31	…	…
…	…	…	…	…	…	…